DATE DUE

Sexual Experience Between Men and Boys

Sexual Experience

Between Men and Boys

EXPLORING THE PEDERAST UNDERGROUND

Parker Rossman

ASSOCIATION PRESS | NEW YORK

SEXUAL EXPERIENCE BETWEEN MEN AND BOYS

Copyright © 1976 by Parker Rossman
Published by Association Press, 291 Broadway, New York, N.Y. 10007

International Standard Book Number: 0-8096-1911-3
Library of Congress Catalog Card Number: 76-9029

Library of Congress Cataloging in Publication Data

Rossman, Parker.
Sexual experience between men and boys.

Bibliography: p. 236
1. Homosexuality–United States.   2. Boys–Sexual
behavior.   I. Title.
HQ76.3.U5R69   301.41'57   76-9029
ISBN 0-8096-1911-3

Printed in the United States of America
Designed by The Etheredges

With love and appreciation
to my wife for all the proofreading,
And to my three children for their patience,
And to the many anonymous persons on five continents
who went far out of their way to make this study possible.

Contents

Introduction

For fifteen years I have been exploring undergrounds—religious, criminal, sexual, political—of which there are many. Bribing one's way across borders and taking midnight jeep rides to mountain hideouts to talk to guerrillas hints at adventure, the satisfying of curiosity, even of titillation, but important issues also are involved. Today's underground may surface as tomorrow's counter-culture, or even may be the seedbed for explosive revolution. An underground may have a profound influence even before it surfaces, as, for example, the impact of the youth drug subculture on music, art and literature. Nor is it enough to examine the behavior of one drug addict or one sex deviant apart from the supporting subculture which shapes his attitudes and behavior. From a moral point of view each individual must assume responsibility for the consequences of his actions, but to change moral behavior requires an understanding of the support systems holding psychological and cultural factors together.

Undergrounds like the drug subculture or the pederast are associations of outcasts which have resulted in part from the failure of established society to help the young cope with certain basic needs. Many persons are driven into one underground or another as a result of what they consider to be oppressive, inconsistent and irrational laws and societal pressures. This decade has seen the surfacing of the gay-homosexual underground as a counter-culture—although many gays are still "in the closet," as are most pederasts. There are other sexual undergrounds—sex freedom groups, wife-swapping clubs, and so on—but none are so mired in a conspiracy of silence and none represent so much potential for tragedy as the one to be described here.

1

Spread across my table are newspaper clippings which tell of the arrests of pederasts for sex play with boys—two state senators with a page boy; a policeman with a youngster he arrested; a junior-high-school teacher, a clergyman, a Scoutmaster, a boy's club worker, a doctor, a social worker, an athletic coach, a reformatory psychologist, an adopted father, a newspaper reporter, a school psychiatrist, a legal-aid attorney, a university professor, a YMCA staff member, a film director, a businessman, a TV star, a youth probation officer, and many, many more—urban and rural, rich and poor, old and young, educated and uneducated. Their arrests represent a surfacing of an underground which is much larger than is generally realized, yet about which very little is known.

The general public seems to prefer to know nothing about such man-boy sexual experience even in those neighborhoods where a map of arrests shows one such offense in nearly every block. And for every arrest there may be a hundred or perhaps even a thousand other incidents that remain unknown and unpunished. Only limited data about this underground have been available to social scientists, whose theories and proposals have therefore been inadequate to prevent the tragedies represented by these arrests. Even the terminology is confused, as illustrated by the use of the term *pederast* to mean diametrically opposite things. For example, Bastin (1970) uses the term to include sex play between women and girls, Katchadourian (1972) for anal intercourse with a child, Clemmer (1958) for anal intercourse between adults, Dorian (1965) for a type of prostitution which "is a perversion of the jet set." André Gide (1965) described himself as a pederast, "a man who loves boys." In this book,* recalling the Greek root found in words like *pediatrician* and *pedagogue* the term *pederast* is used to denote the male over the age of eighteen who is erotically attracted to boys between the ages of puberty and sixteen, and *pederasty* is defined as any sexual experience or involvement between a male over the age of eighteen and one between the ages of twelve and sixteen. This type or behavior has surfaced as minor incidents in many novels[1]† in the last ten years, as well as in films, ballet, opera, poetry, biographies and autobiographies, as well as in legal and psychiatric cases, other scholarly studies and in the newspapers.

Yet lawmakers, moralists, parents, and scholars and scientists

*See definitions of terms at back of book.
†Superior figures refer to Notes at end of text.

alike have lacked adequate validated data about pederast experience, with the result that their views are still largely formed on the basis of prescientific theory. A survey[2] of existing research on pederasty revealed that scholars tend to substantiate their opinions about pederasty by quoting earlier works that were not founded on adequate empirical investigation. It is also noted that even the best scientists often are parents also, and for this and other reasons they are less objective than they should be in dealing with sexual taboos. When it comes to their children, it is human to be concerned with what "should be" rather than "what exists," and scientists are also human in finding it difficult to be objective about the sort of frightening and unmanageable questions which are raised by research into pederasty. It is easy to ignore such questions and let them continue to fester underground, or to discuss them impersonally, with charts and statistics, as if talking about rats or guinea pigs instead of human beings. This reluctance to explore the pederast underground has left it peopled with "faceless, bewildering strangers,"[3] which is also the way we meet sex offenders in the newspapers and in case studies.

Therefore, instead of beginning with hypotheses to prove, instead of categorizing people and labeling them, an effort is made here to introduce the reader to some human beings—adults and adolescents—who are puzzled about their sexual desires and behavior. We search out with compassion the uniqueness of each person, letting the evidence assume its human shape, and give faces to persons who usually have been treated as stereotypes or generalizations.

Pederasty is a subject deserving of serious attention for several reasons. First, because there is evidence to suggest that *one out of every eight men* has at least occasional pederastic inclinations, and that the number of normal heterosexual men and boys who engage in such sex play at least once in a while is large. A study presented to the Legal Psychiatric Society in Amsterdam, for example, found that over one million such illegal incidents take place in Holland each year. Existing statistics are quite inaccurate and are frequently confused with gay-homosexual numbers. Nearly all males have had deviant sexual experiences in fantasy. Society, which often smiles at the discomfort of a youngster when an adult tells a dirty joke, or which frequently considers it only normal for teen-age boys to be victims of sex teasing and horseplay, does not always make it clear in law and elsewhere precisely at what point such teasing constitutes illegal corruption of a minor. Indeed, what is tolerated or even encouraged in one social class or one neighborhood may be taboo and reason to summon the police in another. Nor has the impact and influence of one class or society on another been adequately noted in a world which becomes increasingly pluralistic. American tourists and overseas military or business personnel are frequently tempted in other lands by the opportunities they find for varieties of sex play which are acceptable or tolerated in these other societies. When they return home, men with deviant sexual experience overseas may need counsel and guidance before they fall into difficulty with the law, for there is an increasing minority in Western society which seeks recreational sex purely for fun in any form which is found pleasurable and exciting, as sex is more and more dissociated from procreation.

A second reason for research into pederasty is that *many men fall into it accidentally,* without intending to break the law. A study of such offenders in prison revealed that many such men became involved with boy's organizations through altruism and "were startled to realize that their affection and interest had assumed sexual overtones."[4] This can be a shattering experience to a man who has never been conscious of any homosexual desires or temptations, and who is happily married with a family—as illustrated by Thomas Mann's novel, *Death in Venice.* A man is destroyed in that novel as a result of a sudden, unexpected infatuation with a youngster he sees on the beach, although he never even speaks to the boy. A psychiatrist who has studied such cases calls the novel a "myth of universal validity" and warns that any man could experience such a traumatic experience because society has eliminated traditional rituals for discharging pederastic impulses,[5] and has dangerously sought to repress such inclinations, thus making it difficult to cope humanely with the phenomenon. The psychiatrist points out that the ancient Greeks acknowledged the pederastic temptations of all men; they brought such desires to the surface, and they sought to redirect these impulses into constructive channels. The man who is aware of such a weakness and temptation can be helped and strengthened to cope with it. Indeed, this psychiatrist says that open acknowledgment of the temptation "may be a sign of a particular psychic strength," whereas repression may lead to neuroses, mental illness, and emotional *homophobia*—the rage which many males feel when they read of such sex offenses in the newspapers—which makes it difficult for society to help the man who unintentionally falls into such a disastrous situation. One purpose of this book is to seek an answer to a question so often asked by friends and family: "How and why did a fine man like this get mixed up in illegal sex play?"

A third use for this study is to provide facts for evaluating the opinions of those who are advocating *the repeal of the laws against consenting sexual activity of adolescents over puberty*. Who are advocating the sex rights of adolescents? Not the homosexual organizations which for the most part call for stronger laws against man-boy sex contact, partly to protect themselves from the charge that homosexuals seduce and corrupt the young. Teen-agers themselves by their behavior are increasingly asserting their right to sex pleasure and self-determination.[6] Support for moderating sex laws with a lower "age of consent" is developing, for example, in Holland, where pederasty has been more openly studied and discussed. The Association of Dutch Child Welfare Secretaries, related to the courts, has proposed the decriminalization of sex encounters between men and boys over fourteen, as is the law in countries like Japan. Two associations of Dutch psychoanalysts have suggested that the age of consent—now sixteen in the Netherlands—be lowered to thirteen. The National Council of Young Catholics in Holland proposes the decriminalization of all sexual activity between adults and boys over fourteen, with the proviso that there be no punishment in any case where a consenting boy has reached puberty. The Association of Netherland Youth has taken action to recommend that the age of consent be twelve. The National Bar Association of Holland, to which all attorneys must belong, has called for the abolition of all sex laws involving children except intercourse with a girl under twelve, on the ground that police inquiries and court trials do more harm to children than does the illegal sexual activity. The Protestant Child Welfare Association of the Netherlands advocates punishment for sexual relations between adults and adolescents only when there is evidence of seduction or use of force.[7] It is increasingly clear to social agencies that youngsters are not protected by even the most stringent laws—which merely provide false security—but only by careful supervision, organization and education.

The data for this book come for questionnaires answered by 215 pederasts and by written material from nearly 800 more, and from interviews with 300 adolescent boys who had been sexually involved with them. While this is probably the most comprehensive mass of material ever assembled on the subject, only modest objectives are sought in this preliminary study. The illegal nature of this sort of sex play makes it almost impossible to determine the adequacy of the sample, since for the most part it involves the experience of pederasts who have never been arrested. The secrecy involved made it impossible to secure sufficient corroborative information from family and friends.

There is, supplementary to the bibliography included here, much information about pederasty in court cases, psychiatric studies, fiction and biographies, as well as in sociological and anthropological studies. The taboo on sex research with youngsters places limits and qualifications upon the reliability of much that is asserted in such literature, however. Future interdisciplinary study of such sex deviance must be more comprehensive not only in method but in geography as well. Of 1047 subjects, only a dozen were from Asia, Africa, or Australia. Also, 5 per cent were Latin American, roughly 25 per cent were European. The rest were from the United States and Canada. Since we have no way to authenticate the adequacy of our sample, exact percentages are of little use. It is interesting, however, that more than half of the Americans were married, as were all of the Asians and Africans. The European figure was 40 per cent married. None of the few Australian pederasts were married. As a rule, the pederasts who have had frequent or long-term liaisons with boys are less likely to be married. They are for the most part under thirty-five years of age. Of the total group of persons interviewed, from ages 18 to 91, half were under thirty.

How were these pederasts located? A thousand letters were first sent to a cross section of persons who had ordered pederast materials through European commercial mailing lists. These letters requested newspaper clippings or other information about pederasty and boy prostitution. Nearly half of the persons written to replied with letters or clippings. Through them contact was made with another 600 persons. Over 200 of these were personally interviewed, and detailed correspondence, life histories and questionnaires were received from an additional 200. Questions were asked through limited correspondence and/or interviews with approximately 300 more. In order to get information about how pederasts interpret and understand their experience, 100 of these persons for several years shared their ideas and fantasies with one another, and with a group of scholars from various disciplines, through a round-robin newsletter. Two hundred or so other passed on articles, books, papers they had written, as well as written comments on their own emotions and behavior—all of which were reviewed by these psychiatrists, social scientists, theologians and other scholars. Through this round-robin correspondence people revealed things about themselves they had never dared to tell before. For example, many of them traveled great distances to talk to the author in Paris, Beirut, Tangiers, Sydney, Toronto, and in North and South American cities.

Since the aim was not statistical, but was to listen to pederasts, a deliberate effort was made to seek out articulate pederasts who had thought through the nature and implications of their sexual experience. There is no way to establish whether or not they were "typical." The first draft of this book consisted of twenty-six lengthy case studies, based on the assumption that it would be helpful to have more detailed information about representative pederasts. In later drafts the case studies were rearranged by subject, so that comparisons could be made between their experience at different stages of life.

Limits must be set for a book, yet each pederast must be viewed within the supporting structures of society and in the context of history, as well as in the context of his own experience. If one penetrates deeply enough into any problem so as to begin to understand it, it is found to be related to everything else in existence. There is, therefore, no reason to apologize for the tentative nature and inadequacy of a first discussion, nor for asking questions to which there are as yet no adequate answers. There is also the danger of simple answers and easy solutions. Since the sexual experience of the young, and of deviants who may be involved with them, is of concern to every parent and citizen, the aim here is to avoid jargon and the kind of terminology which seems to solve problems by complicated definition. Our aim has been to put aside pejorative language, and to see if we can approach a controversial subject intelligently, objectively, and with compassion.

This book is not intended as a defense of man-boy sexual involvements. However, pederasts are allowed to speak for themselves in their own words, which naturally includes their self-defense and self-justification. The reader is urged to delay emotional judgment until he or she has had the opportunity through these pages to get acquainted with some persons who may deserve as much sympathy as do victims of alcoholism, for it is the author's firm view that we cannot understand the pederast, or deal adequately with the problem of pederasty, apart from a study of causes as unseen and difficult to cope with as the causes of alcoholism.

Responsible citizens will obey the law even while working for its revision to make it more consistent, humane and enforceable. Seen in that context, this is a moral book in that truth-telling is sought in areas where facts have been obscured and neglected, and where a deeper and fuller insight into sex offenders is required not only for crime prevention but also for the establishment of healthy sexual standards at a time when conventional morality and sexual mores are increasingly being weighed in the balance. A first step is surely an honest and open exploration of an underground where deviation flourishes. If some readers find the subject matter here to be offensive, we apologize by recalling the Italian journalist who was declared obscene for describing the suffering of starving babies. All persons need help and support and, with society itself floundering in a sea of overwhelming problems, we are inclined to propose as our theme the advice of a Scottish preacher: "Be kind, for everyone you meet is fighting a hard battle."

CHAPTER 1

Dimensions of
a Complex Problem

The erotic underground explored in this book is inhabited by persons whose total experience is far different from what you might expect. Only a minority of persons are involved in the kind of deviant sexual *acts* commonly associated with pederasty, but nearly everyone is at one time or another involved in deviant sexual *experience*. For experience involves fantasies, emotions, imaginary acts, avid curiosity and voyeurism, lewd gestures, dirty jokes, sex games, reading novels about deviant experience, viewing films, and even some types of physical violence and athletics when they are unconscious substitutes for sex acts. Laws can be passed against certain sex acts, and children can be protected from deviant sexual activity by close supervision, but there is no way to prevent children, adolescents, or adults from having a wide range of imaginative sexual experiences. This is especially true of persons who are creative and intelligent enough to enrich their lives with fantasy and games. Since there is no way to know for sure what is in a child's or adult's imagination and emotional experience, there is no way to predict with certainty which persons will move from imagining deviant acts into actual experimentation. Nearly everyone, therefore, is potentially a sex deviant before the law. The experiences of some offenders are explored here. These are men who have carefully reflected upon the progression which has led them into pederast desires, temptations, inclinations, and at least occasional deviant acts.

We have the compassionate objective of asking how such tragedies can be prevented as that which led to the suicide of a respected physician in July of 1974. He was charged with having made an "indecent approach to a teen-age boy." One of the doctor's colleagues

9

said that the offense was so minor that at worst he would have received only a three months' suspended sentence had the case gone to trial. This physician probably would have been allowed to keep his license to practice medicine also, for he was not charged with having done such a thing before and it was considered highly unlikely that he would do so again. He was a gentle, loving, and popular physician. No one will ever know for sure what was in his mind when he killed himself. Had his crime been a thousand times worse—but not involving the double taboos of homosexuality and sexual involvement with a young person—his patients would undoubtedly have risen to his defense and demanded a fair hearing for him before his career was destroyed. Even if he had been proven guilty of a more serious sex offense, many of his colleagues would have asked that he be given a second chance. The spirit of the medieval Inquisition, however, seems to still apply to a pederast offense. Reporters who had never seen or talked to the physician or any of his colleagues or patients, or even to the boy involved, described him as a "sex monster," in newspapers on five continents.[1] So he killed himself. It would not occur to a newspaper reporter to feel guilty for his death. The boy, however, who told about a playful moment which he felt had not harmed him in the least, will for all his life carry on his conscience the thought the the blood of the doctor is on his hands. That boy and the friends he confided in have taken a step down the ladder into the erotic underground as a result of this experience with the press; for society has thus taught them that everything about sex must be treated as a dirty secret.

The public is in error, however, in thinking that the men who "interfere with boys" are senile—although some of them are—or mentally ill—although some of them are—or idiots—although no doubt some of them are. In our interviews with these persons we have found they are from every walk of life and of nearly every human type. The words *molest* or *interfere*, when used in this context, suggest something done to a boy against his will. This is rarely the case, however, with adolescents who are involved in sex play with men.

Compassionate and intelligent handling of such cases requires that we listen carefully to men like that physician so that we can ask them to explain their pederasty, how it began, and what the experience means. Such men will serve as our guides in our effort to explore the pederast underground. We will proceed with them step by step through the experiences which have led them to affirm a pederast identity—and in many cases to affirm the value of acts and experiences which society condemns. First, however, we must define *pederasty*, not by combinations of words alone (for words can be a way of avoiding experience), but by portraying and examining the experience of some human beings as to both the psychological and social factors which have affected the development of their erotic desires, character, and habits. To define *pederasty*—as we do here—as "any sexual experience, involvement or act between a male over eighteen and one of between twelve and sixteen," and a *pederast* as a man over the age of eighteen who is erotically attracted to younger adolescent boys, so complicates the process of definition and the tasks of clarification and understanding that many scholars insist the subject be limited to a study of overt sex *acts* between men and boys, so that it will be manageable. To do so, however, is to close the door on crucial experience and on any possible means of preventing tragedies before they occur. The process of definition is more adequate if it begins by ranging the thousand pederasts interviewed on a continuum or scale, so that their complex experiences will define both the nature of the phenomenon and a procedure for exploring it.

HOW MANY PEDERASTS ARE THERE?

Even if there were only a few tragedies of the sort illustrated by the case of the physician, compassion would suggest the need for serious and continued study. Since the subject is not limited here to deviant acts against the law, but to an examination of the experience which provides the context and occasion for sex offenses, it is even more difficult to propose reliable statistics. One psychiatrist[2] is convinced that all males have pederastic tendencies but that most are not aware of the fact because the pressures and taboos of Western society require the repression of such desires deep into the unconscious. If so, then the persons here called *pederast* may be those who somehow failed to repress the inclination, or whose subsequent sexual experience brought such erotic desires back to the surface.

It is probably more accurate to say with Freund,[3] a Czech psychologist who tested sexual arousal in male subjects, that one out of every eight males over the age of eighteen is at least on occasion erotically aroused by young adolescent boys, although, here again the percentage may vary from culture to culture. After sifting the available evidence in light of the experience of persons interviewed for this study, the following statistics are tentatively proposed, to stand until corrected by subsequent research. It should be noted that pederasts rarely admit the truth about themselves on questionnaires, no matter how confidential. It has taken fifteen years for the author to become personally acquainted with enough of them to make possible these tentative and conservative estimates.

1. The number of criminally promiscuous pederasts in the United States, defined as "chicken hawks," who aggressively seek sex contacts with boys age 12 to 16, may be as small as fifty thousand (with perhaps a half million in the world). This figure is subject to much variation according to definition. Statistical confusion exists over the number of pederasts because many are listed among gay-homosexuals, and vice versa.

2. There are, however, at least a million American men who since age 21 have been involved in one or more sex acts with young teen-age boys. If we include among sexually active pederasts the men who seek out and cultivate athletic physical contact with young teen-age boys as a substitute for the deviant intercourse they desire and fantasize, there are an additional half million to million in the United States.

3. There are at least another half million males over age 21 in the United States who value sex play with boys and believe it should not be against the law, and who will on one or more occasions in the future be involved with teen-age boys in illegal sex acts. To these potential pederasts one should add the large number of boys between the ages of seventeen and twenty-one who each year enter the pederast ranks.

4. The number of men over age 18 in the United States who have one or more times been consciously aware of being erotically attracted to, and sexually tempted by, a young teen-age boy may be over ten million. Those appointed to prevent deviant sexual acts may well ask what is different in the experience of the eight million American males who are thus tempted and yet do not break the law.

5. At least 10 per cent of the pederasts may be involved in incestuous man-boy sex relationships. If one includes cousins, brothers, uncles, and more distant relatives, the percentage of the pederasts in Category 2 above who seduce members of their own families may be 30 per cent.

6. Arrest statistics are difficult to come by and even more difficult

to confirm. Only one per cent of practicing pederasts interviewed had been arrested. Less than 3 per cent of men guilty of an indictable pederast offense ever go to prison. Therefore most pederasts tend to view the risk of arrest with the same fatalism which a fast driver has for the risk of an auto accident.

7. The percentage of males in Category 4 above who make sexual overtures to boys while segregated from women, or when they are away from wives and families as tourists or service men overseas, is difficult to estimate, but it would appear that at least two million such American adult males have engaged in a deviant and illegal sexual act with a boy under age 16.

If these statistics were reduced by 50 per cent or even 90 per cent the problem would still be an urgent one. These statistics for sex acts are, in any case, of minimal importance, since our concern here is for sexual *experience*, which may be traumatic even if an incident never moves so far as an illegal act.

EXPANDING THE DEFINITION PROCESS

Labels, categories, even word definitions, tend to shrink people into depersonalized beings, but there is simply no other way to get handles to grasp so complicated a social phenomenon as sexual deviance. Honesty requires, however, the prior affirmation that a human being is rarely ever a "case" that precisely fits a category. The pederasts interviewed here, in fact, belonged in different categories at one stage of life or another. Each pederast at any one time was a unique combination of types. Adequate definition requires the avoidance of Either/Or categories, although it may be helpful to draw contrasts between loving sexual experiences on the one hand and exploitive sexual relationships on the other. Recreational sex may vary from one to the other. The term *homosexual* encompasses such a wide variety of types and behaviors as to cause difficulty for the law, for scholars, and for the public. If one begins with logical definition, uncomplicated by the evidence of our cases, it is convenient to describe pederasty as one type of homosexuality. For example, it is sometimes suggested that all boys go through a homosexual phase and that the pederast is a male who never grows out of it. The latter may be true of some pederasts, but it is probably more accurate to say that all males seem to have a homosexual component, and that this homosexuality may be repressed or expressed in differing ways,

depending upon experience, infant imprinting, conditioning, script-
ing, adolescent self-interpretation, and many other factors.
The nature of pederasty may be clarified by an illustration. The
custom of *bedarche* was common among North American Plains
Indians.[4] *Bedarche* means "catamite" or "kept boy." It was an institution which provided tribal status for males who were homosexual
from an early age. At the same time the custom provided a socially
approved outlet for the pederastic tendencies of Indian men who
were married and basically heterosexual. The existence of this type
of homosexuality—different from gay-homosexuality as usually
understood—is also discussed by McIntosh,[5] who points out the
error in many cross-cultural studies which fail to distinguish between
gay-homosexuality and pederasty, the latter being the homosexual
play of men who are basically interested in women. For example,
McIntosh points out the error of those who wrongly argue that
pederast Pope Julian II could not have been involved in sex play with
boys because he had a mistress (arguing that someone who had a
mistress would never perform homosexual acts). The fact is that the
promiscuous heterosexual is often likely also to experiment sexually
with boys.

A CONTINUUM OF BEHAVIOR TYPES

Picture a continuum: a thousand males arranged on a scale, with
the more passive and feminine types to the far left and the more
aggressively masculine to the far right. Each person's experience is so
unique that it is almost impossible to group them into categories. In
order to talk about "types" we simply draw arbitrary lines at certain
points along the scale, neglecting the continuing movement back and
forth—and perhaps up and down into other varied dimensions of
experience as well. For at any point on the scale there is a wide
variety of behavior, inclination, experience, motivation, and so on.
Nevertheless, in order to get handles for discussing pederasts, we
categorize them by style, drawing lines across the continuum at these
points:

LEFT	CENTER	RIGHT
Romantic man-boy games	Platonic man-boy re- lationships	Substitute pederasty *Paiderastia*: Greek
Passionate games	Innocent horseplay	love

LEFT	CENTER	RIGHT
Gay-homosexual games, explorations	Accidental sex play Curious man-boy sex explorations	Sports comrade The adventurer
The "chicken queen" (gay-homosexual who, at least at times, prefers younger adolescents)		Sensuous pederasty Viciously exploitive Fetish, sadist, etc.

Cutting across such such styles of man-boy sex play are both negative and positive experiences: emotional moods of affection, adventure and excitement, and of erotic pleasure; along with experiences of guilt, anxiety, and jealousy. The process of definition of pederasty will move forward as subsequent chapters explore the underground and the ladders of experience by which particular pederasts descended there. Here, however, we categorize to provide some maps and models in order that the underground may be entered with enough information to make possible some understanding on our part of what to look for when there.

● *First,* it is important to note that when males involved in homosexual play are arranged from left to right on such a continuum, *one finds most of them at the center* engaging in the kind of sex play which society is likely to consider most normal, *i.e.,* teasing, joketelling, "fooling around in the shower." It is confusing to refer to this common horseplay as homosexual, even though such playful sex experience is often a first step into deviant activity. This "normal" play at the center of the continuum may not be healthy if in its adolescent forms it continues into adulthood. However, the interpretation given to this horseplay experience appears to be crucial for determining how it will develop. The reader may well search the data of this study for clues in vain—for it is not yet clear why the same sort of adolescent sex play seems to lead some boys into gay-homosexuality, others into pederasty, and most of the rest into normal heterosexuality. Many gay-homosexuals and pederasts share the conviction, on the basis of their personal experience, that it was all determined before age 5. Many pederasts were, by that age, already conscious of the sort of infatuation for adolescent boys which has since plagued them all their lives.

● *Second,* moving to the left on the scale, the cases become more gay-homosexual. This study neglects the left side of the continuum, for our concern is not with the type of homosexual person who is erotically attracted only to adults of his or her own sex. A majority of pederasts interviewed are either bisexual or are otherwise heterosexual for much of their lives and in most of their sexual experience. An examination of their experience suggests that pederasty is probably both a *form* of repression and a *result* of sexual repression. It may be that when the normal homosexual horseplay at the center of our scale is repressed or driven into the unconscious by punishment or anxiety, there tends to be a movement either to the left or right on the scale—perhaps as a result of the way the behavior is interpreted. If his experience or its interpretation pushes him to the left, the adolescent boy may play some romantic game, role-playing a love affair with another boy or a man, perhaps only in imagination. If he is teased, scorned, humiliated, or otherwise develops anxiety over this, he may overreact with an emotional commitment to, and confirmation of, a gay-homosexual life-style. The "chicken queen," or gay-homosexual who devotes his life to adolescents of his own sex, is thus on the left.

● *Third,* if the adolescent boy's experience or its interpretation pushes him to the right on the continuum, he tends to become one of the more masculine types of pederast. It is more correct to say that he is led into his own peculiar combination of these types of playful sex, athletic horseplay, and/or psychic games. When repressed or wrongly handled, this behavior tends to become increasingly perverse, sadist, violent, neurotic, and/or exploitive.

SUBSTITUTE PEDERASTY

Mutual sex play among normal males temporarily separated from females—as in correctional institutions or historically among young sailors on a long voyage—is a type of pederasty which involves an older and younger male—neither of whom is gay-homosexual at all—in a simulated effort to meet erotic and emotional needs. The style of sexual intercourse is to fantasize coitus with a woman while simulating a male-female relationship as closely as possible. This logically involves the youngest and therefore most female-appearing males in the submissive roles. Evidently, normally masculine young boys can find it amusing and even pleasurable to play feminine roles in such situations if they are not forced. Many men avoid actual sexual intercourse in such substitute pederast situations and obtain their sexual release in horseplay, but such teasing and jokes are directed at the youngest and most attractive young males in view. Furthermore, such substitute horseplay takes its spice from the fact—known to the participants—that substitute intercourse can be highly pleasurable in an erotic sense. There are cultures and situations—as in some correctional institutions—where substitute sexual relations, including oral and anal intercourse, are tolerated or even encouraged. This is probably less true today, however, than in the past as a result of the increase in co-education, the removal of juveniles from prisons and ships, and the decrease in the number of other male-segregated environments.

Substitute pederasty might therefore be limited today to those cultures where women and girls are closely chaperoned and segregated, were it not for the penchant of European and American societies to keep their best and most-cared-for young males in a moral-psychological climate where they are required to find substitutes for happy, loving, and healthy sexual intercourse with girls. There is no real underground of substitute pederasts. Instead, it remains an important step toward other deviant activity, for it can be very pleasurable, habit-forming, and taste-forming—which explains why so many older teen-agers become pederasts in correctional institutions.

PAIDERASTIA: THE TUTOR IN SEX

It may be that nature intended older males to tutor adolescent boys in sex, and unconscious or repressed pederast or homosexual tendencies are intended to stimulate an interest in such tutoring. Some of the dynamics of pederasty are at work in the warm, platonic relationship between boys and men who are unaware, or only dimly aware, of sexual overtones. Within this category it is important to distinguish the practicing pederast who actually seeks sexual relations with boys from those men who perhaps only once slip unintentionally into a bit of illegal sex play with a boy as a passing phase. Such "accidental" offenses most often take place among younger men who are not far removed from the time when they engaged in sexual horseplay as adolescents themselves. This is a constant danger (a sort of occupational hazard) for many men who work closely with young adolescents. All boys need human, companionable, tutoring relationships with men outside the family—be they teachers, Scoutmasters, club leaders, employers, priests—as well as uncles and fathers. Both boys and men should be helped to see that it can be quite normal for one or the other to experience sexual arousal once in a while, even for one to develop a crush on the other. If properly understood and interpreted, this need not be the occasion for actual sexual contact, although it is a type of sexual experience which can stimulate the sexual imagination and create a desire for sex contact—at least for touching and for psychic interplay and teasing. Emotionally, anti-homosexual men may so repress any conscious awareness of the experience that they are unable to interpret it in a healthy way to the boy, sharing instead their homosexual fears and taboos in ways that may lead the boy to fear that he is homosexual. The repressed pederastic temptations, however, may build up steam in the man's unconscious in such a way that he can blow up unexpectedly and unintentionally in some moment of weakness, in an act of violence, or in an irrational sex act with a boy. Less homophobic men may also lack the awareness that a happy platonic relationship may be a first step down the ladder into illegal sex play; as when, for example, a boy gets hurt and needs comforting, or when a moment of wrestling gets out of hand.

Some boys, precisely because they are moral and want sexual intercourse only with girls in a loving relationship, have a strong need for substitute horseplay to resolve their erotic tensions. Others, less principled and disciplined, may be eager for experimentation, which, in turn, may lead them to make almost unconscious sexual gestures to a man in a situation where exuberant wrestling or horseplay may easily involve genital touching and sexual arousal. A sexually aroused boy may practice a form of unconscious sexual blackmail in order to continue something which he finds pleasurable and satisfying. Because pederastic temptations and dangers are repressed by society and are kept secret from both men and boys, most males are simply not aware of where a line should be drawn between acceptable horseplay and illegal sex play. Once a man has engaged in a moment of mutual masturbation with a boy, he is vulnerable not only to the boy's unintended blackmail but also to his own conscience, as his moral restraints are eroded by the knowledge that he is now a criminal sex offender; so he may cynically decide that it doesn't matter any more. Instead of being helped to interpret this sex play as an incident that could have happened to anyone; instead of helping him to strengthen himself to guard against future illegal incidents, society may label him a "sex monster." He may wrongly assume that he is in an Either/Or situation: either he must commit suicide or he must rethink his moral position so as to justify the behavior which he found to be innocent and enjoyable—with a consequent moving into a sex freedom or libertarian position.

The unintended incident may therefore lead into the type of practicing pederasty which is called *paiderastia* (the tutoring man-boy experience of ancient Greece), a mutual, affectionate sex-play relationship between man and boy which is sometimes called "Greek love." In ancient Greece this type of man-boy relationship was idealized philosophically as love for a boy's soul and was intended to lead the youngster into mature adult heterosexuality.[6]

An Episcopal canon, in a book on counseling homosexuals, draws a distinction between gay-homosexuality and *paiderastia,* describing the latter as not being primarily interested in sex but as having "strong and tender love feelings toward one he thinks of as a person, not merely as a sex object." In Greece, the canon says, such relationships between an adult citizen and an adolescent boy were "marked by high principles." The adult, generally married, was pledged by his love for the boy to teach him good citizenship and courage, and it was shameful if the boy adopted an exclusively homosexual life-style as an adult. Other authors also note that such Greek love did not die out in ancient times, but has continued through the ages in various forms and in different cultures down to the present time. Even though U.S. law condemns and punishes such man-boy relationships, they are sometimes defended as having a "therapeutic effect on the individuals involved and a positive influence upon society as a whole."[7]

Consider, for example, this case: A school social worker in a large Northern city was astonished when four brothers all under sixteen years old—young hoodlums, the eldest of whom had been arrested 81 times for stealing, mugging, and other violent offenses against elderly citizens—suddenly calmed down and behaved themselves for two months running. They started attending school regularly and doing good work while there. The social worker reasoned that the explanation must be that some dominant personality had become involved with the young delinquents. Her investigation found that a "boy-lover" (her term for *pederast*) had entered into a relationship with the family which was transforming the boys into good citizens. The social worker asked herself: "Shall I ask the police to tail the man, who is the first constructive influence the boys have let into their lives in two or three years? How important is it to have this type of sex offender arrested, when the result may be a new reign of terror for the elderly of the neighborhood?" The man involved might well have been like Ben Burden—the name is fictitious—who in 1970 was given a testimonial dinner for his effective work in redeeming delinquent boys who had been given up as hopeless. When asked to lecture on his methods, he said to his wife: "How can I explain that many of them are violently delinquent because of their sexual frustrations and that they come to love and trust me because I help them meet their sexual needs?"

Ben later put his reputation and life on the line in order to salvage and change a boy everyone else had given up on. Ben was not the type of pederast who deceives himself about the sexual dimension of *paiderastia* relationships, but this does not mean that this type of pederast seduces his young friend or is necessarily involved in oral or anal intercourse. However, such sexual activity was the price the delinquent boy demanded before he would trust Ben and let him into his life. If, in his adolescence, a man like Ben had engaged in highly pleasurable sex play with boys, this may later strike him with a sort of erotic thunderbolt which many romantics describe as love—in that the touch of an attractive boy causes the heart to skip a beat and the breath to become short, and the discovery that the erotic arousal is mutual may inhibit both common sense and reason. On the other hand, for a man to refuse affectionate and sympathetic contact can be cruel and damaging to a fatherless or affection-hungry boy. The boy who is denied the affectionate reassurance of a good man, frequently seeks this from less principled persons or in more destructive relationships, as vividly portrayed in the film *Montreal Main*. This Canadian film, which premiered at the Whitney Museum of Modern Art in March of 1974, explores a *paiderastia* relationship between a 28-year-old American artist and a 13-year-old Montreal boy, whose father enjoys consorting with avant-garde persons and "gays" (homosexuals), until he discerns the growing closeness between his son and the artist. The American agrees to terminate the relationship before it becomes sexual, but at the end of the film the disappointed boy is loitering in the area of town where less savory pederasts come to pick up boys for sexual liaisons.[8]

Most men of the *paiderastia*-type interviewed (nearly half employed by youth-serving agencies as staff or volunteers) were horrified at the thought of abusing such connections. They take great pride in avoiding any illegal sex play with boys they are responsible for in such programs, limiting their physical contact to the friendly hug or playful wrestling—except perhaps when they are far from home or overseas on vacation. Most of them are angry with the adventurous pederasts who sometimes wreak havoc in the Boy Scouts or Big Brothers. Occasionally such a *paiderastia* type, if he has been involved in sexual intercourse with a boy overseas, will, when he returns home, become heavily involved with a favorite boy, usually a boy who is especially sexy and aggressive. However, this seems to take place with great frequency only in residential institutions such as boarding schools—especially those schools filled with boys whose divorced parents have largely abandoned them.

Even then, this type of pederast—who has the good of the boy at heart—generally does not intend to have sexual relations with the youngster. The recent novels *Sandel* and *The Boys*[9] illustrate pedagogues of this type and portray their dilemma. In the former, a teacher at a British choir school is personally convinced that his relationship with an orphan boy is wholesome. He debates with another adult the moral issues involved in his affection for the boy, who is aggressively seeking a sexual relationship. The teacher is troubled enough to run away each time he is confronted by the possibility of overt sexual intercourse, such as when the boy's knowing aunt proposes that teacher and pupil take a vacation together in Italy. In the novel the boys asks: "If a pederast is a man who loves a boy, what is the word for a boy who loves a man?" There is perhaps something boyish in every pederast of this loving-tutor type. His sexual experience with boys is for the most part at the center of the scale—that is, simply joking, teasing, horseplay. When he takes a step into more illegal sexual activity, it is nearly always because his affection for the boy makes it impossible for him to refuse the boy's overtures and deny the pleasure the boy requests.

THE SPORTS COMRADE

A third category of pederast, radically different from the school-teacher type just discussed, is the super-masculine athletic man who sees his role to be that of training boys to be tough and manly. Among the pederasts of this type that we interviewed, for example, was a burly policeman who is one of the most popular men in his community—an ex-prizefighter idolized by the boys, who say that he has never in his life been beaten in a fair fight. It is his point of view that "all boys fool around with each other a bit" and that this should be the occasion for teaching boys to be masculine—that is, sexually aggressive in their pleasure seeking. The idea of oral sex scandalizes him, but he thinks it ridiculous for mutual masturbation to be against the law, and he publicly argues that it is a natural type of sex education. His pederast activity is therefore a sex step beyond the type of dirty roughhouse which is not uncommon among longshoremen, cowboys, soldiers, truckdrivers and other he-man types. The policeman's position on anal intercourse is inconsistent. He thinks that anyone who sodomizes a "normal" boy should go to the electric chair, but he thinks there is nothing wrong with " 'buggering' [his phrase] a 'queer' boy who enjoys it," especially in a situation where girls are not available—as in jail, on a ship, or "when a sexy teen-ager is too young to talk a girl into it." His self-understanding as a pederast is that of a coach, not only in athletics but also in sex. He believes that sex play between boys, and between men and boys, is normal and should be encouraged so long as it is viewed simply as horseplay, with "no romantic mush or 'queer' talk." He tells boys that there is nothing wrong with "hustling" (boy prostitution) as long as the hustler plays only an active, aggressive, masculine sex role for money.

A psychiatrist[10] who has made a careful study of this type of pederasty, believes that the *paiderastia* of the ancient Greeks often really was of this tough military type, and that their *paiderastia* had much in common with primitive tribal initiations and the roughhouse puberty rituals of the ancient Norse. The goal of such man-boy sexual relationships was to make a hardened soldier out of the boy, much as the sports culture of contemporary adolescence is based—somewhat unconsciously—on tribal, comradely association. American sports culture is frequently erotic at its base, a sort of substitute pederasty with rough physical contact as a substitute for more explicit sexual activity. Boxing, for example, builds up a tremendous erotic energy, as well as an approved mode of release, among many spectators. Metzel[11] notes repressed homosexual energy in all physical-contact sports, with violence as a sublimated form of sexual release, a homosexuality confirmed by the almost total sexual segregation of sports. The psychiatrist quoted above agrees with Metzel that boys want and need to love strong, masculine men in authority roles. Boys have an enormous affinity with sports heroes, and it is no coincidence that sex horseplay occurs frequently in locker rooms. The "relationship cries out for closeness" between males of different generations, and the sports tribe—perhaps in effective ways—must often play the same sexual role that existed in puberty rites in ancient Norse society.

Among the ancient Norse, pederasty was a ritual foundation of tribal trust and loyalty, not a love-type of homosexual play. It was perhaps similar to the comradely affection of two boxers or that seen between a football coach and a star player. Among the Norse and Greeks the erotic aspects of a boy's sexual submission to adult male authority was used for constructive purposes. The use of the body's "chemistry and moulding of erotic energy as a way of maintaining a specific mode of authority"[12] is illustrated by the pederast relation to fascism in the opinion of Sartre[13] and Moravia.[14] This is a thesis also suggested by the prize-winning pederast novel *The Erl-King*.[15] Nazi society at points had strong overtones of this tribal type of pederasty[16] comparable to the institutionalized pederasty of the privileged warrior class of medieval Japan. In its more comradely aspects, such he-man sex play is frequently associated with the military, as is seen in the novel *Mario*,[17] which is about a 14-year-old boy who attached himself to a group of saboteurs in the French underground resistance. The other men justify the boy's sleeping with their chief, not only because they are comrades in danger but also because their chief had once served in the Foreign Legion. In such novels, and in biographies of pederasts such as General Gordon of Khartoum, the substitute pederasty of this type does not involve a simulation of sexual intercourse with a female, as previously described. Rather, this type of man-boy sex play is more sporty, like a friendly wrestling match. As a matter of fact, young boys who attach themselves to soldiers and sailors for sex play do not interpret their sexual activity as gay-homosexual for the most part. Adolescents in such a situation consider themselves to be adults, to be comrades in a temporary quest for pleasure and release from tension caused by war or teasing. Such tribal-sport sex play takes place frequently in the "fooling around" of adolescent gangs, in sports groups, and in the fagging, initiations and teaching of younger boys at boarding schools.

The adolescent boy is encouraged to sublimate his sexual energy in sports, and such a channeling of erotic tension is perhaps one of the most positive and constructive ways to redirect pederastic impulses. Boys are sexually relaxed and confirmed in their masculinity when they seek to please the coach who represents sexual authority, and for whom they may have an unconscious erotic affection, "with their young bodies in close physical contact with other boys." Susan

Fisher,[18] in another psychiatric reference to sex play between men and boys, suggests that such pederasty is almost inevitable in situations where men have the authority to use corporal punishment on boys. Normal heterosexual men not only become erotically aroused by adolescent boys in such situations, but there are perhaps analogies between Norse tribal pederasty and the type of erotic relationship which frequently develops in gangs, at correctional schools, and in authoritatively-administered sports. The boy who submits to the authority of a coach or of a gang leader may not be aware that his resistance to authority is a resistance to sexual submission, and the man who finds himself in a position of authority over boys may not realize why it is that he can find himself unexpectedly aroused sexually by the relationship. In Norse and early Greek society there were ritual, celebrative procedures for interpreting and coping with this tribal sexual exuberance which can otherwise explode into a kind of violent eroticism—not unlike the frenzy of celebratory rape which can overtake a conquering army, and which is characteristic of many of the cheap, rough-house pornographic pederast novels published each year.

The policeman-pederast discussed earlier would have been in prison fifteen years ago if he were a feminine or furtive type, for his illegal mutual masturbation with boys is known by fellow police officers, parents, and prominent citizens who were sexually involved with him as boys. He may be protected in part by the western community's thesis that "boys will be boys," and his view that "all males play around a bit." Mostly, however, he seems to be protected from arrest by the athletic, sports-mystique which is so powerful in the community that a coach can do no wrong as long as his teams win and all his boys turn out to be men. For every brazen pederast of this type there are a hundred others of this sports-comrade type who need help to cope with temptations that are worrisome or repressed, and which may at any time result in an unexpected sexual encounter.

THE ADVENTURER

Sorensen[19] divides human beings into two categories: a) the monogamists who tend to go steady with one sex partner, and b) the adventurers who seek varied sexual experiences. Sex is more of a game than it is loving, paternal, or husbandly, for such an adventurous male who may make sexual overtures to any attractive young person he meets just to see what the response will be. This type of pederasty is rooted in and begins with the more or less normal adventuring of all adolescents in the pre-love or love-seeking and dating phase of their sex life. Most pederast-adventurers do not at first intend to get involved in illegal sex play when setting out to play platonic-erotic games with adolescents, much like the young boy who may pretend to be eager for sexual intercourse when in fact he is still quite scared of the idea. However, the person who sets out on the prowl for new types of sexual experience is likely to find it. Teen-age boys are more readily and easily available for sex than perhaps the adventurer anticipated.

The adventurer's quest is often at first simply a search for new experience in the adolescent spirit of "I'll try anything once." No one type of sexual activity is dominant, except the game of "cruising," which is often satisfying in itself even if no sex partner is actually found. Some pederasts are like adolescents in that they are theoretically searching for the ideal sex partner or for a permanent liaison. Others are more like the soldier or tourist who is simply out for some fun as a diversion. Some are simply voyeurs who sexually amuse themselves by observing the erotic foibles of others.

Of the practicing pederasts we interviewed, less than 5 per cent were promiscuous adventurers, except perhaps on occasion when away from home, for pederast adventurism is an occasional thing in the lives of many men. For example, one pederast, whom we here call Evert Evans, was an adventurer only while he was in Vietnam. He would not risk cultivating his new taste in the United States, but hoped to make periodic visits to Southeast Asia for sexual adventurism—only some of which will be pederast. Americans who are pederast adventurers at home tend for the most part to be younger men, unmarried, who define themselves not so much as pederasts as liberated bisexual swingers. Or else they are men of the *paiderastia* type previously discussed who went underground to avoid arrest or whose lives were in some other way disrupted so as to make them more cynical about the need to be prudent and circumspect in their relations with boys in our society.

By profession, Evans is a scientist who works terribly long hours under great pressure. He is unmarried, and every few weeks he seeks a liaison with a woman prostitute. For a day or so ahead of such intercourse, he relaxes from his work by walking around his city, from parks to playgrounds—any place where he can watch adolescent boys at play. He talks to them until he finds a boy who flirts with him a bit and who will play a few hours of "hunt and chase" with him. He has no intention of touching the boy sexually, but when he succeeds in finding a boy who is sexually experienced with men and who is available, he plays a game of sexual pursuit which is not unlike a fisherman who enjoys the sport whether he actually catches anything or not. In this case he is a fisherman who enjoys trailing an unbaited line behind his boat, perhaps it doesn't even have a hook. For him, and often also for the boy, it is a profoundly arousing sexual experience, building up an erotic tension which makes his sexual intercourse with a woman more pleasurable. Indeed, he usually fantasizes sexual intercourse with the boy when he is in bed with the prostitute.

Of course the man who so frequently goes fishing may sooner or later catch something, even if he does not intend to. The pederast adventurer who enjoys sexual encounters with boys overseas on his vacation may on occasion bait his hook at home to enliven the game. Adventurism may thus lead the voyeuristic pederast who does not dare get sexually involved with the boy at home to risk sex play when he is away from home in another city, especially with a boy of the same age and type as the one he would like to be involved with at home. From fantasizing sexual intercourse with a boy while he has intercourse with a woman, the next step may be to fantasize sexual intercourse with the boy he really wants, while engaging in a sexual relationship with a boy who is available, such as a boy prostitute.

Most large cities have "cruising areas" which at night are full of men looking for either a girl or a boy, and where there are many adolescent boys looking for either a girl or a man. Since the adventurer takes obvious risks in making sexual overtures to strange boys, one might expect this type of pederast to be most often in the hands of the law. Why is this not so? One reason is that if he is a skilled adventurer he may run less risk from the police than the man who has a continuing affectionate relationship with a boy which will be noticed. Also, an intelligent pederast who learns all the tricks of avoiding the law is harder for the police to catch, much as the professional thief who moves from city to city is harder to apprehend than the amateur who bungles a series of crimes at home. The adventurer-pederast of the promiscuous sort soon learns the places which are safest to "cruise"—a route which often varies from week to week. Furthermore, since the boys who are on the prowl to meet him are equally anxious to keep the sex play secret from parents and friends, they are co-conspirators who rarely cause trouble unless they are abused or disappointed. These adventurers are rarely arrested unless a boy or his family press charges.[20] The police have no other way to pursue such a pederast, except to trail him in the hope of catching him in a sex act with a boy.

Casimir Dukhasz[21] has written witty novels about the experiences of a pederast adventurer with a series of boys of all types, most of them disappointingly unable to live up to the expectations of his fantasies. Many pederast adventurers are cruising around, simply amusing themselves by looking for the "ideal boy." Some have found this ideal at one time or another, but young adolescents quickly grow into young men; so the man who seeks his erotic amusements with boys of thirteen or fourteen must continually be on the prowl to find a new boy, no matter how pleasing his last experience may have been. Evans is realistic with himself at this point. Boys seldom live up to the expectations of his dreams, and if they do, it doesn't last long, so he gets his erotic kicks from a type of adventurism which consists essentially of playing courtship games. Sometimes he goes so far as to proposition a boy in order to see what the reaction will be, even offering money as a thank-you gift to the boy for spending some hours playing the game. Or sometimes he may hire a boy to prowl with him, to help him find another boy who may be interested. Obviously Evans is only one type of adventurer, for at least 5 per cent of the pederasts we interviewed prowl for boys until they find a boy who will go to bed with them. Sometimes, however, adventurers like this find a boy with whom they enter into a *paiderastia* relationship or, as their cruising becomes more promiscuous, they may move into the next category.

SENSUOUS PEDERASTY: THE SPORT OF KINGS

Adventurism may lead to a more sensual pederasty which in some criminal and prison environments is often called "the sport of kings," reminiscent perhaps of the Oriental "kept boy" portrayed in such novels as *The Persian Boy*[22] or *Kyra Kyralina*.[23] This was the sensuous pederasty of Roman emperors, Turkish sultans, Richard the Lion Hearted, or the more recent Sultan of Bukhara, who took into exile with him his harem of boys instead of his wives. While the sports-comrade type of pederast indulges only in the sex play his boy desires, the sensate pederast uses boys for his own pleasure, as portrayed in the opening pages of the Kazantzakis novel. Jules Romains[24] describes sexual dalliance in Tunisia with young boys of a "high level of beauty," whose sexually provocative and seductive dancing, freedom from inhibitions, and persistence in devoting themselves to erotic pleasures, made them more entertaining in bed than women, because they had more sexual fire and were always coming up with erotic surprises. The spirit of such sensuous pederasty is present in the ancient slogan, still often repeated: "A woman for love and children, but a boy for pleasure."[25]

A black pimp who trained young teen-age boys[26] reported that he considered a high percentage of his sensusous pederast customers to be jaded heterosexuals who were seeking new types of exotic experience for their party guests and for themselves. For example, they often wanted girls and boys at once. Such behavior, of course, is rooted in the present sexual disarray of Western society, in the cynical self-seeking, pleasure-seeking attitude which easily becomes exploitive. The boy who views girls as "lays" to be used and discarded may quite easily become the man who is willing to "do anything for kicks," as in the spirit of the English king in the film *Lion in Winter* who reported that he had tried sexual intercourse with a young boy. Such men may not be pederasts at all, but simply sensate persons who seek new erotic experiences out of curiosity, like the heterosexual who prowls the homosexual bars just for a new experience.

The pimp of boys, however, is likely to be a pederast of the sensuous type who has developed "a taste for young flesh" while incarcerated in a correctional institution. Many gangsters are pederasts, at least at times, for no environment is as effective and seductive in forming sensuous pederast tastes as the correctional institution for juveniles. Such tastes and habits can also be developed overseas with boy prostitutes who are well-trained in erotic skills, or even through a series of sexual experiences with an ordinary boy who plunges eagerly into sexual experimentation, as illustrated by the previously mentioned autobiographical novel *Kyra Kyralina*,[27] in which a man tells how quickly and easily as a young boy his sexual experience with a man became sensuous and addicting. A similar experience is reported by a cautious and conservative junior-high-school teacher we shall call Mike Milkey, who for twenty years kept his pederastic desires in check, priding himself on having never in his life crossed the line into illegal sexual activity. His many close *paiderastia* friendships with boys had been chaste and platonic until he encountered a boy whose insatiable sexuality broke down all his inhibitions. The heady wine of his unfolding sexual experience with this enthusiastic boy transformed Mike into a sensuous pederast who can write: "This marvelous experience would be worth twenty years in prison. It has been like a conversion experience for both of us. For the first time in my life I'm open now to all sorts of new erotic sensations. My relationships with women are much more satisfying and my boy is now a ladies' man no girl can resist."

VICIOUSLY EXPLOITIVE PEDERASTY

Some pederasts become neurotic, sadistic, perverted, and at the far right on the scale we find a number of pederasts (probably less than 1 per cent) whose quest for sensual pleasure leads them to seduce boys by using drugs and alcohol. Indeed, they may kidnap boys, abuse them viciously and prostitute them. Frenchy is a pimp who first prostituted himself while still a boy as a means of advancing his criminal career. He then enhanced his criminal reputation by supplying well-known gangland figures with young boys, even in prison. He enjoys this "sport of kings" with the abandon of a soldier who seeks sex of some sort on the night before battle. He has no conscience or inhibitions as he preys upon runaway boys and girls, especially those who are escapees from correctional institutions and are hiding from the police, for these make the safest prostitutes. Frenchy developed his sensuous pederast tastes in a reformatory, where he became a pimp of boys under circumstances not very different from those described by an ex-inmate of a Canadian juvenile institution,[28] who tells how the older adolescents were conditioned to enjoy highly pleasurable sexual experiences with younger inmates they called "sweet boys." Such sensuous and erotically trained boys are by no means produced only by correctional institutions. Some sensuous-pederast pimps, such as the manager of a large boy-prostitution operation in Rome which involved young boys from upper-class families, come from privileged backgrounds. For example, one boy left his expensive private school each week end to earn money by prostitution to buy the motorcycle his divorced mother had forbidden him to have. This renting of upper-class boys to upper-class men is much less noticeable to the police than if such men had lower-class boys on their boats.

Exploited boys and boy prostitutes generally come from deprived families and impoverished communities, however, and their customers are sometimes men who are too poor to get married, reminiscent of the widespread pederasty among American tramps of the last generation. Ironically the most abusive forms of boy prostitution thrive when law enforcement and police action are most stringent, for then the price skyrockets, making prostitution excessively profitable for both boy and pimp. Police crackdowns on boy prostitution also tend to drive the amateur hustler into the hands of abusive and exploitive pimps.[29]

FANTASY AND FETISH PEDERASTY

Also on the far right side of the scale are men who seek various substitutes for the sexual contact they desire with boys. For example, there is an underwear cult of men who advertise in gay publications, offering to purchase undershorts that have been worn by young boys. Another largely unnoticed type of substitute pederasty involves watching boys take enemas, which is probably a substitute for anal intercourse. Such pederasts report that many boys at a young age discover this erotic play for themselves, and that they frequently find small groups of young adolescents who give each other enemas as a kind of substitute sexual experience.

Rare in the United States as far as we can discover—though perhaps existing as a yet undiscovered underground—are the spanking clubs, common in some countries, in which boys are paid well for submitting to playful spankings. An overseas pederast admits this type of play is his substitute for the anal intercourse he desires. He says: "Nothing turns some teen-agers on sexually as much as spanking games, being tied up, or playing with handcuffs. A boy who has never been spanked by his parents or at school is often especially fascinated by the prospect. And boys who are too inhibited to allow themselves to be fellated, even though they are eager for the experience, will often ask to be tied up, because they then seem free to enjoy erotic experiences with a good conscience." Another pederast says: "I'm too straight-laced to allow myself to participate in any other kind of sex play with a boy, but spanking can be a highly pleasurable and erotic experience for both of us."

A good deal of pederast pornography appeals to this type of fantasy pederasty. Both books[30] and pictures are plentiful which deal with the subject in this way. Such fantasy substitute eroticism sometimes grows out of the tribal horseplay of adolescents. A number of pederasts reported that when adolescent boys are free to play sex games without supervision, many immediately become involved in

sadist-masochist play—especially those who are too inhibited to experiment with the oral and anal play that really intrigues them.

CONCLUDING OBSERVATIONS

• In addition to those described above, there are no doubt many
other types of pederasts. As a matter of fact, most of the pederasts
who were interviewed do not quite fit into any one of the above
categories. At different times in their lives, each one may represent a
different combination of these types. Each person's experience is
unique and is a flowing process from birth to death, with behavior
varying from stage to stage: at puberty, during adolescence, after
marriage, and in later life. The breakdown into types is only useful,
therefore, to begin the process of description and definition.

• It is incorrect to view all pederasts as emotionally disturbed
persons who seduce or molest youngsters. While there are rapists,
murderers, and pimps among heterosexuals, homosexuals, and
pederasts, the percentage of pederasts involved in prostitution,
sadism, murder, kidnapping, or drugs is probably no larger than the
percentage of such criminals in the rest of the population.

• It is an error to confuse pederasty and gay-homosexuality. The
question remains, however—are there "gay" pederasts? Homosexual
organizations assert that adult gays are rarely involved with young
boys and available evidence seems to support their view that responsible homosexuals can be trusted to do social work, to be foster
parents, and to teach young boys in school—at least as much as
heterosexuals can be trusted to do the same with young girls. At the
same time, gay adolescents do sometimes have sexual affairs with
older men. Who are these men? Probably some of them are gay-
homosexuals who developed pederastic tastes as a result of adolescent conditioning. Others may be either pederasts or gay-
homosexuals who have been charmed and touched by the affection of
a gay-homosexual youngster who is already aware that he is sexually
attracted only to men. Most pederasts interviewed, however, are not
attracted to gay boys because they find them too often to be jealous,
passionate and romantic, whereas most pederasts are interested only
in the sex-for-fun horseplay of the normal masculine boy.

• There is a considerable difference in erotic experience from
one pederast to another. The *substitute* pederast wants to pretend
that a boy is a woman, whereas the *sensate* pederast seeks erotic

sensations different from those found with a woman. The *paiderastia*-type enjoys the sexual pleasure of the boy, sublimating his own to that end, whereas the *sports-comrade*-type seeks to sublimate his desire for coitus by rough play that may spill over into mutual masturbation. In any of these cases, the erotic pleasure may be enhanced and altered by fantasy—in fact, meaningful erotic experience may largely be limited to fantasy.

CHAPTER 2

Rings, Subcultures and the Underground

We frequently read in the press about the police breaking up a ring of pornographers or sexual deviants of one sort or another. Since sex play between men and boys is against the law nearly everywhere in the United States, pederasty only exists underground in sexual subcultures. In turn, these sexual subcultures are defined as "collective solutions to certain contradictions within society," for persons who feel "left out" to make a place for themselves where they can explore "who they are" and why their condition exists.[1] On the other hand, an underground is a step below a subculture, and consists of the secret life of persons who are in rebellion against some aspects of society and its formal institutions. Undergrounds may be simple or complex and also may vary greatly in their structure—it sometimes consisting of networks, hangouts, cells, ideas or ideologies, publications, and sometimes consisting of a formal organization. Having explored many types of undergrounds, we find it incorrect to define them as movements, or even in terms of common structure, behavior or attitudes. Secrecy sometimes nurtures a sort of irrational mystique, seen in the solidarity of fellow-sufferers. In the face of violent repression of sexual minorities such as pederasts, secrecy tends to fester into illegal activities.

For some persons, undergrounds are survival systems; for others they are protest movements seeking to change society, founded by individuals who feel they face an unjust, absurd, or cruel condition. Nearly everyone is anti-institutional, for example, when facing injustice that seems arbitrary or moral restrictions that seek to repress what one feels to be essential and unchangeable in his nature.[2] Sexual repression incites secret rebellion which creates the environment which encourages undergrounds. As long as a pederast is isolated in society and made to think that his sexual desires are peculiar and unique, he may brood in isolation. However, when he begins to discover that hundreds, perhaps even thousands, of other persons have sexual inclinations similar to his, he begins to seek them out in order to discover something about himself, his nature, his desires, and to ask why and how he happens to be deviant. When several pederasts meet for such a reason, the police may consider it as a "ring," or a meeting to conspire to aid each other to break the law. Such an underground group tends in time either to surface as a counter-culture seeking to influence or change dominant cultural institutions, or else it tends to become a criminal underworld, despairing of a place within the legal structures of society. An apt illustration of this is furnished by the difference between the French resistance underground and the Mafia. The French underground was universally respected during and after World War II. Historically the Mafia had its origins in a similar underground resistance movement. Historically speaking, the French underground might well have become similar to the Mafia had the Germans continued to occupy France for several centuries. Fathers would have raised their sons to oppose German law, police and institutions, as fathers in Sicily did during hundreds of years of foreign occupation.

Undergrounds exist not only to do what society forbids, but often also to do what society fails to do; for example, to help unmarried people cope with their sexual needs in a culture in which sexual intercourse is permitted only with marriage. If such a subculture is purely criminal and exploitive, it is called an "underworld," if it has some revolutionary aspects and values, it is an "underground." It may be as difficult for middle-class outsiders to understand a sexual underground as it is for many middle-class whites to understand lower-class black culture. Scholars tend to search for explanations which make sense in terms of their own presuppositions and values, and therefore are poorly prepared to discover that a sexual underground may be quite different from what their presumptions have led them to expect. The word *exploring* is therefore used here to suggest that we must expect to enter a strange world so different from conventional values and behavior as to be difficult to understand. If the surfacing gay underground frequently seems complex and mystifying, as for example when a Catholic nun resigns from her order only to surface later as priest of a gay church, or pornographers surface as respectable businessmen demanding their rights in the courts of the land, the existence of pederast groups which demand "sexual rights of adolescents" seems doubly offensive to law and morality. Most pederasts have few illusions about the value of surfacing in a society which has no intention of officially tolerating them. Only an infinitesimal minority, therefore, ever get involved in "rings" or other such groups. Many, if not most, of them resent a book like this or even any publicity at all.

CULTURE AND COUNTER-CULTURE

The existence of sexual undergrounds presumes a dominant sexual culture, a sexual establishment in Western society, based on Judeo-Christian morality, in which theory has authorized sexual intercourse only within, or in preparation for, heterosexual marriage—and, until very recently, only for purposes of procreation. All other sexual experience and involvements have been taboo, but have of necessity been tolerated underground so long as they stayed out of sight. Both inside and outside marriage, human beings have long valued erotic experiences that were not purely procreative: some in art, some mystical, some playful or tension-releasing, some lustful or simply relieving sexual pressures—especially among the unmarried. Most people seem to assume that this established Western pattern of limiting sex contact to the confines of monogamous marriage is innate in mankind and dominant over all the civilized globe. Nothing could be farther from the truth, however, even though support of such institutions as courtship and marriage is written into the law of most modern countries. Ancient counter-cultures such as polygamy, child marriage, and pederasty were thought to be disappearing. Some of the so-called sexual revolution in this century is merely an awakening to and an acknowledgment of what had previously been kept out of sight. Pederasty is increasingly prominent today, not only in news stories of arrests of pederasts but also in fiction,[3] biographies and autobiographies,[4] films,[5] TV and radio discussions and nonfiction books,[6] legal cases, and in the experience of most adolescents who at one time or another encounter a pederast who offers sexual adventures and pleasure.

Social scientists and law-enforcement authorities point to five pederastic subcultures which are identifiable:

Acquaintance Networks

In the last two decades there has been a slow, cautious, deliberate effort on the part of many pederasts to seek one another out in a quest for self-understanding. In some cases, where groups have been formed, the intent has been to provide support or to help the others avoid illegal acts. There have been Alcoholics Anonymous-type experiments calculated to enlist pederasts in helping one another stay out of trouble. Mostly, however, pederasts have gathered for purposes of conversation, seeking an environment in which they can talk openly and honestly about their needs and desires. Partly because of the peril of becoming known, such groups usually gather ostensibly for sports purposes—as a hunting club, a group to raise funds for adolescent sports groups, or even as a stamp club. How do they find one another? Sometimes by advertising in the personal columns of magazines and newspapers, especially in gay publications. But more often simply by noticing other men with similar habits, especially those who hang around near soda bars, bus stations, all-night restaurants, and other pederast gathering places. Some pederasts say they can recognize another pederast on sight, or by watching him for a few minutes at a youth organization. Frequently, like a "Pied Piper," he will have boys trailing him. Once in a while a pederast may catch another in a compromising situation and come to his aid. There are cases, however, in which two men meet at a boy's club and are friends for years before each discovers that the other is a pederast.

Many a pederast reports that when he was young, or when it first struck him that he was erotically attracted to young boys, he thought he must be different from all other men in the world. Surely, he thought, no other men who are happily involved heterosexually with women would also have homosexual desires for boys. It is common for such an isolated pederast to keep secret scrapbooks, with pictures of favorite boys cut from magazines. A historic event for many such pederasts was the appearance on the newsstands in the late 1950's of an issue of *Trim* Magazine with a naked 13-year-old boy on the cover. Many pederasts reported as did this one: "When I first saw that picture on the magazine cover I was excited, not merely because it was erotic to me but also because I realized at once that there must be other persons like me." Some pederasts got acquainted through correspondence with the *Trim* photographer, who made a small fortune from selling copies of the photograph. The publisher, who had previously specialized in photography and in publications for gay-homosexuals, found that there was a large market for pederastic materials. Several mail-order houses emerged to sell pederastic novels, art books, calendars, joke books, with thousands of men even filling out questionnaries to help these businessmen create the necessary materials to satisfy their tastes and preferences. A study of the mailing lists, however, reveals that they consist for the most part of persons who seek books and photographs to feed the fantasies which they substitute for actual sex acts. Probably such persons are willing to have their names on the mailing lists because, not being guilty of any sexual offense, they have nothing to fear from the police.

Pederast Apologists

A second subculture consisted of networks formed in order to pass along information: news of publications, of arrests and dangers, gossip about well-known pederasts such as film personalities, and so on. Such networks consist largely of a hundred or so pederast newsletters most of which have been published since World War II. The Scholarly *International Journal of Greek Love* survived only two issues because the printer was arrested for counterfeiting. Other pederast publications were sometimes typed and passed from hand to hand like underground publications in Russia. Others were photo-offset newsletters such as *Better Life, Hermes,* and *Puberty Rites,* which featured book and film reviews, legal information, medical advice, and exchanges of opinion. There have been many more such publications in Europe, such as *Billy,* which contains scholarly articles alongside erotic photographs and want ads submitted by men or boys who wish to meet other kindred souls. Between 1970 and 1974, the Committee on Pedophilia of the Netherlands Association for Sexual Reform sponsored four international study conferences in Holland. *Better Life's* staff followed them up with a series of mini-conferences in American cities, largely to discuss mutual defense and law revision. The 1973 international conference concluded that it is incorrect to view pederasty as "an insignificant minority within a homosexual minority,"[7] and urged more serious research into the nature of pederasty, its extent, and its significance in relation to gay-homosexuality.

The Rene Guyon Society, a split from the Sexual Freedom League,[8] prepares legal briefs to help pederasts in court and testifies before legislative committees. A number of gay-homosexual publications, especially in Europe, also attempt to serve pederasts, among them is *The Examiner* in London, which in March of 1975 published a long interview with author Michael Davidson about his "paederastic inclinations." These publications include news of such groups as the "Paedophile Action for Liberation,"[9] which in 1974 helped circulate a letter in Great Britain to selected educators, clergymen, social workers, physicians, and parents of teen-age boys, inviting them to join with pederasts in drafting a document and in founding an organization (which presumably would be half pederast but no one would know which half!) to work for "greater realism in legal practice" and education with regard to adult-adolescent sexual involvements. The proposal called for the creation of a core group of persons who would prepare a booklet, take resolutions to various organizations, and consult with groups of lawyers, especially asking for a review of the "age of consent" provisions presently in British law. Eighty per cent of the persons who were written to replied favorably. Ironically, pederasts were the most negative, worrying about "rocking the boat," whereas non-pederasts generally approved of liberalizing the laws regulating adolescent sex practices, although some had reservations about the maturity of pederasts. As a result of conferences with certain Members of Parliament in June of 1975, this core group anticipated that the age of consent in Great Britain might soon be lowered three to five years.

While the number of books and organizations adopting a more sympathetic view of pederasty seems to be increasing, the networks which disseminate such information include non-pederasts as well as pederasts among their members.

Photographers and Pornographers

A third subculture of pederasts clusters around photography, including those who collect artistic pictures, those who keep souvenir photos, and those who collect pornography. Photography and pornography are substitutes for actual sexual contact with boys for some pederasts—74 per cent of whom collect photos. One of the surprising things about pederast pornography is that very little is artifically posed, in contrast to other types of pornography. Another surprising factor is that whether consisting of movies, slides, or magazine photographs, very few young boys are paid for appearing in such pictures. This fact is of significance in understanding the nature of pederasty. Whether the pornographic pictures consist merely of rough play and clowning around or of more explicit sexual acts, the subjects are generally simply given freedom before the camera to do whatever they enjoy, with their payment being solely the pleasure they receive from the sex act and sex play itself. One would expect young boys to be shy in front of a camera, and to demand large sums before being willing to have pictures taken of them doing deviant acts. The fact is, however, that many boys are excited and aroused by the presence of the camera, and on their own initiative perform in ways they had been unwilling or uninterested in doing before. This excitement at being photographed during sex play somewhat resembles the way in which many boys are released from inhibitions by being tied up or handcuffed. When turned loose on a bed in front of a camera, many schoolboys will experiment with practices one would assume they had never heard of.

Police have difficulty in tracing down and arresting pornographers because a high percentage of the pornography sold commercially, as in magazines, is pirated from private collections which may be many years old, and which frequently came from foreign countries; also because boys involved become co-conspirators. The circulation of such materials constitutes a sort of subculture of interest to many pederasts, but it is not the underground we are seeking, for many of the pornography merchants are not pederastic at all, but simply are in the business for the money. Also, there are many men who would claim that they are not pederastic at all, but who enjoy buying and viewing films of boys engaged in sex play, presumably finding them amusing. On the other hand, the pederast "rings" which gather around a common interest in photography are more likely to take pictures of boys at swim meets, fishing, hiking, or playing basketball or tennis.

Pederast Underworld

There is a criminal pederast underworld, actually quite small, which is inhabited by pederasts running away from the police, by pimps, by gangsters who blackmail pederasts and shake down pornographers. There was, for example, a blackmailer in New York City at the time of the 1964 World's Fair who offered young boys to tourists with the suggestion that they might like to try a "new type of sex kick." Because the blackmailer was well-dressed and well-educated and his boys were clever and charming, quite a few tourists who had never even heard of pederasty were curious enough to try a new experience,—not realizing that their driver's license or credit cards would be taken while they were in bed with the boy. However, there have been very few efforts to organize prostitution rings or blackmail rings in the pederast milieu. This may be, if rumors can be believed, because the "lavender mafia" has framed on drug charges those who endangered its operations by trying to blackmail customers. There were many pederast brothels in the United States before World War I, but as with other sorts of brothels they have been replaced in most of the world by call-boy rings or amateur unorganized prostitution. There are gangsters who operate bars and clubs for pederasts. Some are disguised as juice bars or pool halls; others are night clubs that reopen in the middle of the night as soft-drink clubs where pederasts can meet boy prostitutes. Since 1972 the "meat racks" (street corners where boys stand waiting for men to pick them up) have increasingly been replaced by boys waiting at pay telephones in their own neighborhoods or at drugstores and beaches, with their amateur pimps changing such locations and phone numbers from week to week.

These operations are difficult for the police to track down, for this criminal subculture always seems to evaporate like soap bubbles when it is pursued. Such pimps generally operate as loners, and after arrest or after a payoff to police simply move to new locations. Ironically, arrests among pederasts most frequently take place among *paiderastia*-types who slip into sex offenses out of affection, rather than among the pimps, blackmailers, or promiscuous adventurers who patronize pimps. Indeed, the blackmailer who was tricking the curious patrons of the New York World's Fair was never arrested— even when adequate evidence was submitted to the New York Vice Squad. The police themselves perhaps tipped him off each time a complaint was made to them, reputedly because they found him useful as an informant on other crimes.

In this milieu, runaway boys have been drugged, abused, even murdered. They have been passed from pimp to pimp across the United States, and have at times even been sent to pimps overseas. This criminal underworld, however, is not the pederast underground we seek to explore here. Rather it consists of parasites who hang like leeches on the pederast underground.

ARE THERE PEDERAST RINGS?

A 1966 book entitled *The Boys of Boise*[10] reported journalistically on the aftermath of a pederast scandal which involved prominent persons in Idaho. Since then there have been newspaper accounts of many such rings,[11] while others have been less publicized. A group of Midwestern bankers every other year selected a junior-high-school boy for a full-expense college scholarship, with the understanding that he would take turns sleeping with them for two years. Another group of businessmen ran a boxing club for young boys and these same young boys got high prizes if they also shared their sexual favors. A group of fathers in Los Angeles reputedly slept with one another's sons on camping trips. Runaway boys told of being sent on a circuit which passed them from one man to another for six months, few of whom kept the boy for more than a few days. However, very few of the thousand pederasts interviewed for this study had personal experience with any such ring. Several pederasts who had been arrested for participation in such a ring reported that while at least some of the arrested ring members were indeed guilty of sex play with boys, the ring itself was largely a fabrication of the press, or of a district attorney who wanted more sensational headlines to advance his career. Pederasts of various types have gotten acquainted and have developed friendships on the basis of their common interests and problems. They do, as do other friends, sometimes take fishing trips together and if they take their young friends along, then in that sense there is a ring. Whatever their individual behavior may have been, however, the sole group activity of one such ring, declared by the police to be a "vice ring," had been men taking boys to a Catholic eucharist together.

For the most part, when we descend into the pederast underground we find nothing there like a Mafia or a secret political group. Instead we find pederasts clustered in small groups, each heading in a different direction, as if struggling to find their way out of the darkness. Some, their lives already wrecked by arrest or prison, may be anti-societies existing as survival systems. Others will be seeking to find ways to avoid illegal acts or to get out of the underground. Still others exist as rebels, seeking to do simple human acts of kindness to persons who have been crushed or who are puzzled about a doom which seems to hang over them as a result of forces and desires over which they have little control.

SOME CONCLUDING OBSERVATIONS

● The pederast underground does not consist of criminal or political organizations, but of small groups of men who "hang around where boys are." Even the pimps and blackmailers of the underworld, when seeking to find each other, say: "If I hear he is in San Francisco, I know where he'll show up sooner or later." This insight provides a basic clue for finding the pederast underground.

● The police find it difficult to apprehend pederast offenders because the underground is complex, changing from place to place and hour to hour. It may take an investigator weeks or even months to gain the information and make the contacts he needs, and by then everything may have completely changed and he will have to start over again. Also, the police lack adequate terminology and insight into the nature of pederasty, which is so interwoven with innocent sex play and legal behavior (which often may appear more suspicious than do actual sex offenses) that it is almost impossible for an outsider to get a clear picture of what is really happening, and to decide what can be done about it. In one Eastern city of 140,000 people, for example, the pederasts seem always to know immediately of any new police plans for surveillance or investigation, whereupon everything immediately changes. Boys disappear from the restaurant, the drugstore, and the corner of the park where they customarily hang out, and reappear at a suburban shopping center or at a beach in the next county.

● While pederasts tend to view gay-homosexual organizations as unfriendly opposition, some gay organizations, especially in Europe, are sympathetic to pederasts, even though it is in their own best public interests to oppose pederasty. For example, Dorr Legg of One, Inc., in the Los Angeles *Advocate*, Jan. 15, 1975 was quoted as saying: "Among their immense concessions to homophobia, the so-called liberationists have lumped boy-love into the category of child molestation." He then defended the value of men tutoring boys in sex by saying that such efforts in previous civilizations were "beautiful arrangements" and "could be so again." Pederast and gay undergrounds, however, are rarely if ever the same.

CHAPTER 3

The Ladder Down

To understand the thousand or more pederasts interviewed, it is necessary to return with them to their adolescence, at which time nearly every boy engages in the exploration of many secret, exciting sexual mysteries. Some adolescents successfully avoid slipping into catastrophe, and find their way back into a normal place in adult society. Others, and the number seems to be increasing, spend their youth wandering around in one underworld or another, sometimes finding their way out with great difficulty and cost. Those boys who become adult pederasts in many cases did not intend to go so far down the ladder and those who ultimately join the pederast underground are often those for whom the ladder unexpectedly turned into a one-way slide. Pederasts whose lives and careers are ruined become aware too late of the danger of fantasies and small first steps taken before their long-range implications are known or understood. Some persons choose to be outcasts, of course; others go up and down the ladder so as to live in two worlds at once. Some boys and men undertake adventurous explorations precisely because they enjoy a whiff of danger. Yet those who get into trouble are often the ones who are less clever and competent, which, in turn, suggests that one may gain an incomplete or inaccurate picture of the pederast underground by limiting one's study to those who have been arrested, who are in prison, or who are under psychiatric care. It is convenient at this point to ask the reader to imagine one great ladder which leads down into deviant experience, so that pederasts can be categorized by their locations on that ladder. Some tempted persons merely peek down out of curiosity or explore the first few rungs; whereas others move down into illegal sexual behavior, or even deep into the alienated underground.

The experience of any one pederast in the pederast underground is accessible only by the same ladder he used when he descended into something he did not understand, did not anticipate, and did not intend. It is a mistake to confine the study of sexual behavior to clinical details of sex acts. Examining the life history of a pederast makes it clear that crucial sexual experience began long before any deviant act. Many pederasts remember being erotically attracted to adolescent boys at the age of five or even earlier. Many report sexually charged emotional fantasies as early as they can remember. It is difficult to understand and to interpret this experience, for even the psychiatrist who has skills to probe into the unconscious for fragmentary and twisted evidence of a person's earliest emotional experiences, must finally act on hunches and theories, seeking to relieve pressures rather than discovering what caused them. So we shall seek in this chapter to trace back the steps of a pederast we will call Art Adams. It is immediately apparent that more depth of insight and detail is needed to place his pederasty in a far larger context than sexual behavior alone. His sexual experience is part of his total experience as a child and an adolescent. In focusing on what is unique about his erotic behavior, we risk losing sight of the fact that it is really not unique at all, that the same behavior might well have led him to become a homosexual, or even a normal heterosexual, instead of a pederast. For clues as to why Art became a practicing pederast, the reader may want to watch for evidence of conditioning or preconditioning, for unique aspects of his sexual experience, and especially for the way that experience was interpreted, both by others and in the self-interpretation of child and adolescent.

Art Adams' arrest sent shock waves throughout his community, for he was the last man in town anyone would have expected to be sexually involved with boys. He had a good marriage, four bright healthy children, and was well known throughout the state for sports work which was most effective in "turning sneaky, passive, sissy boys into men." He was known as one of those men who love boys in every constructive sense, and because of the concern and affection they sensed in Adams, the most difficult boys could relate to him when everyone else had failed. His image as a sportsman was so different from what the public expected a pederast to be that his trial ended with a hung jury even after the prosecution submitted photographic evidence of his mutual masturbation with a delinquent youngster. To protect his anonynmity, his experiences are here intertwined with those of other pederasts whose stories are similar.

WHEN PEDERASTY BEGINS

If an arrested pederast is asked about the beginning of his deviant behavior, he may answer that it continues a process of pleasure-seeking which began in infancy and has never ceased. Some pederasts grow up with guilty, anti-sex feelings which frequently keep them from any sexual activity at all. They may feel that their adult involvement with boys is a delayed adolescence because they forbade themselves to have a sexual adolescence at the proper age. Adams, however, was quite the opposite. From his earliest memories he had a pro-sex attitude, erotic pleasures were a gift of God to be enjoyed, and in working with delinquent boys he sought to give them positive views of sex. Because he told them that masturbation was harmless, an innocent enjoyment, he felt free to live as he taught. Did he become a pederast at the age of twenty-one, or eighteen, or sixteen? A different ladder could be constructed for each pederast, but the steps here described from the experience of Adams are typical for many who have followed similar steps down into the underground.

Step 1. Discovery of Pleasure in Masturbation

Adams discovered the narcotic quality of erotic pleasure almost as early as he can remember: "As a youngster I greatly enjoyed my body in sports, in simply living, but I never felt more alive than when my body began to glow with those self-induced orgasms, which I supposedly couldn't have at the age of four or five. But I did!" While a large percentage of pederasts seem to have masturbated early, there is no obvious correlation between masturbation and deviancy. What one does observe in these cases is a fantasy life which may have a special bearing on a boy's self-understanding and interpretation of his pleasure. Another pederast says: "For a brief period I was puzzled and shamed with punishment and lectures about how wrong it was for me to play with myself, but . . . it was so delightful that I decided my parents were wrong, or else that I was different from other boys." Adams, too, recalls: "Some boys enjoyed math or baseball because they were specially good at it, and I decided I had a special gift, too, which I was entitled to enjoy. I suspected that all boys could enjoy masturbating, but I knew how to accentuate the pleasure through fantasies and games."

Step 2. Shared Pleasure With a Chum Interpreted

"I was about eleven before I had a friend I could trust with my marvelous secret," says Adams. "We had played around with little girls until they got old enough to know the facts of life, but then sex play with each other was all we had, even when we were fourteen and fifteen and really hot for it. So I taught my chum types of sex play which were as much fun, as exciting, as doing it with girls." Adams tells of his excitement with his young friend's body, which was fresh, healthy, and physically attractive, but says: "He wasn't as good as I was at psychic games. We enjoyed cruising the girls, playing strip poker, wrestling and teasing each other, but I could arouse him simply by staring at him, a look and a smile could affect him sexually as much as a genital touch. I still often play that game of drawing a strange boy to me simply by staring at him. We played seduction games, too, with ourselves and other boys." If one defined pederasty as the deliberate seduction or molestation of young boys, then most pederasty would be an activity of young teen-agers. Indeed, a high percentage of practicing pederasts limit their sexual activity to boys who have already been seduced by other boys. Even though a sexually experienced boy is more vulnerable to sexual involvement with a man, attitudes developed in conversations with other boys may still be crucial to the development of pederastic tastes. Said one pederast: "I was aware that I could have a lot of fun playing around with boys sexually, but I was shy and afraid, and perhaps I was too moral, until my friend and I began to tease each other with jokes and stories about sex play with boys and men. For example, we passed a note around school which said: 'Never talk while you make love, because it's not polite to talk with your mouth full.' It seemed wrong to fantasize about girls, who were supposed to be kept pure, so we made up jokes and imagined sex play with boys. Soon we were ready to try things we had joked about. We were pointing out the boys we considered to be most attractive: one, for example, whose legs were as pretty as any girl's in the school." Said Adams: "My chum and I decided that there was nothing wrong with masturbation, that it was more fun with someone else, and that it was unhealthy and selfish for me to make love to myself. We decided which were the sexually most attractive boys we knew and made bets as to which of us could seduce them first into mutual masturbation and other sex play."

Step 3: Pleasurable Sex With a Younger Boy

"I was fourteen," Adams said, "when I began a long sexual relationship with my cousin who was a year or so younger. My chum had him first and pointed out how cute he was, but my cousin liked me better. He was very sexy and imaginative in thinking up things to do, so I had more fun with him than with anyone else." The following comments from other pederasts reveal a similar stage in development: "We slept out in the yard in a pup tent all that summer. He came for the first time and couldn't get enough of it. I still tremble sometimes to remember how great it was, each of us discovering how to give pleasure to the other, much more intense than we could accomplish alone." . . . "I'm sure the summer I was thirteen I developed a taste for this type of pleasure which became deeply ingrained. I discovered that there is nothing so marvelous as the responsive body of a young adolescent." . . . "The fantasies I had about what we might have done, had I accepted the invitation to spend the week at his house, may have been more emotional and affecting that anything sexual we might actually have done in bed if I had gone."

It is generally agreed that the impact of a particular sex experience depends to a great extent on the way it is interpreted. For example, a raped girl may rebound with great resilience, both physically and emotionally, unless someone tells her she is "ruined." Much adolescent sex play is simply not interpreted by adults at all, partly because adults—except for some pederasts—know nothing about this secret play. As a result, the child or adolescent is involved in a continuous process of interpreting it for himself, which almost inevitably involves fantasy. He may have healthy fantasies in which he interprets sex play as exploration helping him to understand his sexual experience and as preparation for heterosexual adult life, or because of secrecy or shame he may seek to replace the actual sex play with exciting fantasies or other substitute acts, such as violence. In his case, Adams continued the play, but interpreted it as proof that he was unique or different. His interpretation may make the ladder more attractive for further exploration: "My cousin and I decided that since were were young and didn't know much, there must be even more exciting things to be explored, so he proposed oral sex and enjoyed it so much that he decided we must be 'gay,' although that isn't the word we used in those days. 'We're fags, I guess,' he said. 'I never realized that queers have more fun than other guys.' We argued about it, and I remember insisting that there was nothing queer about it at all, but I was worried enough that I almost immediately started dating girls."

Step 4: Suppression of the Memory and Sex With Girls

"I never found sex with girls disappointing," Adams said, "Just different and hard to get. As soon as I had a steady girl who would let me do it, I forgot all about that 'kid stuff,' and certainly never thought I would be interested in it again." Later he admitted, however, that while having sexual intercourse with his girl, he occasionally remembered how uninhibited his young cousin had been, in contrast to the worry and guilt of his girl friend. Another said: "My first sex with a girl was every bit as good as it was supposed to be, and all I had learned with Freddie was put to good use. I remember thinking to myself that fooling around with Freddie had been O.K. as a way of getting ready for women, but I thought about the fact that Freddie now had a beard and asked myself how I could ever have enjoyed sex with him. I actually found him ugly and repulsive, compared to the sweetness of my girl."

In many of these cases, it would seem that the pederastic taste which had been nurtured by sex play with boys in young adolescence could have been openly acknowledged and discussed. Instead, however, it was repressed in less healthy ways and was thus driven underground where it festered until something in adult life triggered it to surface again in the experience of someone like Adams.

Step 5: Pederast Recall in Adult Situations

Adams was active in sports throughout his middle and late adolescence. While he now recalls admiring the bodies of attractive boys, he was not noticeably aware of it at the time. He was consciously aware, however, of discharging his erotic tensions through body-contact sports—especially with younger boys—and he was highly critical of spectator sports, which so often built up erotic tension without release. He says: "When I was nineteen, little Jim's father asked if I would instruct his son in football, and try to interest him in the sport. The youngster kept hold of my hand when we were introduced and an erotic spark passed between us, which he sensed as well as me. I refused to teach him, because it flashed through my mind that the kid was sexy, cute and sexually experienced. The erotic sensation of his hand holding mine was very worrisome."

Other pederasts report similar flashes of recall: "I hadn't been on the military transport for two weeks before I missed my wife so much I couldn't stand it. I had forgotten how bad it was to be sexy at fourteen or fifteen and seeing other kids have sex fun, until I discovered another sailor in bed with a younger guy. I found it obnoxious but very disturbing, because the gay kid was too old. I bit my tongue when I said to myself: Now if that little sailor was just thirteen or fourteen. . . ." Another said: "In the middle of a thunderstorm the fool kid said he was scared and wanted to get into bed with me. Intuitively, I sensed that the other kids in my cabin had put him up to it to tease a green counselor, but as I turned my flashlight into his face he blushed in a way that reminded me how sexy, how much fun in bed, a kid can be at that age." Another pederast reports emotions at being propositioned at a tourist resort by a boy prostitute who reminded him of a boy he had enjoyed in young adolesence: "Something came surging up in me, maybe habits long forgotten or desires long repressed or simply a beautiful memory of how Joey would do anything I suggested in bed when we were twelve, or a beautiful memory like favorite music I wanted to play again."

Step 6: Erotic Arousal by a Specific Youngster

"I had assumed that once happily married I wouldn't find young boys erotically attractive anymore. I was therefore doubly shocked to realize how aroused I was by a tan-legged kid who turned up in shorts for the first day of Little League baseball. I had to stare at him, shocked that my marriage had been no cure, for this was not the first time since I was married. Some weeks earlier I had been struck by the sight of a kid on the train. I recall the knowing look on the face of the boy in shorts when his eyes met my stare. I had so suppressed the incident on the train that I didn't remember it at all until the boy in shorts started walking toward me. Then a flood of erotic memories flooded my consciousness."

If human beings could be more open and honest with one another, the impact of this sexual experience at the Little League field might have been insignificant for the man involved. He could have joked about it with his wife and friends or could have sought out skilled counsel to assure him that almost anyone can be momentarily troubled and aroused in such a situation, even without troubling memories surging up from his unconscious. In his isolation, however, he had to justify and interpret the experience alone. Another interviewee said: "I said to myself, 'man, I love my wife, but he is something I've been hungry for and I didn't even realize it!" Another reported: "I was at one of those junior military outfits as a visitor, and I was hit with a jab in the crotch when I saw Jerry across the room, for he reminded me of someone I had known. My legs wilted and I almost fainted. I thought it was something I had eaten, but I could hardly keep my eyes off him. My friend noticed it and introduced me to Jerry's father. I blurted out an invitation for him to come and see my boat on the river. He brought Jerry to go fishing the next Saturday, and we were hardly on the boat before the boy asked me to rub suntan oil on his back. His body was overpowering because of what it drew out of me from when I was his age. I was almost fainting again and his fool father was saying: 'I hope a university professor like you can find time to take an interest in a really smart son of a truck driver, because Jerry's smitten with you and I want him to go to college.' "

Step 7: Renewed Awareness of Pleasure in Boy's Company

"The psychiatrist had assured me that those temptations and desires would evaporate in the heat of a good marriage. However, I seemed somehow liberated. The good sex I was having with my wife seemed to turn me on again to all sex pleasure, and I began to dream about boys again. The psychiatrist had said that my dreams showed that my dangerous sex impulses were inhibited and well controlled. I think now that he was wrong. Often when I go to bed at night my sleep is troubled by agitation over boys—more moral than sexual— and during the night my subconscious—or whatever you call it— seems to have worked things out for me while I slept. I'm not attracted to just any boy—mostly I dream about blond kids of about thirteen who are strong and handsome in an athletic way. There is nothing I enjoy so much as watching a boy like that jump with a basketball. Such grace gives me almost as much sexual pleasure as an orgasm. The morning after I had spent a troubled night over a boy I saw at Little League baseball practice, I woke with a sense of peace, and the conviction that there would be nothing wrong with playing sexually with a boy like that as long as he wanted it and enjoyed it. I remember that in my dream I had anal intercourse with that boy—something I had not done since I was fourteen—and in the dream it was a good, happy experience, nothing wrong with it at all. I think maybe my daydreams about boys feed on desires that well up from my subconscious or somewhere, and the fantasies I spin raise problems somewhere in my soul that my subconscious works out while I sleep. My subconscious picks up and elaborates on my daydreams and experiences—like my bedazzlement with that boy—and works them over to give me a point of view, a way of rationalizing that it is O.K. for me to do what I want. I'm sort of mystical about it, too, because sometimes I am attracted to a boy I have seen before, and then I realize that I only saw him in a dream. But he probably looks like someone I had sex with as a kid. It isn't the way he looks that makes me so sure I dreamed about him, but the way he moves. It is the rhythm of bare legs that is so erotic, so irresistible to me." This pederast thus felt that in this way he had worked out a self-interpretation which made it possible for him to understand his erotic experiences with boys, and to justify his sexual behavior with them.

Another pederast reported a similar process in which he rationalized and interpreted his behavior by building on the daydreams and fantasies of his youth: "Good boys don't interest me at all, but a dirty little delinquent who has been arrested many times for stealing can drive me wild, especially if his record indicates that he has been involved in sex offenses also. I was always such a good altar-boy type myself that bored as I was I enjoyed daydreams about bad boys and what they did, especially sexually. I was too moral to do such things myself, but I could enjoy being a voyeur in my dreams. My main experience with bad boys was the way they picked on smaller children, so my fantasies revolved around an older boy who would beat me up and make me do things, such as forcing me to undress a girl and kiss her. As a young teen-ager, and even now as an adult, I am not sexually inhibited with a 'bad' boy or girl, only with good ones. I feel perfectly free to relax and enjoy sex play with a boy who is already sexually delinquent."

Both of these pederasts decided as adults that there was no reason why they should not seek out the company of boys of the type they enjoyed, and while both were aware that their fascination with favorite boys was sexually motivated, they were at this stage convinced that they would limit the erotic experience to talk, watching, and encouraging boys to find happy sexual intercourse with girls.

Step 8: Cultivating Voyeurism and Involvement

"I suppose I've always enjoyed watching boys, but it was an important moment in my adult sexual experience when I became aware of how really pleasurable it is and why. I can spend an erotic afternoon just sitting on a park bench watching young teen-agers play ball and showing off for the girls." Most pederasts stress the importance of this sort of voyeurism at one time or another, and insidiously it seems to lead to more overt sexual involvements. "There is nothing so smashing as watching thirteen-year-olds wrestle, which is why I enjoy coaching. I can tell when two boys are sexually attracted to each other, so I deliberately match them for my own amusement. I have movies of one such pair wrestling, and the film is as sexy as any pornography you can image, when their bodies are flushed from exertion and arousal, the younger one sighs and surrenders as if an orgasm was over." Once such a pederast has decided that boy-watching is his favorite hobby, a next logical step is to organize his life to pursue his hobby, although he is still convinced that his self-control will preclude any illegal acts. "Like any healthy, happy, active boy with a fine-toned body, Charlie was very sexy. I did my best to avoid physical contact with him, because it was becoming clear that boys were going to be a major problem in my life, but I couldn't resist the way he followed me around like a puppy." Another said: "It wasn't enough just to watch boys anymore, so I volunteered to use my station wagon for hauling them to games. There was always some sixteen-year-old crazy to drive, so I could sit in the back with eight or ten of my favorites sprawling all over me." Said another: "I used to hang around the pool to watch, and a divorcee in our block asked if I would take her son along to swim, since I was going anyway. Her son was a cool kid, desperate for a man's affection. He pretended for months that he couldn't swim, so I would hold him in the water to teach him, then he admitted that he did it because he 'loved me.' His mother could not understand then why I was so hesitant to baby-sit when she wanted to leave him with me for a week end."

Step 9: Horseplay With Boys

When is sex play not sex play? A naive, inexperienced middle-class boy or young man may find wrestling and horseplay more sexually stimulating than someone with a different background who has heard so many dirty jokes and has experienced so many sexual gestures that he no longer notices them. Many of the pederasts interviewed were somewhat seduced and misled by the sex talk and gestures of the sexually sophisticated teen-agers they associated with. The man who sat in the back seat of his station wagon, for example, was not prepared to cope with lower-class boys from a radically different sexual culture: "At first the kids were restrained, but after a time, when they see you smile at their antics, they will start groping you like they do each other. Kids from that neighborhood use sex words in every sentence, a sex gesture to illustrate every point. They tell homosexual jokes on each other to provoke fights. They think love means sex, so they ask for your affection with sexual overtures. They make comments like: 'I'm no queer, but I'd sure take my pants down for tickets to the fights,' and the younger boys think the older ones really mean it, so sometimes the younger ones go a step further and one hints privately that if I didn't tell anyone, he would be prepared to exchange sex favors if I would take him on a trip. They then masturbate each other openly and 'moon' passing cars [take down their pants to present their bare bottoms as an insult to passers-by]. It is harder than you might think to keep from slipping into involvement."

Another said: "It is easy to move from semi-sex play into more overt games." He then described the behavior of youngsters in the locker room when unsupervised, and reported on the study made by a non-pederast staff member at a boy's club, who made notes for two months and then reported at a staff meeting on the frequency with which young teen-agers make basically unconscious sexual gestures to men, and which the staff hardly noticed, except for some of the pederast volunteers who were continually dismayed and kept off-balance by behavior to which the staff was immune. One boy, for example, in the course of a month a) sat on a staff member's lap and told a homosexual joke, b) goosed an older boy and told him he "had a cute ass," c) told a fellatio joke to a visitor and asked the man to buy him ice cream and d) told the swimming instructor that his mother had said he could spend the night with him (not true). A pederast member of the staff was so aroused by this behavior that he insisted the boy be given a psychological test, which was done. The boy tested out as a typical, normal boy of his age, a bit more sexually inhibited than most! Observations of other boys over a period of time bore out the psychologist's conclusions, suggesting that a man who is erotically attracted to boys may be more affected by a subliminal awareness of such events than he may consciously realize. If he is close to a boy whose behavior is a bit more sexually curious and experimental, small incidents may add up to a triggering effect upon his desires and emotions. A typical comment: "Watching boys and coaching them in sports seemed innocent enough, but somehow the cumulative effect was an erosion of my inhibitions and self-control." Again, however, it may have been his fantasies about the boys that worked the erosion even more than any behavior, joking, or minor horseplay which the pederast observed. "Long before I ever touched a boy on the team, I was playing with them in the locker-room showers of my imagination, and in my dreams I had worked my temptations through, trying each of them out, so as to come to the point of consent. Since I was convinced we would both enjoy it and find it good, I had already told myself that there was no reason why I should not enjoy myself with a favorite boy when the opportunity presented itself."

Step 11: Incidental Happenings

"Shortly after Charlie's father became paralyzed, his mother asked me to drive him to a swim meet, so he would not miss the event he greatly enjoyed. She said that her sister could put us up overnight there, if I could put up with sharing a bed with Charlie. Our sexual relationship developed so gradually that I can't remember how it happened for sure. At first we simply wrestled in bed, joking and teasing. Then there were more swim meets and trips. . . . It would be a mistake to say that Charlie and I loved each other, but we had a real comradely affection. Charlie was one of those little devils for whom sex play is more like a boxing match than lovemaking. There wasn't a feminine bone in his body. Sex between us was two men enjoying a rough sport together, and it would have shocked us both to hear anyone call it 'queer.' With him I recaptured the fun I had had with my cousin as a young adolescent, partly because Charlie wanted to ask endless questions about sex which he had never been able to talk about with anyone before. I found myself repeating to him, as a philosophy of life and love, the puerile things my cousin and I had decided together when I was fourteen. I realized that nowhere else in my education or reading had I come across any more adequate explanations of the sexual experience Charlie and I were having together. He was worried about being homosexual, and he was reassured because I was married and had children. He wanted to know why it was that anything you enjoy doing is wrong, and I told him that I was more inclined to trust my own body than what other people said who hadn't had the experience."

A pederast with the fictional name of Ben Burden committed suicide after an unusual sexual encounter with a boy. A social worker for the court, Ben was charged one night to care for a near-suicidal, violent, unreachable young criminal who had so disrupted a reform school that he was threatened with the state prison at the age of twelve. The boy was tearing up the room when Ben began hugging him, partly in self-protection. When on impulse he kissed the boy, the young "monster" burst into tears, saying that it was the first time in years that anyone had kissed him. The boy then refused to leave or to go to bed unless he could sleep with Ben. Ben's wife, who was a therapist, encouraged him to indulge the boy, who soon became polite, went willingly to school, and even began to discipline an unruly younger brother and make him shape up. As a result of several subsequent experiences which gained similar success, Ben and his wife discussed the possibility of writing a book about how affectionate sex might be used to help violent and troubled youngsters. When Ben committed suicide he left a note saying: "I'm still convinced that what I did was right in God's eyes."

Step 12: Recurring Sex Play

"I've now had three serious affairs with boys," said one of the pederasts interviewed. "The second boy will soon be twenty and he still comes around once in a while to borrow my car to take his girl out, when his own car won't go. I've helped him some with his college expenses, have found him summer jobs, and he says he's going to name his first baby for me. My current boy is the most turned-on sexually of any kid I've ever known. He's all boy, but he's wild in bed, with his friends as well as with me. It is fascinating to watch him go at it with another boy. If you don't believe me I can show you home movies where it is all written honestly in their expressions. Kids love sex and become joyous when they are sexually happy. I'm not just rationalizing when I say that 90 per cent of the trouble we have with teen-agers is the result of sexual frustrations. When I see a really happy, well-adjusted boy, I say to myself: 'He's getting some good sex somewhere.' As for my new boy, I prefer to judge our relationship by the happiness, contentment and pleasure I see in his eyes, and by the eagerness in his voice when he phones to ask when we can get together. Across a wide generation gap he loves his uptight father, but he also thinks it funny that his dad is so uptight about sex." One can note a gradually shifting in position from first to the third of the boys he has been sexually involved with since he made a decision to be less inhibited. He says: "It seems to me that boys are getting less and less inhibited these days," when, in fact, he is perhaps saying something about himself. "I find that I have fewer fantasies these days, perhaps because I do not need dreams as substitutes for the real thing." Because he is less troubled by his desires and behavior, he is also more careless, although he might not have been arrested had it not been that his boy was increasingly promiscuous with other boys, and his behavior had become the subject of comment in the community.

Step 13: Reconsidering

The quotations above are from the only one of the interviewed pederasts to be arrested during that time. Despite the scandal he did not lose his job, in part because he began therapy with a psychiatrist at the suggestion of the court and his friends. "I've been to psychiatrists at two points in my life," he says. "The first one, before I was married, said there was nothing wrong with me that a happy marriage wouldn't cure. He was wrong. The second said that he was sure I didn't want to be cured of anything, and that he couldn't change a patient who is happy with himself as he is. He further said that he couldn't in any case, probably, cure my pederasty (he didn't use that word) without altering my personality dangerously. What he did offer to do was to help me re-establish self-control, and also help turn my interests toward gay boys of a legal age so I could avoid trouble with the law. I told him I was only interested in heterosexual boys of the he-man type I am: football players, mountain-climbers, sea-divers, and he said I could find gay boys like that. He has helped me do a lot of rethinking of my situation. I really didn't mean to get sexually involved with boys, and with my wife's help I think that won't happen anymore. However, I haven't the least intention of giving up boys and sports. I wouldn't want to live at all on any other terms." He was shaken by the impact on his family, friends, and community of the fact that his sexual experiences with boys had gone further than he had intended. At the same time he was personally convinced that there was nothing wrong with mutual masturbation—just as he feels there is nothing wrong with smoking marijuana—except that it is against

the law. Some other pederasts reconsider their sexual involvement
with boys when an affair turns out unhappily. "He had reached the
age when I knew we had to break up, but I thought we could still be
friends," one said. "So it hurt me when he refused to write to me from
Florida. I decided that if I had hurt his feelings I'd make sure not to
get involved with another boy. I kept that resolution for a month,
until a boy came to my door selling soap. He was such a great kid that I
told him I'd buy all of his soap if he'd come in and play cards with me."

SOME CONCLUDING OBSERVATIONS

● Crucial questions suggested by this ladder revolve around the
nature of the sexual experience men and boys have together, and the
impact upon attitudes and emotions when much of that experience
involves fantasy and games which are substitutes for coitus. A society
which denies coitus with females to developing boys should not be
surprised at their fantasies and substitute experiences. Of all the sex
offender groups in prison, the pederasts show the highest percentage
of masturbation before puberty (57%), and the largest percentage
involved in pre-pubertal sex play (84%), which for 57 per cent continued three or more years. The majority were involved in sex play
with both boys and girls, many with oral and anal experience. This
evidence from Gebhard[1] leads one to speculate that a very strong sex
drive, as indicated by the frequency of masturbation, which develops
before society makes provision for heterosexual activity is a major
factor in pederasty.

● The same Gebhard study points out that pederasts as youngsters had been engaged in the highest percentage of sex fantasies
when boys, and were more frequently involved as youngsters in
imagining sex play with other boys than other types of sex offenders.
Hatterer[2] suggests that such play is damaging if it becomes pro-
longed, intense, and passionate—thus marking habits and personality. Gebhard points out that in comparing pederasts in prison to other
types of offenders the most striking fact is the sudden decline in the
percentage of heterosexual activity among pederasts at about age 15:
"*Something disastrous to their heterosexual ability must have taken
place between their twelfth and fifteenth year of life*" (my italics). It is a
striking fact that these pederast offenders participated in a great deal
of sex play to the point of orgasm in this period of early adolescence,
half of them remembering more than 45 such orgasms a year from
puberty on. During this same period many of them established a

pattern of sexual adventurism with both boys and girls, and found sexual experience with young boys to be highly pleasurable. This runs counter to the theory that boys are seduced by men into homosexuality, and if pederasts are indeed seducers they do most of their seducing of boys when they are still young adolescents themselves.

• A Catholic theologian[3] has suggested that every person must be helped to deal with his "potential for homosexual desires, fantasies and experience." He implies that Americans are ill-equipped to deal with the fact that our "procreation-oriented, anti-sex-pleasure system leaves most people powerless to deal with their own sexual impulses"—which is why it is so difficult to handle pederast acitivity intelligently. It may be true that much of the emotional anti-gay, anti-sex-pleasure emotion in Western society is rooted in what Vanggaard calls "every man's suppressed pederast desires." It would seem that much more information about fantasies—especially in adolescence—is needed if we are to gain a satisfactory insight into pederasty.

CHAPTER 4

Why Do They?

Each pederast's ladder into the underground consists of different experiences. As we peer down into the chasm of possible arrest, prison, or disgrace, we ask why some people are there, while others with the same inclinations are not. Intelligent, well-educated pederasts sometimes attempt a step-by-step analysis of the sexual experiences and fantasies which seem related to their motivation. Psychologists and social scientists have other, differing perspectives on the drives, instincts, unconscious incentives, and reinforcements involved. They will frequently differ with pederasts over the extent to which there is indeed any sort of biological cause or nature which predetermines such sexual preferences. Our purpose here, however, is to listen to the pederast as he explains why he is in the underground. By the time these human beings are conscious of being pederasts, many of them are convinced that they have a nature which they did not choose and which was bred into them by outside forces, but a majority of these same pederasts say they would not change that basic nature and personality if they could. To do so, many of them say, would be like giving up life itself. It is true that at times of humiliation and repentance following arrest, resolutions are often made to change life-style, habits, and illegal behavior, but for the most part pederasts seek to do so by legal substitute behavior. For example, said one: "I can avoid sex contact with boys by enjoying my pictures, my memories, my fantasies and voyeurism."

When reflective pederasts discuss their nature, most of them tend to lose interest in causes of pederasty, even when the examination of their own experience suggests that their pederasty is learned and is socially reinforced.

In the last chapter we found some clues as to how practicing pederasts may move from desires and temptations into actual sexual involvement with boys. At the heart of the question of motivation, however, lies a more basic question: What causes some men to experience a strong sexual attraction to, and desire for, young teen-age boys?

GENETIC BASIS FOR PEDERASTY?

"If you want to understand my emotions," said one pederast, "imagine laws against sexual intercourse between men and women. Would the threat of prison prevent it?" Genetic research is not yet able to say conclusively whether or not there is some combination of genetic factors which may affect sexual preferences. Why are some men attracted to fat women, and others to pubescent boys? There may be genetic factors influencing delinquency, and there are differences in sexual capacity, sensitivity, and gender which are genetic. Genetically based chemical processes cause sexual heat in animals and human beings. A European pederast writes: "My cousin and I have been aware of each other's innate tendencies from an early age. He has become a geneticist precisely to research why it is that as early as we can remember he has been gay. He always wanted to be with men, so his father assumed that meant he was going to be heterosexual. I wanted to follow along with older boys. I tormented every young teen-age boy I knew to provoke him into hitting me, for that was better than being ignored or having no physical contact at all. I was attracted to them like a bee to honey, or as animals are sexually attracted to each other. Gide wrote a book[1] describing male-male sex play among animals to deduce that pederasty is a natural phenomenon. Something similar to pederasty exists between older and younger baboons, and may be at the basis of all male friendship and therefore a foundation for human society.[2] A psychiatrist points out that men and older boys instinctively use sexual gestures similar to those of animals to put down and discipline younger boys who easily fall into the same authority-submission patterns that characterize the younger ape when threatened by a stronger male. Such sexual gestures, symbolic in their human intent and meaning, have a pederast pedagogic role which is innate in masculine society. Tendencies to respond erotically also seem to surge up in men and boys in situations involving corporal punishment. This suggests that research into sexual experience which is not primarily on the male-female procreation model, will reveal innate tendencies and desires for sexual pleasure which may naturally be expressed in play as well as in coitus. Perhaps my cousin was conditioned to be gay as an infant or through other experiences, whereas perhaps I was conditioned or scripted from infancy to find adolescent boys erotically attractive. In either case, however, there had to be something there in the first place to be conditioned. My body responds with joy to certain types of physical contact, in mutual masturbation for example, which seems as natural, innate, and genetically determined as coitus."

PHYSIOLOGICAL BASIS OF PEDERASTY

Those who assert that they have an innate "pederast nature" have varied opinions as to what it is they were born with, but before reporting the views of those who understand their deviancy as socially created, we note certain views which are unusual. One pederast, mentioning Burton's view that pederasty is "popular, endemic, held at the worst to be a mere peccadillo in certain climates,"[3] speculates that the body's chemistry may be upset by the sun's rays or the pull of the moon. He doubts it, and suggests that his body's chemistry was upset by the charms of what Cocteau calls the "third sex," something radiated by what Voltaire described as the "freshness, intensity and sweetness" of the pubescent boy during the period when he resembles "a beautiful girl for the space of two or three years."[4] This same pederast asserts that his body chemistry is continually affected by a sort of musk which some boys radiate much more powerfully than others. It is especially noticeable, he says, not merely when a boy is sexually aroused, but especially in boys who are sexually aroused by men. "If it is merely my imagination, why am I not equally attracted to another boy of equal charm? Is the heightened erotic appeal of a woman to the man who senses that she desires him purely psychological?" Another said: "A boy who is sexually experienced is fascinating, one who is sexually aroused is exciting, but one who desires me is irresistible. Isn't my chemistry involved in that?"

In the last generation an Italian physician[5] conducted a thorough study of man-boy sexual intercourse, giving physiological examinations to hundreds of boys and men who were pederastically involved. He concluded that there is a vast difference between males in their capacity for sexual pleasure with each other, especially in the intensity of eroticism in various erogenous zones. The psychological factors were so complex as to suggest wide and unique varieties of experience; for example, some males find it quite painful to be sodomized and get no pleasure from it, while others have a physiological capacity and anal sensitivity that makes anal intercourse highly pleasurable and exciting to them. He found this to be especially true of many young adolescents, although in a high percentage of cases the capacity began to disappear by the time the boys were fifteen. He further found that this capacity for anal eroticism could be enhanced and sustained if it was cultivated from infancy, as in ancient Greece.[6] One type of gay-homosexuality may result from a conditioning or psychic nurturing of this capacity. Several European pederasts have pointed out that they seem to be able to sense which boys have such erotic sensibilities, and are attracted to such youngsters—especially those who have been awakened to the pleasures of oral sex and are eager to be fellated. One of these pederasts notes: "I was that kind of boy myself. It hardly seems fair but some youngsters are more highly attuned or tunable to pleasure because of the potential they have for nerve and muscle response. My erotic sensations were simply marvelous when I was a young adolescent and I am still powerfully attracted to a boy who has such sensitivities. Sometimes I can tell just by shaking hands with a boy that he is one of those special creatures who, perhaps because he is less inhibited or because he has gifts like those of a musician who gets more out of a symphony, has greater erotic capacities. As for me, I was highly sexed and was so high-tuned erotically in my thirteenth year that I was more than ready for any and all sexual experiences. I could tell instinctively which men—I suppose they were pederasts—'knew' somehow, as soon as we met. How can you say this is against nature? Well, I suppose all that is most human—such as anesthesia and equality—is against nature; but I doubt if it is against nature to enjoy one's honest physiological capacities."

ORAL /ANAL FIXATION

One's human nature is formed in infancy, with both nature and society as partners in the creation of personality. It is only to be expected, therefore, that many pederasts—and especially those who trace their inclination to very early childhood—should propose a cluster of theories around Freudian concepts, seeing sexual preferences as shaped by the way a child is handled at the oral and anal stages of his infant development.[7] Early influences no doubt shape sexual tastes just as they do food preferences. It may well be that the newborn infant is a blank page upon which parents and relatives, as well as other societal influences, early write the script which determines sexual development. Oral and anal eroticism may well be kept alive and cultivated by regular caressing in infancy and throughout childhood, much as Greek slaves were sometimes eroticized from infancy. In some societies mothers and grandmothers deliberately sooth a crying or troubled child with such genital caresses. No pederasts questioned could discover if such was the case in their own infancy. Nor, in retrospect, can they understand the dynamics of family emotions which might have influenced the development of their sexual inclinations and preferences at such an early age.

One pederast writes: "Freud makes sense to me, not so much intellectually, as in my bones." Another says: "I was too early aware of being erotically aroused by boys to accept any theory of pederasty that is not rooted in infancy or very early childhood. Why should society blame me or punish me for having a nature and overpowering desires which developed so young? Even before I went to school I was erotically sensitive to boys who were in the first flush of puberty, especially when they were aroused sexually. When I was three or four I had a crush on an uncle who at that time was about fourteen. I am told that he and I greatly enjoyed each other earlier than I can remember. Isn't there a kind of imprinting—the process by which a chick raised with ducks may come to think he is a duck—at crucial formative emotional moments, perhaps when an infant is sexually aroused? I don't know whether my young uncle played with me sexually or not, but he certainly was the subject of my earliest erotic fantasies. It may well be that I am still attracted to boys who remind me of him."

Sexual experience begins early and many pederasts report discovering erotic pleasures of narcotic quality at a very tender age. Some of them feel that they were "liberated youngsters" who were not so inhibited as to be unable to enjoy themselves sexually from a very early age.

FIXATION AT EARLY ADOLESCENCE

In a book on education which discusses how adolescent boys often provide subconscious erotic problems for male teachers, Friedenberg[8] attributes this kind of pederasty to a "subject eroticism," which leads a man to view a boy as an extension of himself.

Such a man identifies "with them in their growing capacity to love women . . . often taking delight in their young friends' marriages." Such a man feels tender and protective feelings for boys, unless "it is contaminated with a good deal of self-hatred." Such pederasts—one of whom describes himself as having "twisted paternal feelings" for some reason—are in no way effeminate. Rather, their erotic attraction to boys is a jealousy of youth and sexual vitality, leading such pederasts to love "the boy in themselves and themselves as a boy." Such men generally make excellent teachers, although in some cases when this erotic attraction to boys exists at a subliminal level of awareness, the homosexual taboos of Western society tend to turn it into an impatience with the aggressive and boisterous behavior of youngsters. Friedenberg says that sexuality in an attractive and vital boy can provide a double threat to an adult man. The boy's capacity for pleasure stimulates the man's repressed sexuality, and if the boy has sexual problems—as most adolescents do—the sympathy of a concerned and affectionate man may well cause sexual arousal.

One pederast said: "When I love a pubescent boy I am really loving myself at that age, remembering my pleasure then, and the memory of that excitement makes him erotically attractive to me. I love to watch a boy who is stirred by a girl and in my imagination to share his thoughts and emotions. I am moved to help him fulfill the potential for intense feeling which I have, maybe as a result of infant preconditioning which made me vulnerable and susceptible to an intensely erotic emotional experience at puberty or shortly thereafter, but I think something happened to me at puberty to freeze my development at that age, and has led me ever since to be fascinated by a boy in erotic bloom. I love to relive my own pubescent experience over and over."

Another said: "I have no memory of any erotic attraction to a boy before puberty. I was, however, sexually precocious. I was erotically aroused by girls when I was five and six. When I was nine I had coitus with a little girl. I read in books that I was too young for it to be possible, but it was highly pleasurable and successful. I was fascinated by the way the girl—she could not have been more than six—enjoyed it. At puberty I began to enjoy and be fascinated with the way boys enjoyed their sexuality, just as that little girl had, and I'm still touched and charmed by young boys who are erotically aroused and excited. I'm not interested in their genitals so much as I enjoy the sort of aura of pleasure that hangs over a boy, especially the flush of anticipation." Another wrote, commenting on Friedenberg:

"I can understand how a gay-homosexual is responsive to the arousal of another male, but why should a man like me, with all of my interest in women, also be attracted to young teen-agers? If it is their sexual vitality and capacity, shouldn't I be more aroused by older teen-agers? No, I can almost tell you the day and hour when I became a pederast. In my pubescence, around the time of my first ejaculation when I should have been wilting at the sight of a cute girl (which might have happened if girls had been undressing in view?), I saw a thirteen-year-old boy undressing to put on his gym shorts. I was so enthralled by the experience of his bodily charm that I followed him for days, hardly eating, neglecting my schoolwork to daydream about how to find excuses to touch him. Perhaps it would have been a passing moment if I had actually tried a sex contact, for when I finally did find an excuse to put my hand on his bare back it was highly disappointing. By then, however, my fantasies about him, which had for some months concentrated all of my erotic emotion around my masturbation upon that enthralling boy, had become so erotically powerful that I was spying on boys and dreaming only about boys. I wish I had a picture of him, for I'm sure he was in no way as good-looking as I remember. It was my own erotic imagination that turned him into the demon that has haunted my erotic dreams ever since. At that highly impressionable age my erotic sensibilities were irreparably grooved and seared by his impact upon me or—no, by my own experience of him."

SOCIALLY PRODUCED NEUROSIS

Ollendorff[9] suggests that among the Trobriand Islanders the erotic potential of each child is conditioned by that society to move normally into heterosexual channels because little boys are allowed erotic play with little girls without any prohibitions or anxiety. The boy who has an active sex life with girls from a young age, he says, along with warm and supportive understanding from adults, does not need to develop substitute fantasies, neuroses, or sexual deviance. When this heterosexual experience does not evolve naturally and freely a person's sexual orientation and preferences can be redirected as suggested by the following cases: One pederast said: "I grew up in a family, neighborhood and society which failed to encourage my normal sexual development. As a result, as I see it, I was given the wrong erotic diet as a child and I grew up with a sweet tooth which I can't escape now, even if it endangers my health. I refer, of course, to secret types of sex play which developed habits and inclinations which society now tells me are wrong." Another says: "I am a pederast because I had spent so much of my youth in reform schools where, in isolation from girls when I was sixteen, seventeen and older, the younger boys became more and more attractive erotically. I see now that many teen-agers grow up influenced by sex starvation more than anyone seems to notice." Another said: "If I'm neurotic— and I guess everyone is in modern society—the attraction I feel for boys is clearly the result of my being raised to view all sex as dirty and sinful. An anti-sex society twisted my erotic desires out of their normal shape, so that my preferences found new channels when what should have been permitted was forbidden."

Another pederast said: "My psychiatric training and analysis gives me confidence that I was an average and normal boy, perhaps a bit sexier than most, which caused me to chase girls more and younger than most. Because I was over and over punished for sexual overtures to girls, and was made to feel guilty for sexual thoughts about girls, after puberty I turned to boys my own age to meet my sexual needs. I found that boys could be great fun—especially young teen-agers, who, before their growing spurt, could be as erotically charming as girls. Evidently through this happy sex play with boys I confirmed some polymorphous tastes, continuing and keeping alive the tendency in all of us to have diverse normal sexual interests and capacities. Few young people are allowed to grow in sexually healthy ways, and as we are all moulded by society, I evidently got put in the wrong mould—that of a pederast."

SEDUCTION BY OTHER BOYS

Whether or not any man has a "pederast nature," the important question of motivation remains. Why does he choose to take the exploratory steps into the underground by engaging in illegal sex play? In court a judge usually takes into account a person's motives for perpetrating a crime; the assumption being that each man is responsible for his "nature" and his actions. Yet our evidence suggests that a high percentage of pederasts began their illegal activity before they understood the consequences. Society, too, recognizes this fact in a sense by its concern over protecting adolescent boys by law from homosexual seduction, on the assumption that a youngster can be "damaged" as a result of such sexual experience—indeed, that a youngster might be given a second "nature" which is antisocial. What has often been overlooked in debates on such law is the fact that most young adolescents who are seduced into homosexual activity are not seduced by men, but by other boys. A psychiatric study of juvenile experience found that homosexual play is a "mass occurrence" which is "apt to produce major adjustment problems for practically everybody" as a result of "undissolved latent homosexuality in the make-up and conduct of our western civilized life," since "the real problem is the mutual seduction of juveniles by other juveniles."[10]

Our evidence certainly supports that thesis. Not only are the boys who become sexually involved with men most likely to be those previously involved sexually with other boys, but it may well be that a basic cause of pederasty—insofar as we accept the notion that sexual preferences, habits and behavior are learned—is to be found in the sexual experience an older adolescent has with a younger one. The older boy is "seduced" into pederasty by the pleasure he finds in sex play with younger boys in mid-adolescence. This learning is reinforced during older adolescence and into adulthood by the "fantasy replay" of these erotic experiences as well as through "recurring emotional experiences coupled with masturbation, mutual masturbation and other self-seducing activity. For example, one pederast said: "I might have become gay had I continued to sleep with boys my own age as I grew older. I don't know. But I am sure that my pederast inclinations developed through the continuing, highly pleasurable active male-role sexual intercourse I had with younger boys in the all-male boarding school I attended. Maybe a younger boy can become gay by playing a feminine role for a long time during his adolescence, especially if emotions run high. I've seen such cases. But I was aggressive in seducing young boys and it was a highly satisfying erotic game. I have a good marriage, but these inclinations continue to pop up once in a while, especially when I meet the kind of lovely, well-bred younger kid I slept with when I was seventeen. My spine still tingles to remember the magic of that experience."

FANTASY INTERPRETATION OF EXPERIENCE:
SELF-SEDUCTION

Whether the body writes the scenario for the development of sexual inclinations or whether it is written by parents, society, one's peers or oneself, some combination of various factors comes into play to shape erotic preferences and tastes. Whatever those factors are, each person has the task of integrating his experience, of discovering his sexual nature and identity, and of coming to an understanding of his sexuality which makes sense in terms of his possibilities. When one seeks to compare as the cause of their pederasty these different theories which different subjects propose, one finds that each hypothesis may have merit for a particular case. Instead of choosing among them, perhaps one must seek some complex combination of causes, with clues as to the nature of a specific individual being related to his own interpretation of his erotic experience through fantasy and how he understands the explanations of other persons. One pederast said: "It is a mistake to assume that all human beings are the same. If there are five different models for sexual normality: subjective, moralistic, cultural, statistical, and clinical, how am I to define it?" Another wrote: "I resonate to the suggestion that a boy does not so much learn pleasure through sex play, as that if his imagination is lively enough, he fails to repress it as society expects. Through my own imaginative experience I cultivated my own erotic potential, and society ought to encourage the development of each youngster's sexual powers and eroticism, just as cultivation of his mind and calisthenics for his body are encouraged. My profession gives me many opportunities to observe how society inhibits the creative potential of many kids by stultifying their eroticism, which ought to flower to stimulate creativity and imagination. How do I explain my pederast inclinations? Society failed to interpret my sexual pleasure to me when I was young, so I developed my own explanations and interpretations. Despite the rumors I heard, I found out through my own experimentation that sex play with other boys was fun and good. Through my own imaginative fantasies I made a place for such play within my philosophy of life, and free from inhibitions I had a series of delightful sexual experiences in adolescence which I integrated into my personality and self-understanding as they occurred, one by one—some with boys and some with girls. Although I found the female delights were most enchanting, I was not completely wooed away from boys because by then I had already incoporated into my personality and self-definition a kind of bisexuality and philosophy of sex freedom which motivated me to enjoy any and all sexual opportunities that presented themselves. Can anyone doubt that in all areas of experience the tastes we develop when we are young remain with us for all our lives? And tastes are not merely developed through experience, but also through what one hears said about that experience, and how one is led to interpret it."

THE SEDUCTIVE LURE OF NEW EXPERIENCE

If some pederasts are "eternal adolescents" in their erotic life, even more of them seem to be adolescent in their hunger for adventure and their desire for new experience. It is not just in their erotic experience that they are adventurers. Among pederasts interviewed were many who still go on motorcycle exploration of jungles, sky diving, and so forth, even though they are now old men. For some pederasts the quest for dangerous adventure may be another substitute for the forbidden sexual activity which they desire, but for others, sexual adventurism seems to be an aspect of a larger curiosity about life itself. One said: "I'm simply the kind of person that cannot be contained in the restricting institutions of dull, ordinary life, sexual or otherwise. My spirit is too large for that. My wife well understands my need to roam."

Another pederast wrote: "You asked what triggered my first sex play with a boy, after years of adult self-control? I would never have become involved in sex play as an adult if it hadn't been for an overpowering curiosity. It had always been my intention—aware as I was of the erotic appeal of boys—to substitute fantasy and imaginary experiences for the real thing. Perhaps I wasn't so foolish as to think that fantasy would satisfy me forever, for in every other aspect of life I must make sure that my fantasies are really based in reality, on sound experience. I have had to try everything once, so that I could have authentic dreams, so when a friend introduced me to a promiscuous boy, and told me how much fun he was in bed, I simply had to try it. Since then, from time to time, I get curious again when such an opportunity presents itself. I wonder if it would be different with this black boy or with an older one, or... they are all so different. Curiosity is the force therefore which motivated me the first time, and which still triggers the desire from time to time since."

THE LURE OF AFFECTION

Whatever later motivations and behavior there may have been, a vast majority of pederasts said that initially they became involved in sex play with a boy because of affection. There are obvious differences between the experience of single and married men. A single man in his late forties said: "I spend a lot of time with boys because I am lonely. There is this boy I taught to box, who has no father and who is as lonesome as me. I feel no lust, and nothing very illegal has happened between us, but something erotic, nurtured by our affection, keeps demanding more intimate expression. If I do the moral thing and end our relationship before it is too late, it will break his heart and mine." A married man, by contrast, said: "The word 'love' so quickly and easily comes to the lips of kids today. They 'love' cars and hamburgers, so I must be cynical when a boy says he loves me, especially when I've just let him try to drive my sports car and he is experiencing hero worship. Such a boy said to me: 'You're the first person I've ever loved because I wanted to," and then, to prove it, he hit me, which is approved affectionate physical contact at his age. I hit him back and he sparred with me, to hide the fact that he really wanted me to put my arm around him. There's nothing romantic in our love, but I can't resist the way he feels and the way he makes me feel." Another pederast contrasted his love for his wife and the "lure of affection" he felt for a boy: "I agree with Eglinton who quotes Henry Stack Sullivan's definition of love as 'that state of affectional rapport in which someone else's satisfactions become spontaneously as important' to me as my own. Sullivan also said that a boy's first such affectional relationship is generally with someone of his own sex, and is a normal step towards healthy sex with females. It is more harmful in my view to refuse sexual pleasure to a youngster than to indulge him. I think adolescents must have sexual freedom to heal the damage done by the notion that sex is dirty. It is really sinful for persons who work with kids to shame and refuse their affectionate gestures. Nor will I refuse to reach out to a boy when my heart says it is right."

LURE OF EROTIC PLEASURE

When all the reasons given for sex play with boys are examined, one basic motivation emerges: need and desire for erotic pleasure. Sexual needs and desires are normally met by women, even among half of the pederasts interviewed. So when one examines the pederast experience, one uncovers a desire for unusual and exotic experience. One pederast said: "To say that I am foolish for enjoying what I do fails to take account of powerful, nonrational desires. There's no accounting for a person's tastes. It is foolish to smoke, knowing what we do about lung cancer, and certainly smoking is as abnormal as deviant sex play. Perhaps it is even more foolish to drink alcohol. Those who passed the prohibition laws were right that society would be better off if people were self-disciplined and were devoted to work rather than imbibing, but I love alcohol, tobacco and boys. I'm no alcoholic. I'm really not addicted to any of the three, but frankly I feel like someone who has discovered fine wines in a society that approves only of drinking fruit juice. Erotically, as in everything else, my world is full of a rich variety of experiences, sexually and otherwise, and I trust my own taste in sex as in other things." Another said: "For some people the first bite of fudge creates an almost irrepressible desire for a second piece, especially by people who are overweight. My adolescent experience with certain types of sex play was like that, and still is. That is, whenever I encounter a boy who has a reputation for enjoying such play, I find myself like a hungry man on a desert island. Otherwise I scrupulously keep my hands off boys, until I smell that 'fudge.' I don't want to involve a boy in a guilt trip, so I want to avoid even mutual masturbation by rough play, teasing, games. I don't think there is anything wrong with masturbation, however. Two prep-school boys who soap each other off in the shower and playfully relieve each other's tensions may have more common sense about sex than all the psychologists; and the same experience with a man can confirm a boy's masculinity and assuage his homosexual fears. I confess my idea of heaven is an eternity of soaping off boys in a warm shower."

Another said: "Once a boy feels free to let go and enjoy himself, he is infectious and irresistibly so. Boys are satyrs, insatiable, full of fire—I know, I've been burned often enough. A young teenager's joy in sex play is probably more like what life is meant to be than all the stock markets and assembly lines. Someone criticized me by saying: 'But you just play at sex, you aren't taking it seriously.' Not so. I don't just play at life, I live to play, to enjoy myself. Most people are cruelly tortured and unhappy in the psychological chastity belts that society imposes on kids; and when a boy comes to a man to ask sex questions, what he really wants to know is how to get out of that belt! He wants someone to tell him it is all right to have some fun and to show him how. Society's view that I corrupt boys is entirely false. I just open the trap and let them out. They always teach me twice as much about sex as I can teach them. Once free, their imagination soars and they think of erotic games that astonish even me. I haven't the capacity to resist such fun even when I decide to do so. Society plays sex games with me all the time, in novels, films, advertising, and many of society's games are more unhealthy than the fun I have with my boy. Someone, who obviously didn't know what he was talking about, asked if it wasn't a mistake for me to let him get sexually jaded so young. Jaded? Enjoyable sex doesn't jade one's appetite any more than a regular diet of good food. All I really do, in any case, is to whet his appetite. I'm not making him queer, I'm just enhancing his sensitivities so he can enjoy life and women. If you want to envy someone, envy the girl he's about ready for. What a lover she's going to have!"

NEGATIVE MOTIVATION: WHO CARES?

As one reviews the seemingly endless variety of reasons and excuses given to justify pederasty, there is a good deal of difference between men who have been arrested and those who have not. Persons whose lives have been radically altered by arrest may no longer care about their reputation and may more openly join pederast groups because they no longer have much to lose. For example, one pederast said: "My first offense was almost accidental, and I set out to make a serious effort to reform my life, which the court aided by giving me a suspended sentence. I found, however, that my career was ruined by the publicity. A felony record made it impossible for me to do the sort of work I enjoyed and was prepared for. I tried working as a salesman and failed. My probation officer wanted me to work as an elevator operator, and what I am now doing is as much a waste of my graduate school education. Since my life is over, I might as well do what I enjoy sexually. It's all I have left. If I go to prison what would that matter? It was a mistake for me to try to reform my life. I guess I have the criminal mentality now, for I see that the only way for me to live is to be clever and not get caught." Another one who had served a prison term said: "A friend of mine in England was arrested for a much worse offense than mine in the eyes of the courts. He was given a three months' suspended sentence and protection from publicity, if he would go into therapy. Because I had a tax-financed education in deviant sex at a juvenile correctional school— which they called a 'criminal record,' I was clobbered with a long prison sentence with no help at all. The judge said I was sick, but he didn't send me to any hospital or offer any cure. Instead he treated me like an animal. They all did. All the time I was in prison I made plans about the kids I was going to have when I got out. Working for the syndicate as I do, I have all the protection I need, and all the cute kids I want to sleep with. Society made me what I am so I might as well enjoy it!"

CRIMINAL MOTIVATION: RAGE

A number of pederasts with Houston connections have discussed the case of Dean Corll, who sexually abused and murdered many teen-age boys in the Houston area. What motivated him? Was he a pederast? Gay-homosexuals have rushed in to disclaim any relationship between the murders and homosexuality, pointing out that heterosexuality would not have been blamed had he raped and murdered girls. In the pederast context, however, no such easily dismissed implication is possible. Some factors in the case which are circulating as rumors through pederast networks may tend to throw some light on these bizarre and horrible crimes.

Up to the time of the disclosure of the murders, Houston was a city of extensive pederast prostitution, where hundreds of young boys were on the prowl every day to solicit men, largely through hitchhiking.[11] If the Houston police knew, they either ignored it or lacked adequate resources to cope with it, for the problem was so far out of hand that no simple solution was possible. Young boys from Houston hitchhiked to other cities, even as far away as the East and West Coasts, and a good many of them were subjects of pornographic films for sale as far away as Denmark. Some parents were so lax as not to care, and some parents even accepted money for permission to use their sons in pornography. A pederast visitor to Houston could make one phone call and be offered a choice of boys for a night, for a week end, or for a long trip.

Dean Corll, the murderer of many of these boys, was apparently not a sexual adventurer who patronized the amateur boy prostitutes of the city, but was at first simply an arrested-adolescent-type who enjoyed the company of boys. Initially gentle and kind, he was horrified at his discovery that the boys he was fond of were "hustling." His horror, however, was not directed at the boys or their customers, so much as at himself. He was infuriated to the point of rage with boys who sexually aroused him, at his being tempted; for it was typical of people he knew to have a compulsive homophobia which scorned and detested any type of homosexuality as the most vile of sins. To admit even to one's self such homosexual temptations was like admitting that one was a devil. Corll had high moral principles with regard to women and sex, which made his own sexual arousal and temptation by boys even more frightening—as when he tried to lecture a young "hustler" that he had known since the youngster was ten or eleven years old and whom he had always thought of as a sweet and innocent boy. *Stunned* is the right word to use for the changes wrought in Corll's psychological stance when the boy defended his right to take money for deviant sex, and accused Corll of being a "fag" like his customers. Perhaps the boy shouted the accusations out of intuition or perhaps as a weapon to fight back against someone who was much larger. In any case Corll, though perhaps never really a conscious pederast, was wounded by the boy's probing at a sore point. Corll did not know that many men have such temptations and learn to manage and control them. Apparently he became obsessed with the notion that he was "bewitched by evil."

The newspapers suggest that Corll sought out, or sent others to hunt for, innocent boys for his sadist amusements. At first, however, his cunning and rage may have been directed only at boy prostitutes. This explanation of his behavior is considered to be only partly true, however, because it is too simple. If he later began a systematic policy of torturing, shaming, and killing boys he thought to be prostituting themselves this happened only after he had killed the first one more or less accidentally. One rumor says that he had tied the boy up simply to make him tell the truth about which boys had seduced the victim into "hustling." The boy's refusal to blame anyone infuriated Corll and the first killing may have happened when the chair the boy was tied to was knocked over. In any case, once Corll knew himself to be a murderer, his awareness of himself as a "devil" was confirmed. It was then much easier for him to set out deliberately to hunt down and murder the boys he felt to be corrupting innocent youngsters, or those who were 'bewitching' Corll himself.

How, then, could it happen that he also began to murder his young friends? His affection for innocent boys turned into sadistic rage—as a result of the impact of this experience on his personality—whenever he saw signs of behavior which he interpreted as sexually arousing. Corll's mother knew of his indignation about homosexuality and of his disapproval of "sex play for fun," and that he saw red at anything he interpreted as a homosexual overture. As his obsession grew he began to molest boys to see if they were aroused by homosexual acts; for, if so, this would be proof that they were evil and had to be destroyed for the sake of the world and humanity.

Evidently Corll could not cope with his own pederast tendencies and suppressed desires, especially the direction they now took as a result of the torture murders in which he found needed sexual and emotional satisfaction. Yet he kept moving to get away from boys.

Was he running away from his murderous temptations? Or from the more innocent boys he liked and didn't want to involve? When he finally accepted his homosexual tendencies, he made some unsuccessful efforts to relate sexually to adult men, and he evidently continued to blame his homosexuality—his devil character—on the seduction of the young. Had he himself ever been seduced? It is quite probable that he never had any happy or authentically pleasurable sexual intercourse. He was puzzled and sad about that and read a good deal in an effort to understand sex. He was not prepared by education or point of view to accept his pederasty, and nothing he had read or heard helped him accept it and cope with it, so he concluded that he was a "monster." He not only accepted emotionally this self-interpretation but he also acted it out in his murders. His problem, therefore, was not so much homosexuality as being morbidly antihomosexual. His confirmed identity was not "I am queer" or "I am a pederast who is erotically attracted to boys," but "I am a monster and the demon in me can be exorcised only by destroying the corruptors." The process by which he condemned himself was similar to that described by Sartre,[12] who portrayed an adolescent resolved to become "the evil person society says I am." Corll may well have been seduced and motivated by his own homophobia.

SOME CONCLUDING OBSERVATIONS

• Among pederasts interviewed, we found little evidence for the common view that they turn to boys because they can't make it with women by reason of shyness, feelings of inadequacy or impotence, although the range of opinion among pederasts as to motivation is wider than this chapter has suggested. We have omitted some naive theories and some esoteric ones, such as angel-possession. Most of the pederasts who were questioned, however, had concluded that at an age too young for them to have been personally responsible they were overcome by something which radically changed their lives.

• By omitting much data because of lack of space we have lost sight of some complicating factors, such as the difference between the fantasy experience of intellectual pederasts and the rough-play experience of the less-well-educated. It is difficult to clarify the use of fantasy as a substitute for sex play as versus the extent to which fantasy triggers and stimulates actual sexual contact. Fantasy life is not so easily remembered and reported as are sex acts.

• 74 per cent of pederasts in one study were aware of their sexual interest in younger boys by the age of eighteen, indeed 28 per cent were aware of this by the early age of fifteen. Even more striking—whether one is searching for cause or for means of prevention—is the fact that 64 per cent of the pederasts had been sexually involved with a younger boy in their teen-age years, and only a very small percentage of perhaps 8 per cent had their first sexual act with a boy after the age of thirty.

• Most pederasts reported consciousness of a strong erotic attraction to boys long before their first overt physical contact, and in many cases before they had any idea what form of sexual act might take place with a boy. Their first thoughts were often simply of wrestling or games—actions which might not be defined as sexual at all were it not for the accompanying fantasies which stimulated and accentuated genital pleasure.

• Masturbation plays a role in the motivation and triggering process, but there is no evidence that masturbation leads necessarily to deviant acts—indeed, for most boys it is a first step toward normal sexual behavior. Perhaps further study of masturbation fantasies would show a relationship to the progression in pederast experience from mutual masturbation to mutual sex play and games which involve real or imaginary oral or anal experimentation, and the extent to which some boys become addicted to such fantasies as a substitute for coitus.

• For many pederasts, adult involvement with boys is an effort to recapture an experience of erotic pleasure which was so powerful in young adolescence that the memory of it from time to time triggers an irresistible desire to repeat the performance. On the other hand, there are many cases in which the adolescent experience of pederasty was entirely imaginary, and adult experimentation with boys is an effort to see if what was imagined is true, or perhaps to have in adulthood the sexual experience that was denied at an earlier age.

• The factor most often reported as triggering a man to make a specific sexual overture to a boy is his discovery that the boy is sexually aroused, available and experienced—which reminds the pederast of his own sexual arousal at the same age. However, a first incident may also be quite the opposite. In situations where a pederast has great affection for a boy, he may wish to give the youngster his first orgasm and teach him how to enhance the pleasure received in masturbation. The pederast may view this as a type of sex education or as a special gift.

• As our case histories suggest, often there is no one cause for pederasty. The experience of each person is unique in some respects, with a special combination of factors often coming into play. Pederasty probably has more in common with normal heterosexuality than might be perceived at first glance. For example, the reasons a pederast becomes promiscuous are probably not essentially different from the reasons a normal heterosexual young man becomes promiscuous or an adventurer.

CHAPTER 5

Support From Adolescent Culture

What is to be found at the bottom of the ladder? The word *underground* provokes a "kaleidoscope of images":[1] secret societies, publications, illegal political groups. In the course of our exploration of this pederast underground, we will rely heavily on the guidance of three individuals whose stories will be told in detail. In the following chapter, our first guide will point out the structures in the adolescent subcultures which support the pederast underground. Psychological factors may account for a wide range of interior experience and fantasy, but one must look for the social forces which support pederasty in a society which forbids it so strongly by law and the sanctions of public opinion. In later chapters we will examine the support a pederast may receive from other persons in his community, along with the impact of other cultures on Western pederastic experience, but first now—since pederasty cannot exist without consenting boys—it is important to examine in broad perspective the view that the pederast underground has little structure of its own, but is almost completely dependent upon adolescent society.

A TRIBAL SOCIETY OF ADOLESCENTS

Western society today provides two basic supports for pederasty: (a) the increasingly tribal nature of adolescent society, and (b) the conspiratorial secrecy of so many young adolescents, especially on matters of sex. Pederasty thrives not because of "sexual freedom" and "moral laxity," but by quite the contrary because so many adolescents are pushed into rebellion and secrecy by their lack of freedom. Adolescence, of course, is a relatively modern phenomenon in history, especially in its modern form which prolongs immaturity into the twenties for graduate students and others. Earlier and more primitive societies often provided for marriage at the early age of thirteen or fourteen. Since modern adolescents are not integrated into adult society through marriage and careers, they tend increasingly to withdraw from the mainstream into their own subcultures. Some of these are drug and sexual undergrounds. The inhabitants of undergrounds are generally rebels against some or all of the norms of the society, from which they have fled, and a majority of the adolescents of today are rebels against the sexual establishment as they understand it. They resent and reject the unwelcome repression of what they consider to be natural processes and feelings, and their rock music and dancing may well have the same use as did tomtoms in primitive tribes of arousing and expressing tribal emotion and personal frustrations.

Since the pederast underground does not fit into the models society provides for us as we begin our exploration, we must look for a new analogy. It may perhaps be instructive to compare the organization of this underground to the structures and customs of the Lapps—a migrant people in Finland. The Lapp subculture is almost entirely built around the migrating habits and patterns of reindeer herds, which provide nurture for the migrant tribe. Most societies domesticate such animals to serve human needs. The Lapps, however, domesticate their own lives to serve and to follow the reindeer, reminding us of the first rule in seeking the pederast underground: go where the boys are who need help. For insofar as there is a pederast underground it is not only supported and enabled by adolescent subcultures, but also by whatever societal structures there are for shepherding and protecting young adolescents. Pederasts may appear to be outcasts from society, but in fact they frequently live within and take their protective coloration from adolescent groups. The worst pederasts are predators who follow the migrations of adolescents; the best pederasts, motivated by principles of responsibility and service, are most frequently the only men willing to volunteer for the work of shepherding the young, especially the most difficult and obnoxious. It is often pointed out that one has to be the "sort of nut who loves boys" to be willing to put up with them at Boy Scout camps, in junior high school, and in other exhausting positions with young adolescents. What is also largely unstudied is the extent to which such "nuts" are welcomed by many rebellious adolescents into their secret councils and underworld subcultures.

Being no longer integrated into adult society, many adolescent boys are today left to roam in bands during a lengthening adolescent limbo. We should be astonished that they manage their sex lives as well as they do, considering how little positive, constructive help that sort of boy receives from society as a whole. The only advice most such boys get is negative: what not to do. In ancient Sparta the only way a boy could get food was by stealing, with the added proviso that the boy caught stealing food was severely punished. This custom turned boys into cunning and tough soldiers. Western society today feeds its boys well, but punishes them severely if they are caught indulging in sex, which makes many young adolescents sexually cunning and tough. This is true not only of delinquent gangs but also of adolescents in other modern-day tribes, such as sports groups. Pederasts are involved on all three levels of adolescent society: 1) the organizations on the surface which are approved and financed by adults, 2) in the gangs and subcultures which exist just below the surface, and 3) in the adolescent undergrounds which are well out of sight, such as those that organize themselves for prostitution, blackmail, mugging, or exploitation of "queers."

One pederast said of adolescent tribal society: "On the surface such gangs may seem cruel, heartless, aggressive, and phallic as a pack of wolves. But underneath most of the boys in these tribes are sensitive and fragile, with the toughness as a cover for fears, worries, sexual insecurity, and even a good deal of tenderness. If boys share their secret lives with me, it is because they finally come to trust someone, feeling that I am no longer the enemy, because I am willing to play with them on their own terms. The young adolescent is playful, and seductively so if he is healthy and happy. His tribe exists for play. His personality takes shape through play—which is therapeutic, educational, a way the adolescent explores his body, his relationships, his experience and everything which is important to him. There is much play in the sexual experiences of adolescents: courtship games, testing, enticing, pretense, surprises, games to build up sexual tension, a wide variety of psychological games which characterize nonloving or pre-loving erotic relationships. Psychologists caution parents against taking the sex play of small children too seriously, but it is precisely the sex play of young adolescents which should be ignored, instead of shaming it and driving it underground at the very moment it becomes desperately important, and when its interpretation by sympathetic adults is so crucial. In secret or with trusted friends the boy flexes his muscles, explores the erotic zones of his body, acts out emotions and moods. In my judgment it is almost impossible to teach kids in school, or to reach them in their gangs without being open to, and accepting of, their sexual explorations."

This same pederast proceeded to suggest that there is an essentially sexual foundation to adolescent tribal society, from which constructive adult influence is excluded because many boys sense adult disapproval of the private world which they entered when they began masturbating. He continued: "Once in a while a boy invites me into that private world to share his joy and I consider it a precious privilege. I would rather hit him than refuse such a gift. Is there anything more cruel than rejecting the gift a child brings in affection? I consider it unforgivable to shame him and wound him with rejection as most do."

Another pederast spoke of a pederast teacher, who had been effective in penetrating perverse and violent gangs and turning them into more constructive groups: "One of the best men I ever knew, who really helped boys grow up to be fine persons, who scrubbed up their dirty sex lives until they came out O.K. in the end, said that boys caught in masturbation or any other sex play should never be scolded or reprimanded, for it was a holy moment which presented the perfect opportunity for sex education. He would say to a shame-faced gang: 'Go ahead. It's great, isn't it! But first let me tell you something about love and how beautiful it can be with a girl.' He never scorned those dirty jokes they told about merit badges for masturbation, because he seriously argued that kids today need some sex rituals to replace rites of passage which have largely disappeared from modern society."

It would seem from the perspective of those pederasts who have made themselves at home in the adolescent sexual underground that such rites of passage have not really disappeared from modern society. Rather, they have moved underground, since society no longer assumes responsibility for sexual initiation into the adult world. Underground rites of passage often consist of a frank, brutal, and generally incorrect sex education, climaxed with sexual initiations as a precondition to a full adult membership in the adolescent tribe. Said another pederast: "I was embarrassed to discover that my son had to talk a girl out of her panties for such an initiation. In fact, I think it was supposed to be more than that, since when such secrets are revealed one never gets the full truth, not from fourteen-year-olds. He had been forbidden to be involved in that motorcycle club of upper-middle-class kids whose members were sons of professional people for the most part, and who were up to every devilment you could imagine, including initiation into sixty-nine kinds of deviant sex play. They commanded a type of obedience that no father in town could get from a son of that age. They imposed a uniformity of discipline and behavior that would have caused violent protests at school. They copied the Nazis, perhaps unconsciously, right down to the sexual deviance and cruelty which seems to characterize authoritarian adolescent tribes. Some of the eighteen- and nineteen-year-olds in the motorcycle club would have ended up being arrested for serious sexual abuse of younger kids had I not found my way into the group to love some sense into them. One of them said angrily: 'There's not a fag in our bunch. We just tease the younger kids in the shower to teach them to use their fists to defend themselves.' That boy is going to become the macho-type pederast who will never be able to admit the truth to himself, always asserting that all red-blooded boys indulge in homosexual horseplay. He'll still see himself as one of the tribe when he is sixty. His anti-pederasty is another log on the fire of sexual revolt, which at its base is a rebellion of the young against the very condition of their sexual lives at a time when the sexual customs of Western civilization are in a great disarray."

CONSPIRATORIAL SECRECY

Many adolescents have no respect for the law because they feel that its repression of their sex lives makes no sense at all. Some of them get caught up in drugs because of their sexual rebellion, others become involved in criminal activity. Few of them tell the truth about their sexual behavior and experience. One pederast said: "What fascinates me about most young adolescents is the way they know how to live in two worlds at once. Some of them are little angels at home, at school, in Sunday school, at Boy Scout meetings or whenever they are in the presence of the Establishment. Once alone with their tribe they are entirely different kids." There is, of course, a vast difference from state to state, from city to city, and from neighborhood to neighborhood. Goal-oriented middle-class boys are often more open to parents and teachers. However, the conspiratorial secrecy of adolescents on matters of sex and drugs crops up in the least expected places. Even in close-knit families, by mid-adolescence many youngsters are living in a different world from their parents, and they continually lie about sex. For example: "In a junior high school where both pederasts and police attest to the fact that perhaps as high as 90 per cent of the boys have been involved, at least one or two times, in sex play with a man or high-school boy, a careful study of the school and neighborhood was initiated by police-sponsored social scientists, who interviewed every boy in the school, with every possible safeguard and protection for privacy and anonymity. The social scientists reported at the end of their interviews that, while most of the boys were aware that man-boy sex play was common in the community, few of them had personally been involved. Why did the boys lie? In that school on a typical day truancy runs at 10 per cent, and when the boys are absent from school most of them are stealing, using dope, or are engaged in sexual adventuring. So they all lie to protect one another. Sex, drugs, ripping-off cars are not things one ever admits to adults."

Speaking of a similar community another pederast said: "The pederast underground is possible because of this secret adolescent world of sex games and dirty jokes, which facilitates boys in sex play. Man-boy pornography circulates in the schools, even among ten- and eleven-year-olds, and much of it is drawn by the kids themselves. Many of their drawings are clever, even amusing, as are some of the pederastic comic books they prepare, such as Batman-Robin pornography. Since all this takes place in a world which is secret from parents and most adults, it feeds the imagination without adequate interpretation, or it is clarified by the dirty jokes of their peers. Do you want an example? The boy who told this joke said it was not really a dirty joke, but could be told in mixed company! He said that a boy who had consented to go on a boat ride with a man had been sexually abused against his will. When he got ashore he ran to find a policeman and told of all the sex acts he had been forced to perform. The policeman appeared to be sympathetic, so the boy finally exclaimed: 'Well, aren't you going to do something?' Whereupon the policeman replied: 'What else is there to do? You seem to have already done everything in the book.' "

Another pederast said: "Theologians observed the behavior of kids and found confirming evidence of original sin, for until recently sex play between adults and children was fairly common even in Western society.[2] It was considered only natural that adolescent boys would be involved in sex games: some adultery, pinching, suggestive remarks, evenings with prostitutes when a young as thirteen or fourteen. The honest and serious efforts to uplift society succeeded as far as the middle class was concerned, at least in the smaller towns. However, this moral effort also had the effect of driving the playful side of sex underground, leading to double standards and hypocrisy, or to repression and rebellion. In the secret world of the adolescent there was less change than on the surface. Indeed, as sex play became more secret, it became all the more attractive as forbidden fruit. At one time or another many boys become charmed and fascinated to learn that secret worlds exist, and are charmed by reports of pleasure and excitement found by others who dared explore them. Secrecy is not only always enticing but it also breeds even greater secrecy."

This man goes on to point out that it is the boy "who loves a game which involves some danger" who is most likely to become a co-conspirator, who is most likely at least once in his young adolescence to get caught up in sex play with an older teen-ager or a young adult. When a boy takes a step or two down the ladder into an underground things happen in the dark which might never happen in the daylight, and the pederast underground is a very dimly lighted place. It is dimly lighted because adults who should do so "rarely participate in any realistic or effective way in the sex-socialization of youth."[3] An expert on adolescent sexuality points out that most parents and sex educators "find it emotionally impossible to go beyond providing a few biological and reproductive facts,"[4] leaving everything important for the kids to find out for themselves from their peers and by their own experimentation. Most adolescents are in fact lucky in belonging to good tribes, or to tribes that shape up by late adolescence. By then many of them are already "touched by the fire of mysteries which adults seem not to know."[5]

THE HUSTLERS

Adolescent tribalism and secrecy converge at one point to provide the most serious example of how adolescent culture frequently provides the structure for pederasty. No one knows how many boys, as amateur prostitutes, offer themselves to men for money. Two surveys of adolescent sexuality project that of the over six million adolescent boys in the United States aged fifteen years or younger, at least a million of them will engage in sex play with a man for money.[6] The happy hustler is not merely the poor boy who needs money. Often he is the middle-class hitchhiking adventurer or the upper-class runaway, one of the kids who are products of a commercial society where everything is for sale, and of a sexual culture which "shoves kids back underground every time they try to come up for air."[7] It tells them: You are queer if you enjoy masturbation, intercourse with a girl is statutory rape, enjoying youself with your friends is deviant and illegal! So, many boys decide that if it is illegal and punishable anyway, one might as well go for the money. How else explain the impulsive decision of a nice middle-class boy to go hitch-hiking when he hears a warning at school about what might happen? There's a marvelous anonymity to hitchhiking which, from the boy's point of view, fits right in with his decision that he can explore sex, have fun, and earn some money while taking a spine-tingling step down that ladder which others have found so exciting. One pederast has described it thus: "The boy first decided just to hitchhike down to the YMCA and nothing happened, except some friendly conversation and the discovery that hitchhiking is easy. Next, he thumbed a ride out to a lake where a friend had a boat. A nice man went several miles out of his way to take him to the boathouse and offered to pick him up on the way back if he'd like to go to his apartment to see a movie of some girls. "Adult only" films were forbidden to the boy so the opportunity enticed him, with the thought that if the man was inter-ested in girls it ought to be all right. He had been warned that there might be tragic consequences. Young teen-agers sometimes got hurt or killed, but he needed a ride home, stranded as he was at the lake. So by the time the man returned he was waiting impatiently. The tragic consequences? He had the time of his life, more fun than he had ever had before, and his only problem was, from his view, that like his masturbation, he couldn't tell anyone about his new friend, the sexy movies, and his pleasure at being fellated."

SOME CONCLUDING OBSERVATIONS

• The pederast underground is a society dominated by and enabled by the conspiratorial secrecy of juveniles on sexual matters. Paul Goodman's *Growing Up Absurd*,[8] which influenced an alienated generation of the young, shows how society pushes youngsters into the "sexual underlife." The book points out that a boy may have a few sexual adventures which he thinks are great, but when he is caught, adults try by explanations and even punishment to convince him that what he found delightful is not good. The boy knows by the evidence of his senses that nothing could be better. So, in Goodman's view, if the boy gives in to adult pressures he may either lose faith in adults or else decide that he is queer, thus developing a distrust in his own body and feelings. Unable to make sense out of adult attitudes on his sex play, losing faith either in society or in himself and his own sense of reality, a boy become restless in school, rebellious at home, and often become compulsively fascinated by sex, since society has made it a problem for him. Goodman quotes Bertrand Russell as saying that it would be better if youngsters were allowed their sex play so they could then give undivided attention to schoolwork like math. But the important point, Goodman insists, is not whether sex play is right or wrong, or whether it should be encouraged or discouraged; the important thing is for youngsters and their sexual experience to be treated seriously. "It is hard to grow up when existing facts are treated as if they do not exist."[9] This is the climate that enables pederasty to thrive.

• Goodman goes on to point out that if a youngster dares to be man enough to stand up and argue for the validity of his own experience, or persists in the sex play which seems so good, he is declared delinquent and may even be "put away." The real problem, Goodman insists, is that adults do not really believe the boy has had authentic sexual experience. Because adults feel it should not have happened, thus it isn't important enough to be taken seriously. Goodman felt that such alienating experience lies behind much juvenile delinquency and is the basis for the rebellion and tribal society of adolescents which enables much deviant sexual behavior. Most adolescent sexual experience under sixteen takes place in a "sexual underlife"[10] not unlike the subvertive underworld of a prison, and often is characterized by the same anger and rebellion against the authorities which forbids even a wronged youngster to "tell." Many pederasts grew up through such gangs or adolescent tribal groups and still function as "alumni members."

CHAPTER 6

Response to Adolescence: An Educator's Story

One way to understand the underground is to listen to a pederast describe his experiences with enough completeness that we can understand him as a human being. The story of a distinguished man, now dead, is reconstructed in this chapter, using only the material he himself made available in his published journals and other books. Everything is in the first person, told anonymously. The life of this first guide to the underground illustrates the impact of adolescence, as well as serving as an introduction to questions of identity. The reader may detect the heartbeat beneath the words, the mechanisms which trigger behavior as well as motivational factors, as the story is told as it might have been told by the protagonist himself.

I was a poor Jewish boy without a father, smart, healthy, who liked to play ball and who was interested in girls. If pressed to say why I grew up to be a man who enjoys sex play with boys, I must honestly say that it is because sex play with girls was forbidden to me. Once I was put back four grades in school for writing a love note to a girl. Later, when I was a teacher and caught myself staring at young boys, I realized it was because in the formative years of my adolescence I had conditioned myself not to look at girls that way, for girls as future wives and mothers were to be kept pure. My masculine pride was hurt at an early age. It is taken for granted that boys, if they are permitted to grow up naturally, will develop a normal heterosexual adjustment, but my psychological training tells me that this is not so. A good marriage requires a great deal of support from society, friends, and relatives. A boy's unfolding heterosexuality requires special encouragement in the same way. Older friends and big brothers often provide this support, as when I saw a boy of sixteen pointing out to a boy of twelve some of the physical charms of a girl at the beach. Some fathers demonstrate that it is good to make love to a woman, but on the whole our society is pervaded with an anti-sexuality which is devastating to boys. We tease them and repress them in ways that wound their heterosexual pride. We deny them healthy sexual intercourse with girls their own age, and as a result more boys play sexually with other males than most parents realize.

My sexual pride was also wounded by the fact that the girls I liked, the really sexy ones, were interested only in older boys. I also had guilt feelings over the bit of sex play with girls I did manage. My sex habits in adolescence somehow attached themselves to some infant desires that are buried deep in my subconscious. I don't know what my infant need was, but I developed some emotional hungers which somehow became related to my sex play with boys. I am now deeply moved when I sense similar anguish, confusion, need, sexual hunger and frustration in a boy, and I love him deeply. On the surface I think it is his beauty that captivates me, but what I really want is to be to him the loving father I never had. The one I needed so badly when I was being severely punished for normal sexual desires. It is my view that most people will and should have only heterosexual intercourse most of the time, but at the same time I believe homosexual play to be perfectly natural and healthy. This is helpful to the personality and for the enrichment of friendship. It is pathological not to be able to make love to someone of the opposite sex, but it is equally pathologically sick not to be able to experience homosexual pleasure. For a youngster to have a bit of homosexual fun with an adult is of little significance if his normal sexual relations with the opposite sex are not impaired. I speak out of personal experience and also from psychological observation of others when I say that homosexual play under good conditions can be enjoyable and of positive value. For example, when sailing ships used to leave port for months at a time, an older and a younger sailor who had a good time sexually together on ship did not find that it affected their sex with women in port. The neurotic man is the one who cannot enjoy sex play in such a situation.

Saint Thomas said that the chief use of sex, in addition to making babies, is as a way to get to know other persons intimately, and my deepest friendships and personal loyalties began with sex play— which is a way for two males as well as a man and a woman to develop a deep relationship. Sex play does not last long between males as a rule, but the friendship remains. Obviously I'm not very sympathetic to the idea of gay marriages, but I don't object to them for people who find it meaningful; for joy and delight are so precious, and loving relationships are so needed in this world, that we should encourage such precious things whenever and wherever we find them. Lives and personalities are shallow because the sexual dimension is so often blocked off. We would have better community if we all had better sex.

Except for sex play I was a good kid who worked hard, made good grades in school, and helped my mother, yet I grew up with wounded feelings and guilt—which perhaps explains why I love delinquent kids. Why should a grown man enjoy playing ball and sex games with such youngsters? I remember one lovely boy who was mixed up, who badly needed the insight and affection I could bring into his life. As usual I agonized over whether to send him away or take him to bed, which is what he really needed. He not only wanted a warm human contact, but he wanted to submit to me, to feel the dominating strength of a father. Our bodies hungered together for something which risked destroying the affection we both needed, because it would leave guilty feelings. Most people will assume the sexual intercourse I had with that boy was damaging, but what is really obscene is the way our society makes us feel shameful and like criminals for doing human things that we really need. The only wrong thing I did with that boy was fail to love him enough. The best way to change our inhuman sex laws, in my judgment, would be for each person to act out what he thinks right, expressing his sexual emotions as his heart and body tell him to do, and join en masse with others to do as I did with that boy.

People often ask me what is wrong with the schools, what kills the spirit of so many youngsters today, robbing them of curiosity and creativity. As an educator who has written much on the subject, I've never really said what I think, which is that a good pupil-teacher relationship inevitably has sexual overtones. A healthy recognition of, and a creative use of, such sexual experience is basic to the flowering of a youngster's personality and genius. Perhaps someday scientific research will confirm that a sexually fulfilled, sexually happy youngster will bloom in school like a rose. It does the adolescent boy no harm to have a sexual affair with a favorite teacher. Such a master-disciple relationship, as when the teacher coaches the boy in sex as well as in other aspects of the mind and spirit, is successful if the boy grows up to be a mature heterosexual who no longer needs his teacher. Facetiously, this does not mean that I would repeal the laws against man-boy sex play! For youngsters, and many men as well, find it much more exciting and rewarding to have secret, illegal affairs. When everything that is fun becomes legal a lot of the spice goes out of young lives, especially for the kid who needs to rebel. Good sex education is given by example and by shared experience. I think the ban on homosexual play damages and depersonalizes education, and I think the ban on heterosexual play is a catastrophe. A student who blooms under loving praise will shrivel under impersonal, cold relationships.

A critic once wrote that I am "queer for kids." Of course I am, how could I write perceptively about them if I wasn't deeply concerned. I know a man who takes boys mountain climbing, which develops their self-confidence and helps them to become healthy and manly. Everyone says he really loves boys. Of course he does. Why else would he devote so much of his time and energy to them? I once taught at a prep school where most of the kids had either lost a parent or were unwanted at home, and were in desperate need of love. Because I am a pederast I quickly won their affection, since they needed to love. It was a very anxiety-producing relationship, yet they were eager to conspire with me. They became excited about learning, where other kids were bored. Timid educators usually crush kids to keep them quiet, because real teaching would involve a release of emotions and taboo sexual expression. Better crush a kid than admit he is a sexual being. So kids are emasculated, homosexualized, and are systematically retarded—since they are never allowed to ask the really nagging questions.

My career as teacher didn't last long, however. I came across a group of boys masturbating, and school rules said they should be punished. All boys masturbate, but they are not supposed to be caught! It is against the rules to have sex hungers and needs when you are fourteen. We certainly don't want boys of that age to be warm, human, and concerned for each other's problems. Few teachers would even have discovered that the group was trying to help one of the older ones who was sure something was wrong with him and that he couldn't do it. In their friendship and compassion the group stuck with him until he proved to them and himself that he was O.K. and not queer. It was a great human moment that I chanced upon . . . and I was supposed to lecture them for being bad boys. Feeling very guilty, the boy who had been the center of it all burst into tears, which is a shameful thing for a boy in his teens. So, without saying anything, I simply put my arms around him and kissed him on the forehead. It was a fatherly deed, yet because I was a teacher I did something considered as horrible as if I had masturbated with them. I was visibly conspiring with them! Our sense of community in the next hour was so thick you could cut it with a knife. To heal the tension, I told them the story of Agamemnon and Orestes and I suspect it was one of the best sex education sessions the school ever had. You have to hand it to the Greek myths. Life could be permanently soured for a young boy who crawls into a teacher's bed for a bit of warmth and affection, perhaps he needs to cry about something at home. Instead of expelling the pupil and arresting the teacher, the Greeks would have told the story of Zeus and Ganymede, how the greatest god of all took a boy to bed. Why else should such a story be at the center of their mythology, if not to say that it could happen to anyone. Most of the Greek myths are deeply psychological interpretations of human problems, like the Oedipal complex.

To be honest that's not the way I handled it when a boy came to my bed one night. I sent him away, and ironically he was the one who later told on me and had me fired. Had I taken him to bed for a few minutes of affectionate sex he might have been a better and more compassionate boy. He was jealous because everyone knew I had a favorite. I taught him to dance, how to court a girl, and when he was embarrassed at his fumbling attempts at lovemaking and came to me with his embarrassment, I sent him back with confidence and contraceptives.

There have been few days since I was eleven years old that I haven't had an orgasm, and I've certainly had many more than my wife could need or want. Given this sex drive I have had many sexual adventures, generally with boys whose fathers only kick them out for their sex education, boys who turn to a man like me for tenderness and understanding. Fathers in Italy used to take young sons to prostitutes, but in America a father doesn't even dare encourage his son to masturbate, although he may leave *Playboy* lying around for that purpose. In an article in the *New York Review of Books* I said that we can't hide sex from children, but instead we must help them to manage it in creative ways. I once wrote a story about a boy who was invited by a strange man to go for a ride in his car. The boy suspected the man's sexual intentions, so he said: "All right, if you'll buy me an ice cream cone first." Although I called the boy by the name of Horatio Alger, he was in fact really me. Actually I didn't go. If I had, I might have found the sexual experience disgusting, so as to end all my fantasies. Since I didn't go, I enjoyed in my imagination the sexual experience I thought I might have had. If you wish to understand any pederast, or the sexual experience of any human being, explore his dreams. Only in that rich world of fantasy and concealed experience is the truth about ourselves in any way revealed. There will be no honest sex except where there is truth, as well as honest love.

SOME CONCLUDING OBSERVATIONS

• The story above is that of Paul Goodman, who once said that he expected to be arrested sometime for pederastic play, but never was. He was for many people the spokesman and prophet of the underground. His views, which are summarized here, can be found in *Five Years* (1969), *Making Do* (1962), *Parent's Day* (1952), *Growing Up Absurd* (1960), and various articles. Also of interest are other novels of his which are listed in the bibliography.

• Goodman puts sexual deviancy in a larger context, placing an emphasis on *human* nature, suggesting that adolescent delinquency cannot be solved until we provide youngsters with a human society they can be fulfilled in, instead of trying to "adjust" them to a cruel order which dehumanizes them. When youngsters are thwarted and starved for love they naturally invent deviant objects for themselves, since human beings are creative in bypassing the "system" as in everything else. Since sex may lead to trouble, boys substitute violence, drugs, stealing, gambling.

CHAPTER 7

The Uses of History

Pederasts often search through the history of sexual customs in an effort to understand themselves, asking questions. How different are human beings today from those in ancient Greece, where sex play between men and boys was sometimes highly approved? Do we look for the origins of pederasty in history as a learned behavior passed from culture to culture and generation to generation? Or are there certain types of cultures which nurture pederasty? An adequate historical study of pederasty would require volumes, for it would involve a study of sexuality and human nature in each epoch, including the role of women and the family, prostitution and adventurism, religion and morality, and other complexities involved in the development of sexual customs.

Despite a growing volume of research, however, very little is known for sure about such sexual practices in the past. Many of the sources are suspect, having been written either to attack pederasty or to defend it, with little objectivity on either side. While this chapter is dependent upon the research of scholarly pederasts, its aim is not a "pederastic interpretation of history." We must, however, note the danger that the categories used to organize known facts may obscure the truth and lead us in wrong directions, for historians are obliged to impose a point of view in order to fit together the limited data they have. Taylor,[1] for example, fits the facts into his theory of alternating sexually permissive and sexually repressive societies. Some historians use Freudian categories, and others Marxist. Some scholars search for evidence in the past for the type of gay-homosexuality which thrives in urban society today, and confuse pederasty with gay-homosexuality. Karlen[2] suggests they often abuse history. But we are dependent upon our guides to the underground and their perspectives. This chapter focuses on the history of pederasty as we know it today.

THE EARLIEST PEDERAST

Despite the helpful inferences of anthropologists, who may draw wrong conclusions about prehistoric folk from the study of aboriginals today, we can only speculate about pederasty among the earliest primitive societies. While females stayed behind to tend fires and care for the children, men and boys must have huddled together at night when on hunting expeditions. Surely there would have been sexual joking and horseplay in such an all-male society. The man who did not have a warm-blooded young companion when it was cold may well have borrowed one from a friend, as men exchange sons at the Oasis of Siwa.[3] In many societies, in the absence of women, clowning youngsters provided the evening's entertainment around the fire with provocative dancing and singing. All adolescents were adults and in a sense all men were children, ready to enjoy themselves in whatever ways were possible. Youngsters have always been sexually exploited,[4] and evidence from the earliest known cultures shows that captive boys, orphans, and strays from other tribes were fair game to be worked and exploited. The more attractive boys and girls could be sex objects for men without mates, and soon the most attractive captives became slaves to be set aside as servants and entertainers for the pleasure and amusement of the chief men of the tribe.

At the same time there was a great difference between tribes, and far from being sexually uninhibited, many, like aboriginals today, were no doubt highly structured and superstitious. Sex taboos may have developed when, because of its relation to birth, men began to view sex as something sacred; priests laid down rules to avoid making the gods angry, and to prevent tensions between men and families. We may assume that men have always been jealous and protective of offspring of their own tribe, but the young of other tribes were vulnerable. At best, such a captive or slave might have been a pet, a plaything, a toy for sexual amusement, and when older a prostitute or catamite. Many peoples had certain seasons when taboos were suspended, when the entire tribe would be permitted to revel and enjoy sex. Orgies, of course, were religious, and sex play was tolerated at festival times, even when otherwise restricted except among adolescents and the unmarried. So we may conclude that prehistoric peoples discovered pederasty much as unsupervised boys today, without any tutoring from others, frequently discover enjoyable kinds of sex play with each other. Also, it should be remembered that the words *child* or *youngster* no doubt meant something quite different in societies where a boy was an adult at puberty.

In a society of warriors, captured youngsters were raised and trained to serve the victors, which may also have facilitated the exploitation of women. While ordinary people may have been much the same throughout history, the rulers of some of the earliest known societies set an example of pleasure-seeking, in which slaves were trained from an early age for singing, dancing, and sexual amusement. In this context, pederasty became something quite different from playful man-boy sex of a tutoring variety, as may have existed in earlier tribal society. In ancient Persia,[5] for example, as in much of Asia at the beginning of history, pederasty became an exploited vice, typical of exploitive sexual cultures. Captive boys were castrated, depilated, perfumed, and abused in a sensuous pederasty which sought exotic pleasures, with erotic sensations different from ordinary coitus. Pederasty became a cultivated taste of heterosexual men who despised gay-homosexuals, for they were not seeking love, but play and diversion.[6]

THE GREEK EXPERIMENT

This sensuous "sport of kings" had always existed in Greece. Indeed, Alexander the Great's father was killed by such a catamite. Alexander probably indulged in such erotic pleasures himself.[7] The Persians said that pederasty had begun in Crete,[8] which was one of the first civilizations with the wealth and leisure to enjoy such tastes. Aristotle said that man-boy sex play was encouraged there to prevent overpopulation. Varied sorts of pederasty may have existed in Greece from prehistoric times, for Greek gods were portrayed in mythology as being sexually involved with boys in ways which appear to sanction religious and ritualistic pederasty. As Greek civilization began to flower a few centuries before Christ, the Greeks sought through philosophy and science to beautify and elevate all aspects of human life; for example, seeking to transform avarice into industriousness and lust into love. They sought to deal creatively in this way with the erotic attraction of boys for men by ennobling and beautifying the relationship in an experiment aimed at transforming pederastic desires into a constructive force for education. Men who were erotically attracted to boys were obliged to love their souls and to cultivate in boys a beauty of mind which would endure and enrich all life.[9] The Greeks glorified youth and beauty and sought thus to transform the "sport of kings" which exploited boys into the *paiderastia* which would use the erotic bond as a teaching device, enhancing the learning process by a bond of affection.

This Greek experiment in transforming pederasty was probably limited from the beginning by two cultural factors. First, Greek sexual culture degraded women, and second, the existence of slavery inevitably corrupted the experiment. As one pederast says: "It was never as platonic as some writers suggest. The beauty they praised in boys was frankly erotic, as they sang of 'bright laughing eyes,' teasing sex games, youthful skin to massage after a game, grace in wrestling and kissing contests, sleeping entwined." The Greek experiment succeeded in one sense, however, in that it used pederast eroticism to strengthen the bond between soldiers and the apprentice warriors, thus inspiring heroism on the battlefield, but the use of phrases like "frenzied, uncontrolled passion" do not suggest that such sexual experience between soldier and boy was entirely spiritual even at the height of the experiment's success. In Crete it was the custom for a man to kidnap a boy he liked, taking him home for a two-month "honeymoon" after which the boy was rewarded by a gift of armor. Beside this image of the noble tutor who nurtured the soul of a boy, we must place the record of the well-bred twelve-year-old boy seduced by sweet-talking cynics at the gymnasium, who coquettishly asked for gifts in exchange for sexual favors, and the continuing existence of perfumed pubescents in the brothels. A pederast who has studied the epoch concludes: "Then as now the world was peopled by all sorts. Ancient Greece was not a pederast culture, but it tolerated several pederast subcultures, as reflected in religion, literature, and art. There is a continuing influence across history of the Greek experience, with Greek philosophy used by some to justify homosexuality, sensuous exploitive pederasty, and platonic friendship. Man-boy sex play may not have been so different then, perhaps the Greeks were just more poetic and artistic. The constructive aspect of the Greek experiment was an emphasis on *motive*—that the same act could be destructive or loving, depending on how one valued a boy and respected him."

ROMAN SEX EXPLOITATION

Evidence of pederasty is found in Etruscan Italy, so it may not be true that the Romans took over the custom from the Greeks. Many

Romans justified their pederasty by appealing to Greek philosophy, and the most highly sought and expensive boys were Greek boys especially bred and trained in Alexandria. Roman pederasty must be evaluated in the context of the brutal excesses of Roman sexual culture as a whole. The anti-sex attitude of Christianity may well be the result of the way Romans sexually exploited their slaves, with sex circuses, sex tortures to amuse the crowd, sexual abuse of children by animals for entertainment. As conquerors of the world, the Romans exploited everything as brutally as they wished. The Achilles-Patroclus type of love between soldiers in the Greek army was in many regiments of the Roman army replaced by the custom of allowing a soldier to take along a captive boy to carry his supplies, wait on him, and serve as his sex partner.

Horace wrote love poems about boys, scoffing at meaning anything more than the serving of his lust. Martial told his wife that women and boys were separate pleasures, boys for dirty jokes and playful sex as entertainers. The emperor Hadrian erected statues of his favorite boy all over the empire and commanded his subjects to worship them. Upper-class boys were seduced by their slaves, who played with them sexually, and a Roman father might provide a slave boy for his son to sleep with until marriage, to keep him from getting emotionally involved with some slave girl. One pederast has said: "I think the Greek experiment might have succeeded, resulting in a continuing improving pedagogy which would have nurtured science instead of letting it die, if the Romans hadn't conquered the world, and if Alexander the Great's armies hadn't been tainted by the 'sport of kings' when Persia was captured." "The Romans were playful in a bawdy sense," says another pederast, "with dirty jokes, songs, plays, poetry, dancing, psychic games—all of which spilled over into the Middle Ages and Renaissance to fertilize even our own times. Generations of the young have studied the classics. I am told that copies of the *Satyricon* in typescript circulate, for example, in many French and Italian schools as they did in mine—especially the incident where the tutor who seduced his pupil threatens to tell the boy's father if the boy doesn't quit being so sexually demanding. Jokes which were told in Roman times and styles of sexually teasing boys from ancient days continue to be prevalent around the Mediterranean. Is it any coincidence," he continues, "that pederasty thrives most in those countries that were part of the Roman Empire?"

Another pederast wrote: "All kinds of man-boy sex play existed in the Roman Empire, but the worst abuses are recorded in history as evidence of need for change. Although the brutality certainly existed, the Roman pederast literature is really playful, in the sense of the dirty joke as in Catullus. The man-boy sex play in the *Musa Puerilis*[10] is honestly erotic, satyrical, and amusing." Roman violence and sexual excesses made inevitable, however, a radical swing of the pendulum in another experiment in transforming the moral climate.

THE JUDEO-CHRISTIAN REACTION

The Christian religion took over the Roman world, preaching a gospel of love which would transform evil into good. Once in power, the Church sought to transform society's morals by imposing upon all, by law, the view that sex was sinful and could be redeemed and allowed only within Christian marriage. Indeed, it was better to repress all sex desires and abstain from all intercourse—although as St. Paul said, "It is better to marry than to burn." Pederasty, polygamy, along with a positive attitude toward various sexual pleasures had long existed among the Hebrews, but as their vocation as a specially-called people of God was clarified, Jews rejected the sexual aspects of the religions that surrounded them, including the pederasty of Baal and temple prostitution of boys and girls. These efforts at purification never completely succeeded,[11] but nevertheless had a strong influence on the early Christians, who reacted against Roman cruelty and vice. Many early Christians were slaves and would have been highly conscious of the sexual abuse of young slaves. It is not clear whether the New Testament condemnation of homosexuals[12] is addressed against adult deviants, for feminized men were generally despised in the ancient world, or only against such abuse of boys. It is perhaps impossible to sort this out, since the Christian movement proposed the celibate monk as the ideal man. "If the New Testament references to homosexuals refer to gays," one pederast writes, "then it is striking and astonishing that there are no pederast references also among lists of sins, since the world in which Jesus and the early Christians lived was rife with pederasty.[13] Jesus seems to have proclaimed a revolutionary love ethic—as illustrated also by his treatment of prostitutes—which sought to transform vice rather than condemn it. There was a pro-pederast Gnostic party in the early church which taught that within the context of the 'Greek experiment' love of boys could be holy and Christian. A pederast monk told me that such a tradition has come down through the underground in some monasteries, where the Greek and Roman pederast classics were preserved through the Dark Ages. Such monks, and some priests, bishops and popes, have been practicing pederasts motivated not only by the Greek philosophy of *paiderastia*, but also by the view that Jesus intended Christian love to beautify all human relationships. The monk suggested that several incidents in the New Testament may have been censored by minor language adjustments during the Gnostic controversy. When Jesus told his followers to go 'the second mile,' the monk asks, did he not know that to command one to carry his cloak was a common way for a Roman soldier to solicit sex of a boy. Also, the monk reports, this tradition contains the view that the Roman centurion who pleads with Jesus for help in curing his slave boy was a pederast—for why else would such a high official go to such trouble for an adolescent slave? Further, the centurion came to Jesus apologetically, for he knew that the Jews around Jesus would be horrified that Jesus would even speak to a pederast. Yet, said the monk: "Jesus evidently blessed the pederast and his adolescent lover with one of his rare miracles because of the quality of their love. Do we have evidence here of another experiment that failed?"[14]

When the Gnostics were defeated in church councils, the Church took a hard line, "shifting from an ethic of love to one of law, in part because the emperors feared underpopulation, and came to believe the supersition that earthquakes and natural disorders were caused by deviant sexual relationship. In A.D. 390 Emperor Theodosius proclaimed that men guilty of such deviant acts should be burned at the stake. Classic literature was then destroyed or censored; for example, erotic poetry about boys became altered as if to be about girls. The explicit sexual references in the love of David and Jonathan in the Bible were obscured. Such attempts to repress pleasurable sex simply backfired, and sexual culture became schizophrenic, as it is today. Beneath public moral life there is, and always has been, an underworld where any type of sex is allowable because all sex is sinful." Today, as the Church seeks to reaffirm a positive attitude toward sex for pleasure as well as for procreation, gay activists are challenging the Church to re-examine its understanding of Christian love as applied to deviants, and there is confusion in Christian ethics on many sexual questions.

PEDERASTY IN THE NON-CHRISTIAN WORLD

Outside the confines of Western history there are many cultures and traditions. Alexander the Great did not carry pederasty to India

and Pakistan, nor did Muslim traders transport it to East Asia, for it
was already well-rooted in the ancient societies of those areas. Some
of it was the "sport of kings" exploitive variety, but affectionate sex
play was also often seen in Buddhist and medieval Hindu society,
even between monks and novices. In Japan the nobility's pederasty
had a style similar to the Greek experiment; yet, just as in Greece,
there was also the crass side to pederasty in Japan and China, with
boys prostituted in brothels, teahouses and theaters.[15] The customers of boy brothels were "priests, soldiers, police, government officials, writers. . . ."

In the Middle Ages there was a great deal of pederast literature
and art in East Asia. Pederasty was not only cultivated at court but
also man-boy sex play was common with working boys and schoolboys. The same was true in the rest of Asia and parts of Africa.[16]
Muslim scriptures condemn pederasty, but affirm the value of sexual
pleasure, with the orgasm prefiguring the joys of paradise—the
prophet affirming that the faithful will continually make love in
heaven.[17] This fact, and the hint in Muslim scriptures that in heaven
the faithful will be served by beautiful boys, made it possible for many
Muslims to justify sexual intercourse with non-Muslim slave boys and
to "compare the love of boys with the love of God."[18]—especially
since wealth and the slave trade gave them their choice of "the most
beautiful boys from all the countries of the world,"[19] specially trained
to serve any and all pleasures. The finest poetry of the Muslim Middle
Ages was frequently addressed to boys—with the biblical story of
Joseph being a favorite subject, because in Muslim tradition the
youngster sold to the king of Egypt was the most beautiful boy of
history. Greek and Roman pederastic literature was popular in the
courts of all the princes, almost as a fad.

PEDERASTY À LA MODE

Sultan Mehmed II of Turkey, the conqueror of Constantinople in 1453, a patron of learning and, as such, a father of the
Renaissance, undertook a new "Greek experiment" to put pederasty
to work serving the Ottoman Empire, by renewing past efforts to
restore Roman order, the purity of Muslim faith, and the philosophy
and science of the Greeks. His ideal of a pedagogical pederasty was
frustrated, as in ancient Greece, by the general sexual culture's
corruption by the slave system—although Turkish society did de-

velop a type of slavery in which boys were educated, loved and often
adopted as sons. As his armies conquered half of Europe, the Sultan
brought the most handsome and talented captive boys to his court.
He dreamed of a new elite corps, bound by ties of pederast love, who
would be equipped to rule the world by the best education ever
offered in history. He sent representatives to the Christian villages to
draft boys aged 10 to 14 into his armies, and these rigorously disciplined boys were never allowed to marry, so that their loyalty to each
other and to the Sultan would never be diminished by family ties.

The "sport of kings" tradition was too powerful, however, for
Greek philosophy to dominate even the passions of the Sultan himself. He inspired his troops to more conquests by promising them
beautiful boys,[20] and in each captured city he gave the sons of
middle-class parents to his troops, leaving lower-class children to do
the work, and kept the sons and daughters of the aristocracy for his
own pleasure and purposes. He has been described as a "pederast
heroique" who celebrated his conquests in bed, and who spent most
of his time in the company of boys under seventeen—except for his
nights fathering children in the harem. As gifts to Muslim rulers in
Africa and Asia, he would often send as many as fifty young European
boys at a time. His followers and successors took up pederasty so
enthusiastically that it may well have been a basic cause of the decline
in the Turiskh Empire, as its army and leaders devoted most of their
time to passionate play with European children. This is well illustrated, for example, by E. J. W. Gibb,[21] in his seven-volume analysis
of Turkish poetry, including the so-called "city thrillers," which were
on the charms of boys of different nationalities, debating which cities
had the most erotic youngsters. The adventuring Turkish armies
brought home from Europe nearly a million youngsters, with parasit-
ical slave dealers siphoning off many attractive children for sale as far
away as central Asia. European visitors wrote detailed reports of the
pederasty of Turkish armies in North Africa, for example, reporting
that "sexual amusements with young boys" were "the vice à la mode."
Apprentice boys who worked in barber shops and as masseurs offered
themselves to customers, and it was difficult to find a boy in the city of
Algiers who had not been caught up in sex play with a man. Nearly
every Turkish soldier or sailor had a boy who cooked for him and slept
with him, many of them captured in piratical raids on Italy, Spain,
and even Ireland in the sixteenth century. Rich men of Algiers, said
Haedo,[22] kept young boys for their sexual amusement and paraded

them on the streets to show off for their friends; and the sons of the rich also became addicted to pederasty by the time they were fourteen or so, with "lewd boy entertainers."

On the surface—since any handsome boy was considered fair game by Turkish soldiers—it would seem that the old days of Roman orgies had returned, for Turkish pederasty was openly carnal. A scholar pederast, however, privately suggests a counter-interpretation: "While it is true that Turkish men and their boys greatly enjoyed their pleasures, the accusations of orgies may well be smoke screens thrown up by their enemies. There is evidence that Turkish affection for boys at times came close to worship. Their catamite boys were so loyal that a businessman or soldier could trust his boy to die for him. According to Greek sources, Turkish officials like Ali of Ioannina treated boys at court in monstrous and evil ways, yet Greek parents vied for the privilege of sending their sons to his court, as fathers in Bukhara proudly wore gold medals to proclaim that their young sons at court had been to bed with the Sultan. What now looks like exploitation has to be seen in the context of the sexual customs of the age."

Mary McCarthy has suggested that pederasty is characteristic of all virile cultures.[23] It may be more correct to say that pederasty thrives wherever people have leisure and wealth to enjoy themselves. Powerful men, who accept the world's pleasures as their reward, often follow the example of Sultan Mehmed II, in assuming they are entitled to enjoy all the various types of sex play.

THE WESTERN UNDERGROUND

For every European visitor to North Africa and the Middle East who was scandalized by the erotic dancing boys, there was another who brought new tastes and interests back to Europe with him. On the other hand, the Crusaders may well have taken as much pederasty with them as they brought back to Europe,[24] as in more modern times Flaubert, in his diary of a state visit to Egypt,[25] admits that he undertook the trip partly to sample the pederast diversions of the country, where "it is quite accepted . . . is spoken of at the table in the hotel . . . everyone teases you, and you end up confessing that you skewered your lad." Certainly there is evidence of a pederast underground in the Middle Ages in Europe which almost flowered above ground in the Renaissance, fed as it was by the circulation of Greek classics, and by such imitations as *Alcibiades*, a manual on how to seduce a schoolboy. The Earl of Rochester described taking page boys to bed, Christopher Marlowe began one of his plays with a scene of Zeus dandying a boy on his lap, and the motivation of men who paid admission to enter the dressing rooms of boy actors, and those who employed boys to dance dressed as Cupids, was probably not much different from those who paid dancing boys in the East. Boy prostitution was common in nearly every European country, with open brothels in many of them—as in Asia—until World War II. Police in the United States also winked an eye at boy prostitution and consenting mutual sex play between men and boys over puberty, unless parents filed a complaint.

In the last fifty years, with the growing concern for child welfare, laws and their enforcement have been tightened against drugs, prostitution and sexual deviance. If strict laws and their enforcement would prevent pederasty, its history would end at this point.

WHO DARES SPEAK OF LOVE?

In Central Europe in the 1920's and early 1930's there was another effort to revive the Greek ideal of pedagogic pederasty, in the movement of "wandering youth." Modern gay-homosexuality also can trace some of its roots to that movement of men and boys who wandered around the countryside, hiking and singing hand in hand, enjoying nature, life together, and their sexuality.[26] Ultimately Hitler used and transformed the movement—much as the Romans had abused the *paiderastia* of the ancient Greeks—expanding and building upon its romanticism as a basis for the Nazi party. Until destroyed by Hitler, however, the "wandering youth" constituted the "first free adolescent society in history," although there was some pederast precedent among the troubadours of an earlier age. Romantic love and adolescence are both fairly modern inventions, and their implications for pederasty were not noticed until sexual culture began to change under the impact of Freud's teachings and the beginnings of the sex revolution with its emphasis on sex for pleasure. The wandering youth movement was a sex freedom culture, with a strong emphasis on camaraderie among boys, girls, and whomever. It was a forerunner of the postwar, drug-seeking, rock-music-oriented, hippie and related subcultures of adolescent society. Growing out of the German Boy Scout movement, this "friendship and freedom" trend was pederast at its roots, but it also flowered into gay-homosexuality with an emphasis on love. One pederast says of the movement: "Something worthy of the word *love* existed in the 'wandering youth'

and those who oppose pederasty as exploitive may be fighting a
rear-guard action, for the age of sexual exploitation is about over.
Youth will and ought to be protected. Only in areas of great poverty
and neglect do remnants of exploitive pederasty survive; and all
reasonable citizens, as well as anyone who speaks for love, can only
condemn all exploitation, especially of the young. It will never be
ended by law, however, but only as the young organize to protect
themselves and to assert their sexual rights. The wandering youth of
the 1920's, happy in their singing and playful sex, established for the
young the conviction that they are neither to be exploited nor over-
protected out of their right to enjoy life and sex—especially not to be
forced to accept the view that sex, when one is young, must always be
passionate and deadly serious. Sometimes adolescents, and even
adults, feel playful, and sometimes males can love each other. We
cannot now turn back the clock, for adolescent gay activists are daring
to speak of love, and of their right to love whom they please."

SOME CONCLUDING OBSERVATIONS

• The current body of research into the history of sexual customs is not adequate enough for pederasts to be able to find answers
to questions they may want to ask. There would appear to be some
learned pederasty which is passed from generation to generation, but
probably it consists of interpretative ideas rather than behavior, and
most pederasts learn about it only after their tastes are confirmed.
Many pederasts report that the influence of a poem, book, or incident
from the past was a liberating factor upon their pederast experience or
perhaps in encouraging them to admit their pederasty and explore its
meaning.

• This brief historical survey suggests the usefulness of more
research into the history of sex customs. One would like to know more
about its impact on the larger movements of history. For example, is
it pure coincidence that pederasty flowered simultaneously in
Greece and the Far East? or that at the time of the Renaissance it
reappeared in an idealistic form in distant parts of Asia as well as in
Europe? or that sexual reform movements developed in different
parts of the world at the same time?

• Traditional societies have opposed gay-homosexuality in adult
men, while tolerating a virile man's sex play with a developing boy.
Modern society is moving in the opposite direction, tolerating
homosexuality among consenting adults, while placing a great em-

phasis on protecting the young from sexual involvements. There is evidence to suggest that the modern gay movement had its origin as recently as the 1700's. However, since such behavior has always been underground, the evidence to establish or refute several important theses may simply not exist.

CHAPTER 8

Influence of the Past:
An Aristocrat's Story

Carefully researched fiction based on true incidents often presents a truer picture of human beings caught up in something like pederasty than does a clinical case study, for it offers the possibility of a well-rounded presentation of character and emotions. This second of our guides to the underground—again told in the first person—is such a fictional character. As the subject of seven novels he is probably the most completely developed pederast in modern literature. We apologize to his real novelist that our style is not so charming and graceful as his. Also, we have chosen arbitrarily the incidents which we see as typical of what living pederasts tell in their true stories. Many of the pederasts interviewed have come to accept their deviancy with a self-understanding based upon the discovery of a previous period in history with which they can identify. Georges de Sarre, hero of this series of novels, here in a reconstructed biography reflects upon his pederasty as from the chair of a Trimalchio:

I attended a boarding school where my fellow students were from prominent families, I was faithful in my religious duties, and I read widely about sexual matters. Today pupils may talk more openly about sex, but I think my pre-World War II generation was more romantic. My father made a point of telling me that I was a man when I went off to school at fourteen. For me that meant I was ready for the pleasures of sex. I was immediately jealous of the sex play between the boy whose bed was next to mine and a handsome older athlete. Though they warned us against "vice" and "polluting friendships," one of the teachers left open on a table where I could read it, a translation of the *Satyricon* and I hunted for other classics with similar pederast episodes. It was pointed out to me how often the older boys proselyted in the younger division, as, for example, the athlete who went camping with my neighbor and who met him regularly in a seldom-used greenhouse. Jealous, I planted a note the athlete had written to the boy in a place where the Rector would find it. Although the older boy was expelled, the door was not opened for me to tryst with my neighbor, so I began to look elsewhere. In chapel I noticed a choirboy from the younger division, not yet thirteen, who had a dazzling smile and golden curls, and I began to play erotic games with him, maneuvering to be able to kneel beside him at communion so I could press my knee against his bare leg, staring at him, sending him secret notes. He knew what I wanted and, flushed with excitement, soon was responding coquettishly. I sent him poems by the pederast poet and steel heir Fersen, and he replied with little love poems which he wrote himself. He bought a red tie just like mine, as a surprise message of love, my first intimation that Alexander was ready to be passionate where I intended to be playful. "Be careful," I warned him. "Red is the color of fire. Aren't you afraid of getting burned?" As I said this, my caressing fingers closed to clasp his hand.

Our play at the greenhouse was innocent and affectionate. I kissed and caressed his bare legs as he sat above me. He was shy but marvelously responsive. We played other erotic games: traded bathing suits, mixed our blood, had a lover's quarrel, and when he became convinced that I wasn't one of the older boys who simply wanted to use a younger boy sexually, he began to adore me. All might have gone off well if the school authorities hadn't had such dirty minds. One of the teachers who was himself erotically attracted to Alexander noticed the furtiveness of his favorite pupil, and demanded at confession to know what was going on. Accused of something evil, we both became more deceptive. Alexander wrote me a note saying: "Aren't boys human? Don't we have rights to love? Don't worry, it will take more than parents and teachers to keep us apart." But we had a new surveillant, a pederast teacher who played sexually with various pupils by awakening first one boy and then another with a flashlight in the middle of the night, and taking them to his room for food and intimate conversation. This teacher spied on us, and told me that we couldn't fool him, for he knew that the so-called purity of boys was a delusion. He proposed that the three of us could be friends, for he also found Alexander erotically attractive. This worried me, so I framed the surveillant as I had the older athlete by an anonymous note to the Rector. On a surprise visit in the middle of the night, the Rector found a young boy in the teacher's room, so the teacher was promptly sent away. Later in life I ran into him twice—once marching in a parade with his Boy Scout troop, and again, later, in Vienna, where he had been arrested for sexual involvement with a boy.

Other teachers had been alerted, however; so when Alexander and I were caught lying together, smoking forbidden cigarettes, we were told that we would have to be separated, to attend different schools. Alexander sent word to me that he would die first, while I pretended to repent and agree with the plan, even turning over to the authorities the notes he had written to me. He felt betrayed, and later, after I was home, I read about his suicide in the newspapers. It was the most decisive event of my young life. At first I thought to kill myself; then I realized I was obliged to live for both of us for, in dying, Alexander had united his life forever with mine. Since then, I've devoted my life to his memory, dedicating my career to him. At the university I had affairs with girls, but always I was haunted by his love. Had he lived, we would have grown apart, gone our separate ways, but now there is no way for me to escape his spell, since he died for our love. I was delighted that my first job took me to our embassy in Greece. Alexander and I had dreamed of exploring Greece together, so I explored the places hallowed by pederast associations. In those days, before World War II, many pederasts came to Greece for sex play with boys, not only because of the lure of history but also under the influence of Lord Byron, for the pederast underground of Europe was full of stories about the poet. Young friends in the diplomatic service introduced me to the swimming pools where pederasts gathered, and were amused when a boy knocked on the door when I was changing clothes to ask if he could come in. One didn't need to go to such places to find boys, for the hotels swarmed with them. For example, the little groom assigned to me spoke only Greek, so with sign language I asked him, soon after my arrival, to draw water for my bath. Immediately he took off all his clothes to bathe with me uninvited.

I had the unusual diplomatic assignment of rescuing a thirteen-year-old boy from the yacht of a wealthy pederast who had taken the boy on a yearlong cruise with the parents' permission—later they had repented and wanted the boy home. The yachtsman told me that he went each spring to Morocco to contract with a family for a boy as his year's companion. The one I rescued had been delightful, he said, except for one problem. He enjoyed the sex play so much he refused to wear clothes most of the time. We had a picnic at which the boy performed for our amusement a naked dance in the moonlight with a girl his own age. Later, during the war, enquiries were made as to whether or not the yachtsman was a spy, and it was reported that he then had two young foreign boys on his boat. My own troubles, which dramatically ended my diplomatic career, began when I slapped a boy in an Athens hotel, and climaxed elsewhere when I was arrested (I was released with a reprimand and warning) after the police had followed me and a boy all day, although we had done nothing illegal.

I became a writer, beginning with a novel about Alexander which won a large audience of sentimental women who wept over his suicide. I also received many fan letters from schoolboys thanking me for championing their cause. Many confided in me that they didn't see anything wrong in their sex play, some wanted to meet me, and one wrote to say he had fallen in love with me through my writings. I knew better than to reply to his letter, but once in Naples at a hotel a family from his town in Belgium checked in with a charming boy of the right age. When later I learned that the boy who wrote the letter had committed suicide, my grief over Alexander was rekindled and I resolved that the next time a boy made overtures to me, I would accept. At that time I was in Greece with a woman, and we went together to Pergamum where Julius Caesar as a teen-ager had shared the bed of a king. Here we discussed the puzzle of pederasty.

Some time later a friend invited me to go with her to visit the boarding school which her son attended. The Rector greeted me warmly, saying that the sex play I had described in my novel no longer existed, for they now had sex education courses and allowed boys to smoke. The teachers were, indeed, so self-confident that my novel was used as a model of good writing! I found, however, that boys weren't so different as they thought. A youngster hovered near me as if waiting to speak to me alone, and we met in the chapel of all places. He told me that perhaps boys no longer wrote romantic notes, but there was as much sex play as ever, and he kissed me while we were behind the chapel door. Since he lived at home and was not a boarding pupil, he could come to see me each week. He came from a well-to-do, liberal family and had freedom of a sort that even university students did not have in my day. We spent our afternoons looking at photographs of naked boys in an art book, and he admired their physical charms with no embarrassment. I need not tell you that we had fun in bed, but our close ties were intellectual. We discussed Jean Genet and my books, for the boy had been charmed by their spirit, originally nurtured perhaps by the lovely statue of a Neapolitan fishing boy in the vestibule of the house where I grew up, and by the Greek classics which freed me from the necessity of sexual conformism. As he has grown up, we have remained the close friends that Alexander and I should have been. Our love differs now that he is a man, but neither of us regrets a moment of the happy hours we spent between the colored sheets I bought especially for him when he was a schoolboy. He too has explored Greece, for we share a fascination for that time of history when men and boys were free to enjoy themselves, sexually, affectionately, together.

SOME CONCLUDING OBSERVATIONS

• This story illustrates the need for more adequate ways to interpret male-male sexual experience to the boys involved. It further illustrates the power of a sexual experience which never actually involved deviant coitus to influence a man into becoming a practicing pederast. Much of the sex play between the older and younger boy, while full of arousal and psychic games, was as innocent as wrestling. And yet it was a powerfully emotional erotic experience.

• Another pederast frequently quoted in this book tells a similar story of discovering the Greek classics when he was a young adolescent, at a time when his own erotic attachment for a younger boy was distressing and threatening. Reading about Greek pederasty caused him to relax, quit worrying, accept his emerging pederasty and continue a happy sexual relationship with the younger boy. Similar influences from history appear in the experiences of some of the other pederasts interviewed.

• Although there was every opportunity at the school for the boys in this story to be seduced by adults, they seduced themselves. While it is important to make the point that seduction is more often by another boy rather than by an adult, these novels also report cases of adult seduction, as well as great variety of experience in these cases.

• The reader who wishes to examine this story in greater detail may consult the following books of Roger Peyrefitte: *Special Friend-ships* (1958), *Jeunes Proies* (1948), *Les Ambassades* (1951), *La Fin des Ambassades* (1951), *Notre Amour* (1954), *L'Oracle* (1948), *Les Amours Singuliéres* (1949), *L'Exile de Capri* (1959), *Une Musée de L'Amour* (1972), and a book by Giannoli (1970).

CHAPTER 9

The Impact of Other Cultures

The investigation of pederasty in other cultures would be exhausting even if we could limit the survey to the peculiar national styles of sexual deviance found in such regions as East Asia, the Communist world, South Asia, the Middle East, Black Africa, North Africa, Latin Europe, Northern Europe, Western Europe, Latin America, and the South Seas. We would want to ask how ancient pederastic traditions or undergrounds are changing under the impact of the modern world, what types of pederasty exist, what supporting structures exist, what about religion and moral attitudes, class differences, view of pederasty in literature and art, and laws and their enforcement, and much more. Fortunately we have limited ourself to a simpler objective, that of exploring the impact of other cultures upon pederasts, and of examining evidence for cultural conditioning of pederast experience—since all experience is culturally conditioned one way or another. Our method will be to report overseas pederast experience of the men interviewed for this book, with corroborating evidence cited in the notes.

There is, of course, a great variety of sexual cultures and attitudes toward pederasty from one part of the world to another. Some social scientists[1] find few if any contemporary societies where any type of homosexual practices is approved. Others, like Ford and Beach,[2] find homosexual acts of "one kind or another" approved or tolerated in 49 out of 76 societies studied. The difference depends on how homosexuality is viewed. Tolerance for adult men playing feminine roles is rare, and maintaining a lifelong exclusively gay life-style is still only rarely approved. Sex play between men and boys, however, and between older and younger boys—at least among unmarried males—is tolerated in many cultures. To take one ex-

111

ample, a University of Pennsylvania anthropologist tells of a Melanesian society where nearly every male is involved in pederast activity at one time or another.[3] That culture recognizes the erotic needs of adolescents, encourages masturbation, and openly tolerates and discusses man-boy sex play, although there is no gay-homosexuality. When a man marries he is expected to give up masturbation, but he may continue to play sexually with boys so long as he sexually satisfies his wife. Men whose goal is pleasure frequently report more fun with boys than with wives, and Suggs[4] says that the most acceptable and approved form of sex play is with the youngest adolescent boys, as they are more playful and have more appealing skin. Little or no stigma is attached to sex play with boys, including anal intercourse, and adults frequently tease a young boy in public, asking who he has been playing a girl's role with.[5] The only thing considered wrong or queer is for a young man not to marry when he reaches the appropriate age. For him to continue amusing himself sexually with young males is approved so long as such sex play is mutual and playful.[6]

The impact of such sexual cultures is clarified in a review volume on the *French Encyclopedia of Sexual Life*,[7] which described the "flourishing pederast tourism to places where sex play with youngsters is tolerated or even promoted for reasons of business or hospitality." Aware that sex play with minors at home can lead to prison, many European and some American pederasts solve the problem by regular trips overseas (50 per cent to Mediterranean countries; 6 per cent to the Far East) where sexual approaches to youngsters that would lead an American to be lynched at home result only in "approving smiles from ambitious parents." Other men have become aware of their pederast inclinations and desires as a result of their experiences as soldiers, businessmen or tourists. Still others, inhibited at home by laws, morals and customs, are freed from their inhibitions as a result of overseas sex play. The purpose of this chapter is to examine such experiences as reported by pederasts interviewed.

VIETNAM AND SOUTHEAST ASIA

The culture that most recently has influenced large numbers of Americans is the Vietnamese. Many Frenchmen came back from Indochina with newly acquired pederast tastes earlier in the century.[8] Grant[9] reports on the recruitment of twelve- to fifteen-year-olds to serve American troops in Vietnamese brothels. Views of both European and American men are presented here. A European pederast said: "The Thais and Vietnamese accuse the Chinese of pederasty, much as the southern Europeans say that the Germans come down to corrupt their boys. In both cases, as I have experienced it, the sex play is both willing and mutual, for many Buddhist areas are very relaxed about pederasty. The impact of Western society and United Nations standards for protecting women and children have tightened laws against prostitution, but man-boy sex play is nearly everywhere tolerated as an acceptable substitute for the unmarried man or the man away from home—as long as there is no cruelty or vice, by which many of them mean the use of drugs. I first went to Indochina when the area was still under French influence, and many Europeans out there had learned to take life as it comes, including a bit of hanky-panky with willing boys. But when the Americans arrived, everything seemed to turn commercial. I am reminded of what Malaparte[10] said about the corruption of Neapolitan boys when Allied troops arrived there in World War II. The Americans were so open, affectionate, and generous, that it was corrupting to boys who had only their bodies to offer when they wanted to solicit what their families needed. My favorite boys are the Thais, for they are clean, sweet, lovable and sexy. You can talk openly to schoolboys there about sex with no problem, for if they aren't interested, they'll tell you or introduce you to a friend. I got acquainted with a whole Boy Scout troop that way and a friend and I conducted a sort of Junior Kinsey study with them. Only 35 per cent of them would consider sex play with 'a foreigner or teacher,' but over 70 per cent of them said there was nothing wrong with man-boy sexual activity, so long as there was no anal intercourse. Only 10 per cent of them thought it would be right to take money from a man for sex, but most of them said that friends should exchange gifts. They must have told their parents about us, for soon we were politely asked to stay away from the Scouts."

An American thus reports his experience in Vietnam: "When I left for Vietnam my wife said she knew me too well to ask me to stay away from other women for so long, but she really had less to worry about than she thought, for I intended to be faithful. At first I stayed away from places other guys went to for girls. Because I liked the people I made friends with several 'gooks,' including a sergeant who taught me some Vietnamese and Chinese words. He had been a teacher, but couldn't support his family so he went into the army where he could graft. I'll call him San. San was half Chinese and his children were beautiful. He introduced me to girls and, when I said I wasn't interested, he took me one night to a sort of gay bar-brothel where a half-French boy was dancing. He had long hair and was trying to win the obscenity prize, if you know what I mean. San asked me: 'Is that what you want?' I said No and I meant it, but I was curious to meet the kid, as I had never seen anything like him in my whole life—not in Texas, man. San invited the boy whore over to talk to me, although San was anxious to leave because the place had a bad reputation. The boy was wearing a sort of sarong and I put my hand on his bare knee. The boy laughed and in English said: 'That'll be five dollars,' so I left it there, astonished at how great it felt. I guess San saw my expression, for a few days later he took me to visit a cousin of his whose husband had been killed in the war. She was very poor and we took gifts to her children, a boy of thirteen, who was cute as a monkey, and several girls.

"We visited the family several times to take the children on a jeep ride, and I noticed that the boy, Chonny as I called him, had no shoes. I asked San about buying him a pair and Chonny was thrilled when San told him, saying he would work for me to pay for them. I said that was not necessary, that I would buy him clothes, books, and pay whatever was necessary so he could go back to school. This pleased San, who said he would take Chonny to live with his family in order to go to school, if I would 'adopt' him in that way. It didn't dawn on me that I was making a sexual contract, but from then on whenever I went to San's house, Chonny waited on me like a personal servant. San saw my dismay and embarrassment, so he asked: 'What's the matter? He's a sweet boy and wants to love you. Why don't you relax and enjoy him?' So I did. I'd been gone from my wife a long time and I was ready for something. I figured that this kind of jacking-off with a boy was more loyal to my wife than chasing after girls as all my friends were doing.

"From then on, I slept with Chonny a couple of night a week. It was fun teaching him English and snuggling with him. At first he was very docile, eager to please me. As he grew older—I think he was a late developer—he became more aggressive himself. I grew so fond of him I wouldn't do anything to hurt him for the world. I talked of helping him prepare for the university, but all he wanted was to be a mechanic. He had marvelous hands for repairing anything, or for making me feel good. I'd never been much for massage, and so forth, but I swear he was so good he could give me an orgasm just by massaging me. Chonny was also very religious, and he said the body is holy—by which he meant something different from what I had been taught at Sunday school in Texas. He said that when we enjoyed each other sexually we were worshipping. Sometimes he would sing religious songs to me as we made love, and he would pray each time he came—which for him was several times a night. I tried to think what my friends in Texas would say about prayers during orgasms. I grew up thinking of myself as a pretty good kid, so I knew it was sinful when I played with myself—with Chonny, however, it was just the opposite, a gift of the gods or something like that. The sin—in Chonny's eyes—was to fail to please me, and that blew my mind. I was really on the other side of the world where everything was upside down!

"I found I wasn't the only American sleeping with boys, but nobody talked about it, except a friend of Ernie and me. We talked about how much we enjoyed it. He had a boy he was supporting at an orphanage, only it was a sexual arrangement from the start. A pimp had taken him to the orphanage to help him find the boy he wanted. I had scolded Ernie for picking out a kid so young, a regular little doll, but Ernie said he had no intention of using him as a woman, but simply wanted someone to hug, kiss and cuddle. When Ernie and I went to Australia together on R and R [rest and recreation], Ernie was the first to point out to me how beautiful the blond kids were. As fond as I was of Chonny, I had to agree that he whetted my desire to get my hands on one of those Sydney kids who were built like young gods. We talked to some teen-age boys at a Sydney amusement park and found they had been runaways for some days. Just for kicks we told them we slept with boys in Vietnam and asked if they would be interested. They said No, but one of them said that when he was older he might visit Vietnam and try it for himself. Then, on one of the rides at Luna Park, the same boy confided to me that in London, before emigrating to Australia, he had slept with a man and he would consider doing it with me for ten dollars—which he badly needed—if I wouldn't let his friends know. Knowing Sydney was more like Texas than Vietnam, I decided it was too much of a risk, so I gave him the ten dollars for nothing. He must have told his friends, however, for one of them told Ernie he was interested in mutual masturbation for ten dollars. Ernie took off with him, and the third kept telling me he was cold and the cops would pick him up if he slept in the park. So I offered to take him home if he would go. He turned out to be from Malta. His father was very Italian-looking and welcomed us like prodigal sons. The family served me a feast and entertained me—no joking—with stories about a lynch mob that was about to be organized to find a man who had been propositioning boys on the beach. I wondered if it was a warning, but as I left the father said: 'Don't worry! Those were very small boys who were bothered on the beach. I sometimes slept with boys myself when I was your age. At fifteen my son is an adult now, and quite free to decide such things for himself.' He was so nice I felt cheap about it.

"In Thailand Ernie and I met a teen-age boy who wanted to serve as our guide, and right off he told us his life story. At the age of ten he had a job washing the car of a businessman each week, and afterwards the man always used him sexually before paying him. He didn't like that, but thought it was part of the job, so he told no one. Then he made friends with a pederast 'teacher'—a college-age guy, perhaps Peace Corps?—who took him to bed more pleasingly, and 'taught him that sex didn't have to be dirty.' He wanted us to swim in the canal with him, but I decided it wasn't clean enough, as they used the same canal for a toilet. The kids are a beautiful golden brown in the water, their skin shining like satin in the sun, and they clown around sexually for their own amusement as well as for spectators like us. I met a dark-eyed wonder of a boy in the canal, and no one at the hotel batted an eye when we took the two boys to our room. Neither Ernie nor I were prepared for the new type of fun they provided, which was to put on a show for us. I've seen pornographic movies, but nothing like that! It was a wild night, and I was surprised how much two kids could teach us that we didn't know. They really knew how to put on a show to get the studio audience involved."

This ex-service man told of many other sexual experiences with boys during his time in Asia, especially when on leave. He said: "I know I'm an entirely different person as a result of this experience." He developed a taste not only for casual recreational sex but also for varied types of sexual intercourse, which led him to become a practicing pederast and establish a sexual relationship with a boy when he returned to the United States. He belongs to an angler's club which is comprised of a group of ex-service men who are pederasts and who go fishing together. One of them is Ernie, who adopted and brought home his little orphan.

NORTH AFRICA

Another area of the world where many foreigners have had pederastic experiences which resulted in radical changes in their sexual behavior and life-style is the Barbary Coast, from Tunisia to

Morocco, as reported in many novels,[11] travel books and historical studies. For example, Gavin Maxwell,[12] in a footnote about the pederasty of a royal family, points out that sex play between men and boys "was never in any way considered abnormal or shameful," and the omnipresent existence of "Greek love" has been commented upon "either directly or obliquely by nearly every French writer on Morocco," who said that sexual relationships with boys were considered normal and a harmless convenience. Until quite recently, for example, the Moroccan army always traveled with young boys for sexual entertainment in the evenings. During the years of French occupation of North Africa, Frenchmen with pederastic inclinations found North African youngsters most irresistible—they had no hangups about sexual deviancy, were clean, and were "passionately loving as long as they were not being exploited." For example a teacher assigned to a Moroccan village (not one of the cases interviewed in our study) said: "I had never thought about sex play with a boy as being fun and possible until my pupils invited me, the first week I arrived, to join them at the public bathhouse. It was operated by the father of one of my pupils, and was in fact the only place in town where one could take a bath. We were no sooner in the building before the sex play began, right in front of me and the proprietor, who said he would leave so I could join in the fun without embarrassment. My pupils chased the younger boys, undressed them, pinched them, sexually teased them—amidst hilarious laughter—and then they came for me. At the first few times I refused to join in the play, but gradually across the months I began to let them undress me and soap me—and I do mean all over—and of course I was affected by the giggling of the younger boys when they were held down for anal intercourse, hardly against their will.

"Soon," the Frenchman continued, "my pupils were presenting themselves at my little house, one at a time, to sleep with me. They were sweet, sexy, naively innocent, and delightful. I'll remember those nights as among the happiest in my life. I would like to marry, but I'm sure my wife would not approve of such play, and I have no intention of giving up boys. Since returning to France I nearly always have a teen-ager living with me. Currently I have two boys whose mother is quite aware of our sexual relationship. She is only too glad to have them off her hands so she can entertain her lovers. I have had only two troublesome problems with the police. The first was when the postal authorities intercepted some photographs I had ordered from abroad. Ironically, it was at a time when, not wanting to embarrass my family, I had decided to lead a more prudent and moral life. The pictures had been intended as a substitute for sex play. My second problem was more amusing. In my third year in North Africa the chief of the village summoned me to his house. I went trembling, sure that I was to be punished for my sex play with the boys. He received me kindly, and over a cup of mint tea asked me why I had never taken his son to bed? It was true that I had rebuffed all overtures from the son of the headman of the village, fearing trouble. 'Of all the boys in your school,' the chief scolded me, 'My son loves you the most. It is important for you to encourage that love or he will lost interest in his schoolwork, and I am ambitious for him to be the first boy from this village to go to the university. I promise you that if you love him as he wishes, he will be your loyal friend for life.' It was true. The boy writes me every year and invites me to return for a visit. He says all my former pupils will welcome me warmly, and also their wives and sons. The chief's son did an unusual thing when he came to France on a visit. He not only brought his young wife along, but he brought her to my apartment for dinner. I appreciated it as an expression of friendship more significant than his warm kisses when he arrived and as he left. I have a few friends in France who know my secret: *that in my personal and emotional life I am secretly a citizen, not of France, but of that village.*"

AN AMERICAN IN NORTH AFRICA

A businessman, sixty years of age, reported that since his twenties he had been aware of a strong desire for sexual contact with boys, but until ten years ago his pederastic experience had been limited to his imagination, except for one fleeting incident when he had been with the American forces in North Africa during World War II. His memory of an evening on a beach with a young Tunisian boy had so haunted him across the years that when he was divorced he resolved to return to North Africa for his first vacation. He said: "I went with Mac, a British friend, who a number of years ago had met a beautiful lad who, wearing only a bikini, was dancing in front of a jukebox in Tangiers. He took the lad home and met the kid's widowed mother, who said she could no longer support the boy and quite literally gave him to Mac. He paid the boy's school fees, fixed his teeth and supported him for several years until the lad went into the army at the age of seventeen. The mother understood the arrangement to be sexual, for when Mac would arrive on a visit, she would say: 'I'll go visit the neighbors so you can go right to bed.' Mac showed me the love letters the boy had written, always with a picture of a rose clipped from a magazine, since the rose 'is the flower of love.' Mac had so enjoyed the experience that he wanted to search for another lad like that.

"Mac has gone to North Africa so many times that he has dozens of interesting stories to tell. One time a friend of his was awakened in the middle of the night by the police, when he was in bed with a young boy. The police asked if they could borrow his car to chase a thief, apologized for interrupting his sex play and wished him a good time as they left. Another time he was talking to a lad on the street when a policeman called him aside to warn him that the boy was a blackmailer and undependable. The policeman then introduced him to another boy who, he said, 'is more your type.' Mac said that the real danger a pederast faces in North Africa, even though the police are vigilant in enforcing the law, is from older teen-agers who are also interested in the younger boys. They can be insanely jealous. For example, Mac and I rented a car and drove south, stopping at a town where it had been common for pederasts to pause to employ young-sters as companions for their journeys. When we sat in a park we were immediately joined by a delightful boy of fourteen who looked more like twelve. He told us his father was chief man at the mosque, and asked us if we would like to meet his father, which Mac understood to be a sexual invitation. I didn't think it likely, as he was a well-dressed schoolboy, so I asked him questions about tourists stopping in the village to pick up boys to go traveling. He said that the police no longer allowed that, even with written permission from parents, because some boys had robbed the tourists and others had been left stranded far from home. He called some friends over to meet us, and we sent one lad to buy refreshments. He came back with small green oranges and honey cakes. The boys asked us if we would like to stay to teach them English at their school, as boys who could speak English could get better jobs.

"We walked over to see their school, whereupon we were met with a hail of rocks from a young man who was jealous, so we were told later. The youngsters fled, but when we got back to the car, the first one we had met was there waiting to say goodbye. We felt bad about the rocks, so we gave him some money and a coin for each of the others. Then he whispered: 'If we go in the car I can show you a good place to make love.' We didn't take him, however, as we were afraid of the young man with the rocks. Mac said I would like Fès better,

anyway, for 'the Fassi boys are scandalously loving.' When we got to
Fès I set off by myself to look for the swimming pool. I soon attracted
swarms of street boys, amateur guides, shoeshine boys, young prostitutes. I sat on a curb to talk to some of them, and soon two hand-
somely dressed schoolboys, about fourteen years old, paused to
watch. When I smiled, the younger of them said to me: 'They're
niki-puts (whores).[13] Do you like dirty boys like that?' I said No, that
I was interested in love, not sex; so they pushed the street boys aside
and sat down, one on each side of me. We talked about their school,
and the older boy introduced me to his 26-year-old lover, who then
took him off on a motorcycle. Raymond, the younger—not a very
Moroccan sounding name—whispered to me: 'What do you like to do
in bed?' I said I wasn't interested in going to bed with anyone unless I
liked him very much, and then I would do whatever pleased him.
Evidently this was the right thing to say, for he then took me to a
private place to kiss me, whispering: 'Wouldn't you like to meet my
father? He would let me go traveling with you, because I have a
passport.' When we stopped by my hotel to get my coat for the
evening, the doorman looked at Raymond and said to me: 'You are
very lucky, monsieur.' He was right. Instead of dirty experiences
with money-grubbing street boys, I spent several delightful days with
an intelligent boy who considered sex play to be as natural a way to
spend time with a friend as eating or talking. All my fantasies were
fulfilled with Raymond, and I came to understand and accept myself
and my sexual inclinations. It was as if I had for the first time in my life
looked into a mirror, to really see myself and approve of what I saw."

These two pederasts rented an apartment in Tangiers when they
returned from Fès. The American was curious to learn more about
the sexual attitudes and culture of young adolescents in that part of
Africa, which was so different from what he had experienced elsewhere. His tale continues; "When Mac left to check out a call
service that had replaced Morocco's last boy brothel, I stood at the
market, leaning against a car. I was astonished at the number of
well-dressed schoolboys who stopped to talk, to ask for a cigarette or
to introduce themselves. I quickly discovered that the secret of my
popularity was the expensive sports car—not mine—that I was leaning against. As a result of this experience I resolved to get acquainted
with more such lads, instead of the shoeshine boys that interested
Mac. With the help of a student I invited large numbers of youngsters
from good families, a few at a time, to our apartment for coffee and
cakes. I began each conversation by telling them quite frankly that I

wanted to know what they thought about foreigners who came to their country looking for sex play with boys, and asked them to tell me about their own attitudes and affairs. They were astonishingly frank. One lad admitted that he had gone to bed with a jeweler, to try out for a job as apprentice. Older boys told me how they courted younger ones, and sometimes brought their 12- and 13-year-old lovers around for me to meet. They told me that if a youngster in their neighborhood accepted a ride on the back of an older boy's motorbike, for a ride into the country, he knew it was for *niki;* and if they had a quarrel, the youngster would have to walk home, with sometimes the older boy even taking his shoes so that he would arrive home with sore feet. The younger lads were wooed with little gifts, but few of them could resist motorcycles and automobiles.

"One young lad kept returning to our apartment to get something he had forgotten, and he always forgot something else so as to have another excuse to come. When I didn't invite him to bed, he brought around his bicycle, saying he needed a few dollars to have it fixed. I had seen him at the beach with his family, so I was sure he wasn't short on money, nor could I find anything wrong with the bicycle. When he was gone, the student who had introduced him to me asked how direct I expected the lad to be? To ask for a loan was the only honorable way a lad from a good family could hint at his desire for sex. So I sent him a note asking if he would like to go for a ride in my car. I found him to be frantically passionate, for he was used to regular sex with an older boy, who at that time was in Europe as a student. I think he would have come twice a day to our apartment had I encouraged him. At one of my coffee hours I found that I had in my apartment a leading revolutionary politician's 15-year-old son who, indeed, was a bit shy and embarrassed. When I asked him what he thought about foreigners coming to his country for young boys, he grew angry and very indignant, saying: 'It's terrible! Tourists give boys alcohol and drugs, corrupt them with money, abandon them. Certainly I would never go to bed with any foreigner!' Then he added, 'Except of course with a gentleman like you to whom I had been properly introduced.' This explains why I am addicted to North Africa, and spend all my vacations there."

AN ENGLISHMAN IN SYRIA

The tradition is that the Arabs of the desert were untainted by pederasty until they conquered Syria and took over its luxurious houses and sexually-trained slave boys. Tradition also is that Emperor Hadrian was seduced into pederasty by a boy he met in a Syrian garden, which was also a kind of brothel-amusement park. Until recent years the city of Tripoli had a large community of pederast foreigners, all in the same neighborhood, each living with a young boy. It is not yet clear whether or not a Marxist society will be more successful than Christian and Muslim theologians who earlier sought to end pederasty in the Middle East. It would appear, from reports of recent pederast visitors, that as elsewhere in the world, stricter law enforcement and a police state mentality simply drives three thousand years of history underground. A tourist who tried to talk to a boy at a Damascus swimming pool was told that it was not wise for them to talk beside the pool, but they could meet at a private place afterwards. And when another visitor stopped a young teen-ager on the street to ask directions, the boy shook his head, pointed to a nearby policeman and crossed his hands as if in handcuffs. An Englishman said: "Once you speak the language, you meet teachers who worry that the age of marriage should be lowered, there is so much sex play between older and younger boys. There isn't much gay-homosexuality, but man-boy sex play is pretty much ignored unless a parent complains or unless a tourist is involved, as they do not want a bad press in Europe. I got acquainted with, and used to sit and talk with, a boy who ran an amusement stand. He told me all the gossip about men and boys, and offered to 'fix me up' with almost any boy on his street if I would meet the boy privately at the end of the bus line. He said there was a great difference among boys of different neighborhoods, by which he really meant different religions and social classes.

"I would ask boys who were walking hand in hand if they were lovers. Sometimes they would blush and say No, sometimes they would say Yes, or the older would say: 'I can't tell you. His father would kill me!' I got acquainted with a pimp and asked him if boys were available. Not to foreigners, he said; the boy brothels were all gone, the last one having been at Aleppo. Later, when I had earned his trust, he took me to see various establishments catering to pederasts. One was a coffeehouse where men and boys played games and sipped soft drinks together. Upstairs were private rooms where boys came in the middle of the night. Some were street boys who had no other place to sleep. They would dance to amuse men and many would be selected as partners for the night. Others were boys who worked as apprentices and clerks. They came to play cards and often ended up sitting on men's laps and going to sleep with them afterwards when the entertainment was over. The shop boys didn't dance for the crowd, but they often played a kind of strip poker which involved a great deal of hilarious sex play.[14]

"At this coffeehouse I met a Syrian who spoke excellent English, having for many years been employed by the British Army in some capacity. He had two wives, he said, and wasn't much interested in boys, although on occasion he had slept with a young Armenian who was great fun. I asked about meeting the Armenian, and he said that if I wanted to meet some boys who were a cut above the semi-prostitutes at the coffeehouse, he would invite me to his home for dinner. I was warmly welcomed by his own 12-year-old son, a fascinatingly handsome boy with deep black eyes, who promptly installed himself on my lap. During the course of the evening the boy's eyes grew increasingly glazed, he showed obvious signs of sexual arousal, and he played with me sexually in full view of his parents. When I prepared to leave, the father invited me to spend the night, saying his son wanted to sleep with me. I declined, with a sodomy gesture to suggest that something unfortunate might happen. The father laughed and said that the boy was of an age to have a mind of his own and was a very sexy boy. When I left, the boy was in tears. As we walked to the bus, the father said: 'He's a lovely boy and you could have great pleasure with him. His 14-year-old brother is living with a man in Istanbul who enjoys his favors very much. Why don't you take him with you for a week or so?' I replied that I was not a rich man, and the father's face flushed with anger as he said: 'My son is not for sale! And while I would like for him to find a foreign friend who would later help him go overseas for an education, the main thing is that he likes you and wants you. Have you no love in your heart?' "

AN AMERICAN IN LEBANON

A young American who went to Lebanon with the U.S. armed forces, said that he would never have had the courage to make sexual overtures to a boy, even though he had long been tempted, had it not been for his experience with a 13-year-old Lebanese boy named Samir: "Actually it began the very first night, when two brats offered to carry my baggage and stay with me at a hotel if I wished. I discovered that the late buses were often met by young boys for that purpose. I got quite well acquainted with one of them. His father, who had five wives and dozens of hungry children, had placed him with a pederast barber whom he hated. He said he would be pleased to come live with me, as houseboy, for twenty-five dollars a month. I found him delightful company, and since I couldn't hire a houseboy, I got a car and took him on a good many all-day trips. His uncle, a cabdriver, could not understand why I wouldn't take the brat home to live with me, saying he had been to bed with his nephew and could recommend him highly. Out of curiosity, I propositioned the cabdriver for his own 9-year-old son. 'He's too young,' the driver replied. 'Touch him behind my back and I'll kill you, but make an honorable arrangement to educate him in America and you can take him any time you wish.'

"He then introduced me to a boy named Wafi who, at the age of thirteen, considered himself to be a man, for he had a good job in a shop, supported his mother, and went to night school to study English. Wafi's mother told me he had a passport and would be pleased to take trips with me. Wafi was extremely jealous of his best friend, who spent libidinous week ends with a German sea captain whenever the ship was in port. Wafi and I had a fine experience together as equals and friends. He was very proud of our friendship and paraded me before his friends as an uncle from America. Although we didn't have any real sexual intercourse, there was an erotic relationship between us that was powerful, so much so that it still moves me when I see a boy who looks like Wafi. One day I took him to a private swimming club, where there were only men and boys. Suddenly in exasperation he asked: 'What's the matter with me? I love you and you treat me like a little boy who doesn't know how to please you in bed.' I replied that I had so much real affection for him that I didn't want to spoil it with homosexual intercourse: 'Wafi, I feel like a father to you.' He scowled and then grinned, saying: 'When you're my age and don't have a woman, a father is no help when you get sexy.' "

A CANADIAN IN CENTRAL ASIA

There are areas in Iran, Afghanistan, Russian Central Asia, and Pakistan where man-boy sex play is considered to be merely "a pleasant and amusing experience, a necessity just as food and drink."[15] A German newspaper[16] reported that in 1963 alone almost 3,000 boys were prepared in secret Pakistani brothels for male prostitution, many of them for export. Novelists like Michener,[17] and explorers from years ago have described the popularity of boys as sex partners in the region: " . . . the young men of Boukara enjoyed three types of amusement: hunting, music, and sex play with favorite boys. I was astonished at the open way, without any shame, that they spoke of the latter."[18] An Italian mountain climber wrote: "Everyone here talks about it [the sex play between men and boys] quite openly. If you want a girl you first court her younger brother." He tells of the almost mystical spell cast upon his audience by a sexy dancing boy, and then reports: "A father is jolly proud here if his boy goes with one of us."[19]

A Canadian reported on his experiences in the region: "At home I had an affair with a youngster when I was in my late teens, and then, sadly, I thought I had to give that all up as 'kid stuff,' however much it was in my blood. But then my job took me to Central Asia. I thought I could only be a voyeur there because of language problems, even when I found that there hadn't been much change in sexual culture in the last thousand years or so. By the age of ten or twelve a boy is considered an adult who can decide such things for himself. While girls are highly protected, it is assumed that boys must learn to cope with the constant banter about homosexuality, the songs, folk tales, ballads and folk sayings. With the coming of motion pictures, it is no longer true that dancing boys are the favorite entertainment. As the region has become westernized, pederasty has tended to go underground to remain largely as prostitution. I met a cabdriver in Lahore who spoke some English. He offered to help me find a boy who would go for a ride into the country with me, indeed we simply drove until I saw a boy who appealed to me, and then the cabdriver made the arrangements. He wouldn't talke about sex matters though, when I sought more information. He said that was personal and private. He helped me find a student who was willing to take me to some villages—we would call them towns—where people were willing to talk openly about pederasty, although we had to charm a few palms with silver to get things started. I met several fathers who invited me to take their young sons back to Lahore with me for a few days. The student introduced me to two different types of boys, aged twelve to fourteen. Some were passive youngsters who were available for employment as houseboys, cooks or whatever. He said they would be very docile, obedient, and dull. Others—by far the vast majority— were hardy, tough, fiercely independent and masculine, mountain boys who take a comrade on sexually with the same rough spirit with which they play a brutal kind of polo. All this is lots of fun, like playing with a tiger. Since the girls are segregated and, besides, have a kind of rigid puritanism to overcome before they break free to express their sexual desires and needs, such boys 'build up almost unbearable erotic tensions.' In bed, once they have proven they are strongest, the wild tigers become playful kittens. I've decided it is somewhat the same at home, too. I would have thought I was afraid of tigers, but now that I've become an adventurer, I'm ready for and seeking all sorts of new surprises."

A GERMAN IN GREECE

South Italy, Sicily and Greece have been the playground of northern European pederasts since the eighteenth century, as we reported in the last chapter. One observer of the region[20] states that this popularity stems from a positive attitude toward sexual pleasure, which comes down from pre-Christian times; combined with the sensible attitude that all youngsters pass through a homosexual period in young adolescence which is normal, healthy and enjoyable, if treated naturally. Along with this, in many of the more impoverished communities, it is accepted that young persons use whatever talents they have to advance themselves, including their physical charms. For girls this has meant advantageous marriages, but for boys it has often meant finding a pederast patron or sponsor who, in exchange for sexual favors, would help a boy advance his career in ballet, the arts, business, or through aid for an education. Families not infrequently make contracts with wealthy patrons which are almost temporary marriages. For example, a nonpederast businessman went to a school in Athens to inquire about employing a boy as guide to help him find his way around the city for a few days. The principal pointedly asked the visitor if he was sexually interested in the boy. When the reply was negative, the principal relaxed and helped him find the right boy. When the youngster took the visitor to meet his mother, a day or so later, she suggested that the businessman take the boy to the hotel for the night: 'It would save you time in the morning,' she suggested. 'And if you like him you might decide to take him to help him get a good education.'[21]

A German pederast explained: "When I was a boy, just after the war in the 1940's, I had a happy sexual experience with a man who had been a Scout leader before Hitler. With him I had a beautiful relationship but, despite that, I was afraid to indulge my own pederast inclinations in Germany. I knew a teacher who went to Greece at every possible vacation, having been aroused to a fever pitch by working in an Italian junior school for boys. He would go to a rural pension, where the proprietor would let him sleep with one of his sons. This was not considered to be prostitution (a scandalous notion), but affectionate sex play between friends, plus an opportunity for the boy to improve himself by associating with herr professor. I assumed that no such experience would be possible for me, since I spoke no Greek, but still I traveled with a sense of high adventure. On my first day in Athens I met a young Greek soldier in a park who asked me to buy him a drink. When I realized I was being propositioned, I told him that he was too old for me, so he said he would find two young boys and we would 'take them to the mountain.' That may have simply been a slang phrase for erotic pleasure, I wasn't sure. It took only fifteen minutes for him to go and return with two schoolboys who seemed elated to be of our party. We took them to a movie, and the film had hardly started when the boy I was with put my raincoat over his lap and pulled down his pants. Instead of guiding my hand to play with him where I expected, he raised up to sit on my hand, so I could titillate him in an unexpected erotic zone. He then slipped his hand under me, in the same way, and I saw his other hand was under the other boy sitting beside him. The finger play, which was as far as it went, was a very erotic experience, and I suppose it is one of the sixty-nine pederast games mentioned in a medieval book.

— "On another day I went to a small factory on business and at lunchtime I talked with a dozen apprentices, aged twelve to fifteen. After I bought them drinks they grew very friendly, and I played with my dictionary in an effort to communicate with them. Finally, throwing caution to the winds, in light of my experience at the movies, I slipped my hand under the youngster sitting beside me and tried to ask if he would be interested in something like that. Two of the boys signaled for me to follow them to the men's room, where they proceeded to play with each other sexually to ask if that was what I meant. When I said Yes, they went into a huddle. I didn't know but what they were debating how best to deal with a deviant like me. But no, they were drawing straws. The winner, a bright-faced boy with a handsome smile, politely excused himself and departed on the run. I continued talking to the other boy until the first one came back with his father, who spoke a bit of English. He had gone to ask his father if it would be all right for him to take me to their apartment, since no one was there during the day. As the father gave me the key, he said the boy had to be back to work in an hour and a half, but that the others would cover for him if we had such a good time that he was late.

I could tell that it was not the youngster's first time, for he was very experienced. When I returned the key, the father asked me not to let his wife know, as she was very religious, and would feel it necessary for the boy to confess to a priest. However, he said, if I wanted to take the boy for a week end, he could arrange it. During the following three years I spent so much time with that Greek boy that he could speak good German by the time he was sixteen, which helped him to get a good job. We remained close friends, so I made a special trip to Greece for his wedding. Since then I've had a dozen other such experiences, each different, but even when disappointing they've been exciting enough to spur me on to hunt for more."

SOME CONCLUDING OBSERVATIONS

• Mariani[22] points out that pederasty seems to flourish in two radically different types of society. First, there is the spartan military society with a good deal of comradely pederasty. Perhaps, he says, such all male societies want to keep petticoat influences out of camp. However tolerant such a society may be of man-boy sex play, it is secret, private and excludes foreigners. The second type is a pleasure- and luxury-oriented society with an indulgent, sensate sort of sex play, because, despite religious sanctions, there inevitably seems to be a good deal of pederasty in societies which are pro-sex pleasure.

• Most pederasts report that they found boys to be more interested in sex play in countries *other than their own*. It is intriguing, for example, to note that a German pederast who visited New York City in 1971, after surveying the pederast scene on four continents, reported: (1) there were as many boy prostitutes easily available in New York as in any other city in the world, and (2) that the typical post-pubescent American boy was as immediately responsive to sexual overtures as those of Southeast Asia or North Africa. The German generally talked to boys who were with their families in tourist areas, in arriving at the second conclusion. He found these boys initially fearful, but hardly inhibited at all after they found him trustworthy in keeping their confidences.

• An interesting recent reversal is evident in North Africa where pederasty is being driven underground by strict new government measures;[23] in sharp contrast with France where, as portrayed in current novels,[24] there is now what one observer has called a 'veritable invasion of pederasty from North Africa.' Whereas previous generations brought pederastic tastes back from Africa with them (which caused a scandalous amount of boy prostitution in France[25] until the French social work profession achieved close supervision of abandoned and neglected youngsters), there is now evidence of a new sort of cross-cultural influence, somewhat like that which the Puerto Ricans have brought to New York City, with hordes of sexually playful North African youngsters now in France to fertilize the seeds of pederasty long seen in French art, youth movements, and novels.

• There is no adequate evidence on Communist societies such as China, or Albania where pederasty was well-rooted,[26] as to the success of Marxist societies in rooting out sexual deviancy. Certainly, if pederasty exists it is deep underground.

• A hundred other stories similar to those told here could be included about other countries such as Senegal, Colombia, Sweden, Indonesia, Mexico, and so on. The obvious evidence as to the impact of another culture in stimulating the desire for new sexual experiences, as well as providing the opportunity to indulge in sexual activities a tourist would not risk at home, and awakening latent pederast tastes is present in a large number of these case studies. There seems to be little question, after one has examined the data that (1) the availability of exotic types of sexual experience to tourists has an impact on their sexual behavior after they return home, and (2) that sexual cultures are modified, and law enforcement is made difficult, as a result of cross-cultural influences in a world which does not yet have a world society and world law.

• All that is said in this chapter should be tempered by the reminder that in such colonial and tourist areas it is the common view of local persons that pederasty there is caused by persons from England, Germany, etc., "where pederasty is rife."

CHAPTER 10

Experience in Another Culture:
A Nobel Prize-Winner's Story

Our third guide to the underground gives us an insight into his childhood that helps us to see that sexual experience and its interpretation (rather than just sex acts) is crucial to our understanding of pederasty. A British psychiatrist is exploring the hypothesis that men who are erotically attracted to youngsters may well be of unusual intelligence and sensitivity, whose inversion came earlier in their lives than gay-homosexuals' because they were precociously perceptive of the emotional deficiences in their early experiences. The life story presented in this chapter supports the hypothesis and illustrates as well how the same creative intelligence devoted itself to working out artistically a self-understanding and sense of pederast identity. The experiences of persons interviewed for this book tend to substantiate the psychiatrist's hypothesis in that the fantasy experience of highly intelligent children is creative in elaborating and interpreting their emotional and erotic experience. Their masturbation fantasies may be more effective in influencing their erotic and personality development because that is richer and more imaginative in relating to the erotic level at a particular age. It is crucial to note that lust is a product of fantasy, whereas love and wholesome relationships involve physical contact with real persons. As we listen to this pederast tell of his experiences we wonder if there are differences between his day and ours? What was his understanding of his pederast nature? What triggered his first sexual experiences with boys? What role did his interpretation of that experience play in his decision to become a practicing pederast who did not enjoy traveling unless "there were opportunities to fornicate with boys"? He wrote thousands of words on hundreds of pages, and thousands more have been written about him; so only a selection of detail is made here to present a picture

*which helps clarify the experiences of other pederasts who have not
revealed themselves so thoroughly.*

I was a virgin until the age of twenty-three, which may suggest
that if one has too chaste an adolescence he runs the risk of a dissolute
old age. I was born at the convergence of two stars, and my inner
tension results from being a child of two races, two cultures and two
faiths—although I was raised to be strongly Calvinist and puritan, a
pure and innocent child. Under the other star I was a sensuous boy
who could not believe that the sex play I found so pleasurable was sin
enough for me to be expelled from school, as I was at the age of nine.
My life was shaped by the love I had for my Bible and my parents, but
from an early age I also knew that I had to trust my own sensations and
experience on such matters as sex. From my earliest years I knew I
was somehow different from other boys, and sometimes I thought this
meant I had a special calling from God to be an artist who would be
able to describe and illuminate his experience. Certainly no other
pederast has ever given so many hours and pages to self-
interpretation. Sometimes it seemed that my feeling of being different involved some dark secret: a mystery of being that I was
conscious of only in the hours of the early morning when half awake
(this is the time when one get glimpses into the unconscious). I knew
myself to be sexually different from other boys before I knew anything about sex. How could I, at an age when I knew nothing of the
sex thoughts of others, be so sure mine were strange? I see how a boy
can think himself unique if in his adolescence he is attracted to males
rather than to females, but, although I have give a lifetime to thinking
about it, I have no idea how at so young an age I could feel that my
enjoyment of sex was special. Probably the fantasies which accompanied masturbation played a role or perhaps some severe scolding
for masturbating at an age too young for me to remember led me to
make a first self-assertion of independence against authority that
would deny the reality and importance of my pleasure. In any case,
my sex play was a secret, as far back as I can remember.

In many ways I did not have a normal childhood. For eleven
years I was an only child, sheltered by my mother, lonely without
satisfactory friends or playmates, because I was frail and often ill. My
father was warm and loving, but also he was very busy and absent
much of the time. I loved reading, and my literary career no doubt
began as my parents read to me. Perhaps I was a literary pederast in
my imagination—greatly influenced by what I read about exotic

climes—long before I acted upon my inclinations. Yet many boys and
even men must have read the same books, without becoming
pederasts. When I was young I not only masturbated alone, but also
played sexually under the grand piano with the little son of the
janitor. My sex play was not nearly so elaborate as my fantasies, for I
really didn't dare do much, but those daydreams no doubt played an
important role in the development of my pederastic character. Yet I
probably would not be a good novelist without them, or even a
serious artist at all, for it was precisely those erotic fantasies and that
sex play which freed me from the rigid constraints which limit so
many lives and which inhibit so many artistic imaginations.

As an old man I am still youthful, finding my greatest pleasure in
being with the young. I might well be a sour old man otherwise. A few
minutes of joy in hearing the laughter of a boy as he plunges into the
water, his skin shining, his body bright in the sun, is preferable to a
thousand years of frozen, inhibited dullness. Now that I am eighty, I
live by proxy through boys I watch, sharing their sense of wonder,
and as a result of my pederast desires my total self is as alive as sixty
years ago—for I love boys with a sensual curiosity, a voluptuousness,
a foolishness, which has often led me to run after them as if I were
their age, staying out too long in the rain to help find a ball. I
remember E., who had such grace because he spent his afternoons
swimming. He looked so awkward in his working-boy clothes, but
naked he was perfect. His skin was blond and downy, and with his
snub nose and saucy face at fifteen he looked like a fawn. I remember
tarrying with V. in a haystack, my clothes full of bits of straw because I
could not resist his pure blue eyes. The law would have arrested me
for playing with him, but when I had to leave to catch the bus, his eyes
were full of tears because I could not stay longer. Then there was that
naughty little tramp who was looking for a job as a cabin boy. I gave
him money to go to another man who would keep him, aware of a
special mania in myself, a lust which grew out of my awareness of how
pederast sailors played with boys like him on a ship. Lust, Shakespeare said in *Hamlet,* will grow weary of a celestial bed and go to
prey on garbage. I'll not speak of the mania I have for going out in the
evening to follow boys like that.

In the Capitoline museum is a bronze statue of a boy with a thorn
in his foot which delights me more than any work of antiquity. Such
art, with boyish grace and slimness, did not move me to sensuous-
ness; it was surely the other way around. My demon was already lying
in wait for me when I was a child, ready to convince me that what

others said was forbidden was essential for my well-being. I did not yet understand that the tempter is an active, positive, energizing force—and never the way you expect. Most people think they are weakened by a sudden surge of temptation, where actually it is the other way around: the demon intertwines himself with everything good and beautiful in your life, so that to reject pederasty is to reject all you value. To destroy the pederasty is to destroy you as well, your whole nature and personality. In other words, the only cure for pederasty is death.

I have always been surrounded by angels, the chief of whom was the cousin I eventually married, and whom I began to love at thirteen. I was never homosexual in the sense of finding men attractive. I was aware, however, that from an early age there were men who found me attractive, and this erotic experience fired some fantasies. Once I felt a real passion for a Russian boy who came to a school party dressed as the Devil, in black tights with steel spangles. Through all of this I was perfectly normal physically, although I may have been more strongly sexed than most boys. Through my youth I was half Protestant minister who bored myself and half small boy playing games. I was deeply affected by the myth of Tristram, including the ideal relationship between a man and his chaste and perfect love. It became characteristic of my life, under this spell, to want love from a woman without sex, and sex with boys I did not love. I was on one hand intoxicated by feminine purity, and on the other by an erotic vision of naked boys playing in the river. Even now, with my wife long dead, I don't know whether my pederasty was caused by my idealization of her, or whether it was the other way around.

In my adolescence it was all toss and go, for I had two types of fantasies. Not until I had my first pederast intercourse in my twenties was the emotional decision made that I was truly a man who loves boys—a pederast in contrast to an invert who does not care for women. I think pederasty is a good thing, that such affection can spring up between man and boy to stir affectionate friendship wherein each can find exaltation, protection, and challenge. I see all orthodoxies as error, especially our sexual orthodoxies. It is unworthy of an educated person to have dogmatic opinions about what is right and wrong—that is, to judge an experience without testing it personally. The harmony between man and woman is lovely, as the meeting of negative and positive polarities, but so can the electric spark between two positive poles be exciting—and that is one way to describe the man-boy sexual experience. Everything in God's crea-

tion is to be enjoyed, and to supress honest love is to deny God—
indeed, one can only suppress false gods. The need to play, as with
the need to worship, lies at the center of a man's heart. If it be sin to
respond to the touch that moves one's heart and body, then I can only
say I regret not having sinned more. To give joy to the young and to
share their joy in return is to celebrate life and cannot be sin.

I mismanaged the courtship of my darling wife both before and
after marriage. First she refused to marry me, perhaps even then
being aware of a private dimension to my life which troubled her.
Rejected, I went to North Africa with a friend, looking forward to
some sexual escapades there. Both of us had decided it was time for
our chastity to end, and I wanted an experience with a girl to rid me of
those fantasies of golden boys bathing in a clear stream with me. A
conversation with Goethe had convinced me to separate love from
pleasure. So I left my love behind and set off for Tunisia to have fun,
not knowing I would there meet a famous man who would open both
my mind and soul in devastating ways by showing me that those
imaginary boys of mine really existed and were waiting to share with
me the voluptuous play I had fantasied since early childhood. From
the moment we arrived in Tunisia everything was exciting, the sultry
climate, the exotic atmosphere, the charm of the people, the smell
and taste of Arabian coffee. I was both elated and troubled when the
youngster who carried our baggage to our rooms half undressed
himself to show me how to drape myself in native garb. The morning
air was delicious, and while my companion got out his canvas to paint,
I set out to explore. Each time I left the hotel a boy would appear to
carry my coat and rug. This time I signaled to one whose bare knees
and legs were enchanting. When we reached an expanse of sand from
which we could view the countryside, he spread out my rug and
threw himself upon it with a laugh, raising his arms in clear invitation.
I sat watching him, wondering what this charming youngster would
do next, my heart pounding at the realization that he and I had the
same desires. When disappointment clouded his face, and he stood
pouting, I seized his hand to tumble him back onto the rug, whereupon he threw off his clothes that were fastened with no more than a
string. The touch of his naked body pressed against me was as exhila-
rating as the lovely splendor of the sunlight on the sand.

When I returned to the hotel my friend guessed that something
had happened from the rapture on my face, but I said nothing. Day
after day I found answers to questions about myself that I had never
known to ask, in experiences with those youngsters who played

around the hotel, their beauty filling me with an erotic and lyrical joy. I was ill for a time, and I delighted in familiarity with their health. My friend and I then employed a servant boy of fourteen, who came to have a great affection for us. He had dreams like Joseph, was obedient and good-tempered. I used him as a character in a novel I was writing about an unconscious pederast, although by then I was perfectly conscious of my own inclinations.

In my illness my thoughts were mostly with the girl I wanted to marry, and I begged her to join me in Tunisia. Then one day my friend came home with exciting news about a darling girl he had met who was from a village where girls prostituted themselves for dowry money. She was amber-skinned and with an almost childish figure, having a savage beauty. We went to a cafe to see her dance, and on the platform beside her was her younger brother playing the casta- nets. Half naked under his rags, slender as a demon, open-mouthed and wide-eyed, he was as gorgeous as she was. My friend whispered to me as a joke: "He excites me as much as she does." With me it was no joke, more than he knew. Later, when I made love to Miriam, I imagined her young brother in my arms. Yet that first intercourse with a woman, and my pleasure with her, convinced me that I was no invert. She was going to come to sleep with us regularly, and things might have shaped up differently had I continued to make love to her, but a telegram came, announcing the arrival of my mother for a visit. I remember my mother's tears when she saw my friend with Miriam, for she must have suspected the truth about me also. Mother per- suaded me to return with her, and although I had another pleasurable intercourse with a woman in Naples, my mind was with boys in North Africa, full of memories of a cafe where boys came to see *Caracous*, an ancient and obscene play which probably began in Constantinople. In Europe the police would have forbidden it, but in North Africa it was performed each night during the Muslim fast of Ramadan. The same men showed up each night for the play, for it was merely an excuse for assignations with the boys. Under the happy eye of the proprietor a strangely beautiful boy played the bagpipes, and the men mostly came for him. He seemed to smile at everyone without favoring anyone, his music giving the cafe its erotic atmosphere. Some of the men would recite love poems to him, but in public nothing went on but a few caresses, for this was not a brothel, but simply a place of amusement where first one boy danced and then another. They were erotically playful, like young animals frolicking in the spring.

The next year I went to Algeria, trying hard to get my beloved cousin to go with me—especially since my hope to marry her had new reasons for renewal—but she would not. I fell under the spell of a friend who insisted that I go with him to another such cafe, which turned out to be an empty place with only a few old Arabs smoking *kief.* I wondered why we had come until the music began. A marvelous boy then appeared, sat on a stool, and began to play delicious music on a reed flute. He had large, languorous eyes, long shapely fingers, and slender bare olive-colored legs. The music and his charms made me forget time and place until I was asked if I would like to meet the little musician. When I said Yes we were escorted to another part of town, to a house guarded by two huge policemen. My friend said for me not to worry, the policemen were there to protect us and knew full well what was going on. One officer led us upstairs to a small apartment where we were followed by our guide and two young figures wrapped in burnooses which hid their faces. The memory of that night has been at the center of my erotic fantasies across decades ever since. If my love belonged to the cousin I wanted to marry, what word can I use for the emotions I felt as I clasped in my arms that playful, wild, ardent, lascivious musician? After the boy had left I spent hours in a state of quivering jubilation. Although I had come to a climax five times in his arms, I relived my pleasure over and over again, prolonging the echoes of that delight until morning. At the light of dawn I got up to run, feeling no fatigue after the night of sex play but, on the contrary, feeling a lightness of body and soul that stayed with me all day. I wrote to my mother to tell her how marvelous I felt, since she always worried about my health, and I wrote to my beloved that we could delay our marriage no longer. Only marriage, I was convinced, could cure the fever in my blood.

I was concerned enough to go to a specialist to tell the doctor about my pederasty, how I hungered for such sex play, and I asked him if I should get married. He assured me at once that since I was deeply in love, my cousin and I were healthy young people, I would soon discover that my pederast desires were a thing of the past, only having existed in my imagination. He said I was like a hungry person who until then had lived on a starvation diet, but as soon as I married, my sexual health would blossom. He was right about my imagination, which was more powerful than he realized. At the center of my life as a writer it is not easily pushed aside. I now think it would have been better had I had more sexual experience as an adolescent, even homosexual activity. My fantasies would then have been rooted in more realism. As it was I was prepared to enjoy with boys the thousands of erotic masturbatory dreams of youngsters whose bodies were gilded with the pollen of the gods. After I was married I did not need the African boys to feed my dreams. Let me tell you of the boy I adopted, how I remember his tangled hair, his languid, sensuous eyes, his bare legs coming out of homespun shorts—all of which made me a pagan whose heart's secret occupation was viewing this very special boy as a work of art. He was my traveling companion and his soul offered rapturous perspectives.

I was in anguish to discover that even on my honeymoon I was surrounded by such boys. Because of the love and joy I was experiencing with my wife, my mind and body seemed to come alive to every erotic sensation in the world. Instead of satisfying my erotic hungers, my wife seemed to enlarge them so intensely that I loved everyone in sight. I had been perfectly honest with her before we were married, with allusions to my pederasty and glowing descriptions of boys in my letters, so she could not help but notice the boys who responded to my smiles, and how upset I was by handsome youngsters. She began to get headaches, which weren't helped by the boys I brought to our rooms to photograph. I was frank with her about being two persons: one, the loving faithful husband; and the other, an adventurer and wanderer whose hunger for exploration was never to be satisfied within marriage. My work flowered in the midst of this conflict, which seemed to spur my creative imagination all the more. Two years later when I went back to Algeria I saw the little musician again. He had hardly changed except that his figure was even more graceful, and he had become so lascivious as to be shameless in his play. No one should make remarks about sex who has not observed breeding animals, thus to see what great variety there is in the world—not only of species, but of varied behavior within species such as mankind. What people consider abnormal would then be seen as a natural part of existence.

With my adopted son as photographer, I explored some of the lesser known corners of Africa. In one country the Sultan sent two boys along with us as pages, both of the young teen-agers wearing only a smock which came to mid-thigh. They looked as if they had stepped from the fresco in the Campo Santo in Pisa ready for the grape harvest. They walked with a spring in their step as if ready to dance, and it dawned upon me that the Sultan had sent them not solely for the pleasure of my eyes—yet it hardly seemed likely that he knew of my tastes. Had I requested women would he have sent along two girls? I doubted it. Boys involved no risk. They were there as a gift if we were interested, and there was no problem for the Sultan if two servants accompanied us. After a day or so the boys seemed hurt by our lack of attention, so I asked the chief steward what their function was. He was quite amused, finding my embarrassment hard to understand. Evidently everyone but me knew what the boys were for, that they had expected to be invited each evening to come inside the mosquito netting over my bed to fan me. It was quite impossible to see through the net, and the heat was so stifling it would be pleasant to be fanned. Sweet little Mala, how I would like to hear his elfin laugh and experience his joy again. He destroyed all pretense by preparing himself with an hour or so of bathing and beautifying before coming to "wield the punkah." My memory of the sensual delights I experienced inside the netting are not merely those of the transports of Mala's swooning body, but also of the whole mysterious and fearful landscape. I left Mala out of the book about my African journey, but now I publish my notebooks which speak frankly about my sex play with boys, such as at Luxor, not hesitating to say that my interest is to go where I can meet such boys, since tourism is for enjoyment.

I have never exploited anyone, such as paying a boy to do something he didn't really want to do. I restrain my desires toward someone who does not respond with equal desire. One difference between homosexuals and pederasts, I think, is that the more I love a boy, the less I desire him erotically. My first flash of desire is born out of curiosity to experience another person, and of an affectionate wish to meet his erotic need—for it is better to give than to receive. It may seem odd that I use biblical language, yet when I ask myself who I am, I think of the story of the Prodigal Son. God's view of deviation is a puzzle to me. Did he create me a pederast? I did not make myself this way, although I allowed myself to fall under the influence of a pederast at a crucial moment in Africa. But by then my pederast nature was already created. I know that if I could live my life over again, I would give more time to sex play with boys, even in the adventures that caused pain and regret. I would spend even more time in Africa, which to me is a festival of sensory memories—every smell, sound and taste. My Africa is both a past and a future, a nostalgia for what is gone, for the sound of the little musician's flute and laughter; and a grasping of the future, when men and boys will more openly be able to play together as comrades.

How shall I describe my erotic experience with boys? My comrades are on many shores: elegant, tanned boys on a beach, whom no ballet master would dare recruit, for their dancing would be considered too provocative if they danced as they swim, with their natural exuberance. I meet these comrades as I prowl at night when all nature seems to conspire—until I would like to kiss the flowers, or embrace any ardent young body. I understand that each person is different, that somehow we crush the human spirit by failing to allow each child or adolescent to follow the call of his own senses. The mystery remains, the link between my dark childhood, my restless adolescence, my young adventurism, my writings, but the moment of death will find me in a state of ecstasy, for the green and blue water of the river at the end of life has been known by me from the beginning; and the boy who waits there to guide me has eyes as blue as a sea of ice, skin like lilies, hair as a cloud colored by the sun at dawn. He is mysterious, waiting there, sketching his dreams in the sand. Is he the angel I have sought through life's voyage? Or is he the child I was, born of two stars?

SOME CONCLUDING OBSERVATIONS

● To expand this story of André Gide's experience, which illustrates the impact of another culture, see his *Journals* (1956, (1926), (1951), (1952), (1964), his autobiography (1934), *Corydon* (1926), and his novels: (1951), (1930), (1969). On his youth: Delay (1957), on his old age: Michaud (1961). Also of interest: Guerin (1959) and Lambert, his son-in-law (1958).

● As we will notice later with many other boys, if Gide was seduced, he seduced himself with his own imagination. We note that this story is directly the opposite of Chapter 6, where adolescent sexual experience seemed to play a central role in pederast development. Note that Gide was a virgin until his early twenties.

● Does Gide assume sufficient responsibility for his own acts? It would seem that Gide's pederasty surfaced because in Africa he met boys who were available, but if a boy is to be blamed, it would seem to be the boy hidden inside Gide as a grown man.

CHAPTER 11

The Consenting Boys

The pederast underground is inhabited by boys as well as men, and the boys are there by choice, despite the public's view—largely held but incorrect—that pederasts solicit and molest innocent and unwilling boys. No doubt some do, for human behavior is almost unbelievably varied, and the world is full of all kinds of people. Of the three hundred boys we interviewed, however, who were sexually involved with men, the majority took an aggressive initiative in seeking the relationship; while most of the rest had role-played in their imaginations the sort of erotic play that might be possible to the point of consent and readiness. When one asks which comes first: presumably there would be no consenting boys if there were not men seeking them and vice versa, the evidence leads to the conclusion that men and boys are equally responsible, at least in present-day society. This may be puzzling and difficult to understand, partly because adolescent behavior varies so much from region to region and from class to class. It is also true that boys have varied sexual experiences, and many more than is commonly realized are one way or another erotically, emotionally, and/or sexually involved with men.

When placed on Chapter 1's continuum or scale, the vast majority of normal boys are in the center, where their homosexual experience is largely innocent, limited to jokes, horseplay, and fantasy. Most of the sexual activity of younger adolescents is playful, and the first step into mid-adolescence is the first experience of passionate, emotional, serious, or loving sex. If such a first experience is homosexual, and especially if there are several such experiences with other boys, it may be a step toward affirming a gay identity. This is especially true if the adolescent is scorned, punished, or scolded for the homosexual activity in such a way as to drive him into a homosexual group for support and friendship, or if it incites him to flaunt his gayness as an expression of rebellion. The dynamics of homosexual commitment are far more complex than that, but it is apparent that society fails many youngsters at crucial points in their adolescence, by failing to understand and properly interpret their erotic experiences. Society wrongly assumes that through a process of normal development all youngsters will move in healthy ways from young adolescent playfulness to responsible heterosexual courtship and finally into marriage. In fact, however, the structures of society which support such a normal process are crumbling, and they have never, in any case, functioned adequately for a large minority of youngsters. From the center of the scale, depending upon their experience and opportunities, many boys move left on the scale into loving relationships, but many others move to the right on the scale into sexual adventurism, affirming and elaborating a playful style of sex relationship which may persist into adulthood. The boy who becomes a pederast is an example.

Our concern here is not with the boys who become pederast or gay, but with the wide range of youngsters who become involved with pederasts. It is a mistake to assume they are gay, neurotic, from impoverished or broken homes, or neurotically delinquent. Like the men they are involved with, they come from all races, classes, social groups, rich and poor, urban and rural—and most of them can be characterized as normal, healthy boys who will marry and have families. Perhaps they are a bit more sexy than the average and more sexually sophisticated and experienced than other boys of the same age, but one is surprised to find that they do not seem to be problem boys. Logic and theory seem to collapse under the evidence of rebellion, secrecy, adventurism and cultural confusion. It does seem to be true that the boys least likely to be sexually involved with men are those who are strictly chaperoned and sheltered, who are highly job- and goal-oriented, who are passionately caught up in sports and hobbies, who spend a great deal of time with their fathers, and who are shy and slow developing. What such a statement implies is immediately overturned by the evidence from the boys themselves.

CHARACTERISTICS OF CONSENTING BOYS

There are obvious differences between upper- or middle-class boys, and those from poor or neglectful families. But certain assumptions, held in both situations, are wrong:

1. The least vulnerable boys are those who are closely supervised by their parents? Not so, agree pederasts and boys. Boys are sexual creatures and will have sexual experiences of some sort, no matter how closely they are supervised. When boys feel imprisoned, they play deceptive games, often deliberately seeking out whatever their parents forbid, be it alcohol, drugs, or sex. "Boys from the strictest families, as far as sexual morality is concerned, have to be the most secretive and often are the sexiest," one pederast says. Oversupervision, as one boy put it, is what makes kids rebel and sneak off. Since most adolescents have their crucial homosexual experiences with other adolescents, protective parents will find it difficult if not impossible to protect boys from sexual experience with other boys.

2. Is it true that boys whose sex education has been adequate and wholesome and whose parents provide good models are less likely to be involved in pederastic experiences? Perhaps that question is unanswerable, because so few boys have such a sex education. One boy came close, however, when he said: "Most guys figure that sex is something you learn only from experience. You've got to try out everything for yourself if you want to know the truth. You can't believe anything adults say about sex." It would seem that most boys are vulnerable to what they learn from their adolescent "tribe," and that their only really effective sex education is what they learn there. For the most part the "tribe" is the place where sex play takes place, of a sort which paves the way for pederastic experiences or which may gradually fall into such sex play. A father's warnings evidently fail, in many instances, to counterbalance a friend's whisper of "It's fun!"

3. High principled boys, who are committed to Establishment patterns of courtship and marriage, are surely the last to be involved with pederasts? Not so. The boy who wants to respect and protect girls, who accepts the view that masturbation is a sin and unmanly, may decide to be pragmatic. Since all sex is sinful, the best compromise, he may decide, is some male-male sex play that at least doesn't run the risk of pregnancy or corrupting a nice girl.

4. Boys who are most heavily and emotionally involved with girls are the least likely to be engaging in man-boy sex play? The answer seems to be Yes by midadolescence, but the boys most often involved with pederasts are the younger adolescents. One says: "I've got a girl but she won't *do* anything." Another admits that he is still too shy or unsure of himself for coitus with a girl. Many boys whose sexual appetites are strongly awakened through heterosexual play

have a need to discharge surplus sexual energy, as pointed out by one pederast: "Never underestimate the potency of many 15-year-olds. I knew one who would ejaculate with his girl twice in one evening and then would be at my house within an hour of taking her home, acting as if he were sex-starved. Most boys of that age, in any case, have sexual intercourse with a girl only rarely, just enough to arouse their appetites." A boy said: "Where can I get enough money to take a girl out that often? I'm too young to drive a car." Many such boys are involved with pederasts for sexual reassurance, tutoring, and for money to take girls out. The vast majority of boys sexually involved with pederasts grow up to marry and have families.

5. Boys who are athletic and well-adjusted socially are less likely to be involved with a pederast? The shy, withdrawn boy may never meet a pederast except if it be his teacher or librarian, and even then he may reject overtures because he is fearful; whereas the athletic, extroverted boy may in fact come closer to fitting the description of the typical boy we found to be involved with a pederast:

- He has more freedom than the average to take athletic trips or to go hunting or fishing with someone other than his father. He may come from a broken home.
- He is self-confident and willing to take risks for adventure. He has above-average intelligence.
- Or he is rebellious and "fun oriented," frequently seeking kicks from drugs, alcohol, stealing-for-fun, and sex.
- He is bored with school and conventional activities. Some of this boredom is probably sexually based.
- He expects to marry and have children, but has accepted the "fun culture" notion of recreational sex. In this context he accepts a certain amount of homosexual horseplay as normal: "There's nothing wrong with having some fun, with playing around a little."
- He is sexually sophisticated and experienced, first with other boys. He probably developed earlier and has a surplus of sexual and other energies.

The lower-class boys involved grew up in an environment more conditioned by dirty talk and sex jokes, and they lived in an adolescent environment which was inevitably double-faced with adults. They tended to lie more to parents, teachers, and, indeed, to nearly all adults. Middle-class boys were also deceptive when it came to sex.

TYPES OF PEDERAST RELATIONSHIPS

Before discussing why boys become sexually involved with men, we here note the most common types of man-boy relationships. It is important to point out that these relationships exist and are not noticed because for the most part they are natural, platonic, and take place with parental sanction. Most man-boy sex is episodic, *an occasional experience as a part of a meaningful relationship which essentially is not sexual at all*. It is characteristic of boys to minimize the sexual aspects of a relationship even when its intent is largely erotic.

1. Most common is what has previously been called the *sports comrade*. A man and a boy spend a great deal of time together because of some enthusiastic, common interest, such as baseball, fishing, or stamp collecting. Most such relationships are platonic, rarely involving intentional sexual activity, and certainly no seduction. Programs like the "Big Brothers" seek to encourage such platonic relationships, to make constructive use of the possibility. Once in a while—no one knows how often—some sexual activity develops as a result of mutual affection.

2. The *employee-employer relationship* is the second natural structure for man-boy sex play. The pederast who goes overseas seeking an erotic relationship with a boy is likely to employ the youngster as servant or guide—as the medieval gentleman had his page or squire; as early businessmen in Brazil brought boys from Portugal for bed companions by hiring them as shopboys; as master craftsmen have sought apprentices who interested them sexually. While more true overseas than in the United States, and more true on the Continent than in England, the largest single category of boys we interviewed were those who were employed in some capacity by a pederast. Not all were grocery delivery boys or yard-workers by any means. Some were actors, models, vendors at sports events, or were involved in other unusual and enticing work.

3. A traditional form of pederasty is the *"patron" relationship*, whereby a man sponsored a boy, trading his help in getting an education, learning a trade, or advancing in a business in exchange for sexual favors. Patronage continues in many forms even today, especially with disadvantaged boys. Sometimes such an arrangement begins with a sexual contract, more often the relationship is authentically what it seems to be, with sexual incidents developing later, and perhaps only occasionally. We found it true over and over again that when deep friendship and affection developed in such a relationship,

the boy often took the sexual initiative as an expression of appreciation, not knowing any other favor he could return, when and if he
became aware that the man was sexually aroused or interested.

4. Another pederast structure is the club of one sort or
another—and it may be a delinquent gang or a baseball team—where
a *man becomes a volunteer leader of a group of boys*. More often the
pederast is an older teen-ager who takes a group of younger boys
under his wing and plays with them as an equal, including their sex
play. One such group, in which the sexual activity gradually descended from group masturbation to mutual masturbation, and then
to oral and anal intercourse, began when the pederast was only
sixteen, but has continued until the present across fourteen years,
with boys dropping out as they reach the age of fifteen or so and
younger boys continually taking their place. This sounds like a slum
gang, when in actual fact it is an underground group in a wealthy
suburb, and the sex is apparently incidental—the boys are really
attracted to one another by a common interest in playing rock music
and glue-sniffing.

5. *Hustling and hitchhiking*—with the former more likely to be
lower-middle-class and ghetto boys, and the latter upper-middle-
class boys—are two forms of the same adventurism. Some boys seem
to have an undisciplinable desire to explore what lies beyond the rim
of consciousness, to have new experiences, which, according to
Zweig,[1] is not tamed by duty or law in their quest. Apparently they
are spurred on in part by a sexual restlessness which in a sense makes
every adolescent a predelinquent. Such desires and drives lead boys
into sex games with girls, prostitutes, older women, other boys, men,
into "beating up queers for kicks," smashing windows, stealing. As
one boy said: "My parents tried to keep a close rein on me, but I broke
loose when I was about fourteen, and now they've given up. All they
ask is that I stay away from hard drugs and keep out of jail. My dad
plays around some with girls, just like I fool around some with my
uncle. Mostly I hitchhike for the excitement. You never know who
you'll meet next, or what will happen when a driver asks: 'Where are
you going?' and I answer: 'I don't know. You got any good ideas?' I get
wined, dined and you know what, but not until I've been to the races,
or skydiving, or to an amusement park." This seems to confirm what a
pederast said of such boys: "Like teen-age soldiers at Times Square,
they go prowling not merely to meet sex needs but also to have a good
time in the spirit set by the entire entertainment industry, which
glamorizes sex games as the sport of the glamor set—the movie stars

and others who are the idols of youth. Those who are adventurous and loners prowl around, at least in their imaginations, looking for adventure, excitement, sex, anything. Increasingly they constitute a subterranean society, another world of their own that no one knows is there."

6. The hustling boy who directly or indirectly solicits men is often seeking a relationship as an adventure. Duvert[2] points out that it is true that such adventuring may have sex or other varied experience as its goal in some cases, but that more often a boy is seeking money to take a girl out, or simply wants to exchange his favors for tickets to sports events or a trip. Such an adventuring boy would be horrified at the thought that he is a boy prostitute, for what most of them are really looking for is an *uncle relationship*, which is Duvert's phrase for the "secret friend" who will take a boy to exciting places which his parents either forbid or cannot afford. On the East Coast of the United States, such an "uncle" is more likely to be called a "steady" and, as Duvert says of Europe, it is by no means only poor boys from broken and deprived homes who seek such relationships. Boys from good middle-class and upper-class families also seek out such "uncles" as a way to escape from the close supervision of parents who forbid masturbation as well as intercourse with girls. Such an "uncle" is often the relative who takes a young boy to a prostitute, who lends him a car before he is old enough for a license, or who in other ways becomes a conniving co-conspirator. More often, however, with middle- and upper-class boys the "uncle" is himself a boy who is only a few years older than the younger boy, who may provide drugs, sex experiences and instruction, and exciting adventures such as hustling or fast driving. The susceptible boys are most often seduced either by this first older male friend or by someone they meet through this friend. Such is, in fact, also true of those lower-class boys who are involved with pederasts. Through an older teenager who may take him hustling, or introduce him to a friend he met while hustling, a young teen-ager meets the "dirty old man" his parents and school have warned him against. His break with the sexual morality of his parents and society, and their authority, begins when he finds that the man he was warned against is in fact the understanding and trusted friend he desperately needs.

Such a "steady" or "uncle" relationship is more often sexual, in contrast with the employer, patron, or sports companion relationships listed earlier, which might be so only occasionally or incidentally. For example, there is a medical student who takes a 14-year-old boy on a trip every other week end, and for two years has also taken the boy on a one-month camping trip in the summer. The boy says: "Of course I do whatever he wants in bed. I'd be a heel otherwise. Why else do you think he takes me?" Or, to take another example not essentially different from the one Paul Goodman describes in a novel,[3] there is the relationship of an businessman with a young Puerto Rican boy upon whose family he lavishes expensive gifts. The family has made it clear that it understands and tolerates the sexual relationship as long as there is no anal intercourse. Of all the possible illustrations, these two are mentioned here because in both cases the boy solicited the relationship by asking an older boy, who had a "steady" to help him find such a friend also.

WHY DO BOYS DO IT?

1. Of all persons in groups in society, adolescents are probably the least likely to tell the truth about sex,[4] for they have everything to lose and little to gain by truth-telling—especially if they are sexually involved with men or something else which is taboo and illegal. Many scholars are inclined to take them at their word when boys say they are primarily involved in sex play with men *only for money*, for there is some obvious truth to it. Hustling increases, for example, in periods of depression, and is least prevalent among youngsters who have jobs. Nor should one underestimate the impact on a boy who discovers that from hustling or from an "uncle" his friend has fifty to a hundred dollars a week to spend. The boys involved with pederasts are generally those under sixteen, too young yet for legal work, who almost universally feel the need for much more money than their allowances or odd jobs can provide. Hardly without exception, however, and especially among the boys who most loudly proclaim the fact that their only motivation for sex play with a man is money, when one probes further into their experience and gets better acquainted with them as persons, it becomes clear that money is actually only a minor factor. Gifts and money are important in many cases, so that a boy can retain at least for himself the pretense that he is not seeking affection or sex pleasure, because of the homosexual threat implied. A boy can say to himself and others at any moment of questioning or doubt: "I'm just doing it for the money."

2. In fact, however, many boys are *seeking affection and friendship*. Some, for example, out of a deficiency: "My father was the type who believed boys should never be hugged or kissed, and I used to

feel sad and jealous when I saw other fathers wrestling with their sons. In fact, it aroused me sexually and I decided this was why Dad would never touch me. That was taboo, but I allowed myself fantasies, such as being kidnapped by a man who would make me do things I really wanted to do. My first sexual overture to another human being was when I was about twelve. I asked a 16-year-old boy to tie my hands to see if I could get loose without help which was acting out my favorite masturbation fantasy. I hoped he would take some advantage of my helplessness. It was the boldest sex act I had ever made, and I next tried enlisting a young man who boarded at our house. He wouldn't tie me up, but he did go along with me in playing sex versions of some card games I made up, in which instead of gambling for money, the loser had to *imagine* that he was paying sexual forfeits. But the thing I really wanted, even when I was fourteen or so, was his arm around me." Another boy said: "I was tired of being treated as a kid. When I first met Joe, even though I was thirteen and he was twenty-six, he treated me like an equal, like an adult. I thought to myself, I'd do anything to have a friend like that. Then another kid warned me that Joe was the sort of fag who would try to get me to bed. By then I had decided that I liked and trusted Joe enough that I didn't care. If he wanted to go to bed I was prepared to do so, and I told him so." The affectionate "uncle" thus plays varied roles in the lives of different youngsters, but it is no coincidence that youngsters seek physical reassurance and affection in young adolescence when they are at a stage of life when no one else is hugging them any more.

3. In addition to money and the quest for affection, the third and more important conscious motivation seems to be the *need and desire for adventure*. Youngsters are often more eager to escape from home than their parents realize, and they may seek to escape through drugs or alcohol, or some other undesirable activity. Why do they feel the need? Homes are comfortable, and many youngsters have been given every expensive gift they ask for—stereo sound system, pet, motorbike. School may seem boring, but it is generally better than the schools their fathers attended. Youngsters stay out all night, hitchhike, steal for fun, prowl into other parts of town to hunt for girls who might not be as moral as the ones they know at school. Boys from good families are intrigued to discover and explore worlds which are astonishingly different from their own. A dentist's son, for example, at the age of fourteen stumbled accidentally into the underworld of his city, which he explored much as his mother had browsed around

the bazaars of Hong Kong. He found street corners in front of bars where one had only to stand to be offered almost anything one could imagine. "I never knew what exciting sex things went on, and it was for me like playing with fire was when I was four or five. The first time I went with a man my spine prickled and my hair nearly stood on end. It was like swinging out from a cliff on a rope and looking down at the rocks in the sea." Even at so young an age he realized he would have to cope with any person—male or female—who would use him sexually to abuse him, so he learned to protect himself. He admitted that he didn't know what he was searching for. In another age he might have gone on a pilgrimage, in olden times boys of thirteen often did; but in our age the pilgrimage of many youngsters seems to be sexual rather than religious—as Malaparte has said: men used to care for their souls but now they seem to care only for their skins.

The adventurers and explorers from good families usually return, like tourists. The unwanted boys from disadvantaged families, however, often become immigrants into the underground. Ten million boys have run away from home in the last twenty years. Most of them soon return—although 80 per cent of them are sexually propositioned if they remain away from home as long as ten hours.[5] Also, a great many of them disappear and never return home. Probably as many as 30 per cent of them are able to stay away as long as they do because they exchange sexual favors for food and lodging. For example, a runaway boy told his family that he had been camping out in the woods, when actually he had been staying with a man and his wife on the other side of town, and sleeping with both of them. Another runaway reported: "I said No to the first man, but a couple of days later I was cold and hungry, it was night and raining and a nice guy invited me to a motel, offering money and to drive me where I wanted to go the next day. He didn't want to do anything I hadn't already done with kids. I ended up going clear across the country with him."

4. Underneath the wish for money, affection and adventure, there is an undeniable element of *sexual desire*. Whether boys are seduced by men or they seduce themselves, the lure of pleasure, especially curiosity about oral sex, is a primary factor. For example, when asked if he had been seduced, one boy replied: "I was really on the prowl for girls. When we were in the seventh grade we tried to organize a sex club of boys and girls—only we never did anything but talk big to shock the girls. I had heard about getting blown [fellated], but it had never really interested me—I guess because I thought no one would really do it. Until one day a man came to our school with

slides to lecture on the danger of getting into a car with a strange man. He showed slides of kids who had been beaten and killed, and he lied when we asked questions, although it was whispered all over the room that such men would blow you and give you money. He also warned us against the bad boys who hang around the fountain downtown and the bus station and the sort of men who pick them up. After the lecture some of the toughter boys teased the rest of us about being scared to try it, because we were sissies who couldn't fight and take care of ourselves. So of course we found it exciting to hang around the fountain some, just to show we weren't cowards. One of the big boys who had been to the state school said that being blown was just another way of jerking off, and that it was one way to prove you were a man, that being blown was a lot of fun, and there was nothing queer in letting a man do it to you. I'd never have been down there at the fountain if the man hadn't come to school to warn us."

A French writer—discussing the way that youngsters are warned against strange men who may be exhibitionists, torturers, kidnappers—points out that in the process boys often come to realize for the first time that there are "men who wish to make love to them" and give them pleasures that society otherwise denies.[6] Another boy reported schoolboy conversations about "Linda Lovelace"[7] and expressing curiosity about oral sex. "Word swept through our school like wildfire that there was a man who would pay you. No one wanted it known, but a lot of guys sneaked off to hunt him up. We soon found it wasn't just one man, but a lot of them." It would appear that such boys are often the ones who have aroused themselves sexually through extensive masturbation, have grown weary and dissatisfied with that, and yet are still too young and insecure to get far with girls. Oral sex is most tantalizing to the young boy who may be embarrassed and worried about coitus. It is easy for inexperienced boys—and for old men who are impotent. There is also the titillation of seeing a man take a submissive role, which is psychologically exciting to many boys who have grown up always having to submit to these giants. Furthermore, the experience opens doors to new psychic games and fantasies, which may be as addicting as alcohol to some youngsters. Novels about the oral sex experience of young adolescents describe the mystery, delight, and fascination found in such pleasures.[8] It is for many boys a type of sex play which involves the possibility of masculine role-playing and fantasizing coitus with a girl, with little homosexual threat.

TYPES OF SEXUAL ACTIVITY

As a rule playful sex does not long remain content with any one game. Either a relationship grows in depth—that is, it becomes loving—or it must continually search for varied experience, for new games, beginning in the imagination and perhaps never moving far beyond it. A naive, inexperienced boy may find wrestling and telling dirty jokes to be as stimulating and exciting as overt sex play might be to a more sophisticated person—as, for example, a boy from a slum where sex play is more genital and where youngsters play dirty in their normal play. Teasing there generally involves sexual molesting of one kid or another; fighting and revenge include sex threats; and not infrequently there is an erotic climate established by the way sissy boys or pretty boys (who are generally small in stature) are continually teased and propositioned, to the amusement and fascination of other boys their age. One 13-year-old said: "I don't dare use a toothpick, for example, for someone will say: 'Got hairs in your teeth again?' I've been expelled for fighting, when the showers in the gym got wild."

It is not only in such a situation as that, however, in which younger boys may come to expect to pay a sexual price for their association with the older boys they admire. The sheltered middle-class boy may be overwhelmed the first time he encounters such an environment, and it may well shock him into experimentation and sexual involvement to prove himself. One such boy said: "They kept talking about raping me, and while I wasn't really worried, because I knew I could take care of myself, I was fascinated." There is a sense in which he had the emotional experience of rape, as a result of the talk, the continual banter and teasing, because it led him into a near orgy of fantasy and masturbation. Another boy described a similar sexual experience at summer camp which evidently had a profound emotional impact, where the older boys teased him by saying things like: "Watch out for your cabin counselor. Don't let him get into bed with you, for he's likely to get your clap!" Or "Do you know the counselor's favorite cookie? Fag Newton! Last year one of the guys went to the chief and complained that their counselor was queer and the chief told them last year's guys hadn't liked it at first, either, but they got used to it in time." Or "You know why I call my cock Cracker Jack? Because the more you eat the more you want."

Such horseplay can easily move beyond verbal teasing, as in an unsupervised moment at the gym of a private school described as follows: "Abe came lunging across the room and dived onto Ben's back as if to ride him. Perhaps to demonstrate his strength, Ben encouraged it until the others tried to pull down his shorts to spank him playfully. Ben jumped them and as they wrestled someone shouted: 'The loser has to kiss the winner's ass.' A small new boy arrived and asked: 'What's going on?' Someone replied: 'They're fighting to see who has to kiss ass.' The wrestlers fought more intensely. The new boy asked: 'Why ass?' Everyone doubled up with laughter as Abe replied: 'Where would you rather be kissed?' Ben shouted at him? 'You're a faggot!' 'He's the faggot,' Abe retorted. 'Hit his head on the floor until he admits it.' The new boy asked: 'How can you tell who's a faggot?' Abe replied: 'By taking his pants off to see if it makes him hard to wrestle with a boy.' In the general uproar the boys were grabbing at each other's crotches." The play would probably have become even more explictly sexual if a teacher had not then arrived.

Such horseplay is partly curious, partly simply play, some of it is substitute sex, in which boys stop short of what they might actually want to do, and sometimes it is actually a disguised sexual overture or proposition. Disguised so a boy can laugh and say it was just a joke if rebuffed; or it may be, as with girls, an experiment to see how far one can proceed before being challenged. Much of it also, of course, is simply a natural overflow of exuberant youthful energy, which turns out to be sexual in unintended ways—especially when some boys are naturally uninhibited. Its importance, however, is determined by how it is interpreted and understood, and by the type of sexual experience it is for each particular boy who experiences it. The boy who habitually masturbates may experience physical contact in such horseplay in a different way from one who does not. The boy who at times indulges in mutual masturbation may naturally make overtures in a moment of excitement. Younger boys may be tricked or forced into oral acts, something which needs to happen only once for all the others who learn of it to be more strongly and erotically affected by such threats and talk thereafter. Only a small minority of boys enjoy fellating, but the distaste may well be largely moral and psychic; for, if left to their own devices (that is, if given freedom and privacy to amuse themselves as they wished), most of the subjects in a European experiment,[9] who enjoyed being fellated, turned in time to mutual fellation as a favorite pastime. The role which had otherwise often seemed degrading or unmasculine became acceptable when it was mutual. A majority of normal heterosexual adolescent boys found great pleasure in being fellated, and were highly aroused in watching the act.

The same research suggests that at least 30 per cent of pubescent males are highly sensitive anally, although this capacity for pleasure begins to fade in mid-adolescence, or perhaps when they begin regular heterosexual intercourse. One experiment consisted of giving boys a battery-operated vibrator, penis shaped, and to take motion pictures of their anal play with it. The delight in a third of the cases was unmistakable, which may explain the impact of jokes, physical contact such as 'goosing,' and sodomy threats upon the erotic imagination of some young boys. One man reported: "When I was thirteen a man kept staring at me. I had many fantasies about him wanting to bugger me. I played a sort of cat-and-mouse game with him, pretending to be interested in him until he would start to follow me. Then I would disappear. I played this game with him every day for several weeks. Then I'd go home and bugger myself with a carrot, trying to find out what it would be like."

The Boy Who Thinks He May Be Gay

Butch was articulate, intelligent, and moody. His father, although busy, apparently had a good relationship with his younger son. Butch's mother was dead and the housework was done by a harassed older sister who was deeply resentful that Butch did not help more. He lived in a neighborhood where some boys "hustled" and sometimes discussed it at school, but Butch didn't need money. His older brother employed him at a store. He earned enough to buy what he wanted. He avoided sex play with his friends because he worried that he might be gay. When he was thirteen, he decided to find out. One afternoon he approached a man who was sitting in a car reading a magazine, whom he had seen pick up other boys. He suggested the pederast buy him a hamburger. Butch was thin and gangling and the man did not find him especially attractive, but the two of them spent an enjoyable afternoon in conversation. When it was time to go home, Butch asked: "Can I spend the night with you?"

The pederast asked why, and Butch replied: "I want to find out if I'm gay." The boy took the initiative that night in various types of sex play, and decided that the only thing he enjoyed was masturbating while having his back rubbed. Once he was reassured that lots of boys were anally sensitive, Butched decided he was not gay at all, and almost immediately started dating girls. This story might have ended otherwise, of course. It is unfortunate that not enough could be learned about the boy's preconditioning and experience to determine for sure what made the difference. Some boys may decide they are gay because they enjoy oral and anal sex, when in point of fact perhaps 50 per cent of young adolescents can find such play highly stimulating, at least when girls are not available. The European research project reported that considerably more than 50 per cent of young adolescent boys get as much pleasure out of active anal intercourse as from coitus with a girl. Again the percentage declines as they grow older, except perhaps in those cases where anal play is continued regularly into late adolescence because girls are not available. Again, however, the act may be experienced in widely different ways depending on the fantasies and interpretations which accompany and follow it.

What a Boy Told the Police

The impact of sex play on a boy is strongly dependent upon his self-image, on how he thinks other people view it, and upon his own interpretation of the meaning of the experience. For example, a boy may tell varying versions of the same experience as is illustrated here by what 14-year-old Mike told friends, the police, and those who finally determined the truth. A pederast we shall call Van was arrested and charged with sodomy, which under the laws of that state includes any type of sexual contact with a minor of the same sex. The district attorney's office reported the incident to the press as follows: "The police were summoned when a young man found his little brother in bed with and involved in deviant sexual relations with Van Jones, XX West X Street, who had solicited and sexually molested the boy in a movie theater at XX West Street, before taking the young boy to an apartment. Jones has pleaded guilty and will be sentenced in six weeks."

What happened from Van's point of view? He went to a movie theater where one was allowed to smoke, and when he lighted a cigarette, Mike, who was sitting behind him, moved up and asked for a smoke. Van gave him a cigarette, shaking hands. When Van then left the theater, saying nothing more, the boy followed and asked for a ride home. They had a friendly conversation, but nothing sexual was discussed or hinted. The boy urged Van to come upstairs to meet his mother. They found the apartment empty. In showing Van around, the boy took him to his bedroom and showed him a sex magazine. Van got worried and started to leave, whereupon the boy began to wrestle with him playfully. The boy told him that he used to fellate his older brother, who was no longer interested now that he had a girl friend. This worried Van even more, although he admitted that he might have become involved in sex play with the boy had the older brother not arrived. The older brother joined in the roughhouse briefly, then demanded that Van fellate him and give him money. When Van refused, the brother left angrily. Van also left immediately, but delayed long enough to allow Mike to apologize and ask when they could meet again. Mike followed him to the street, where a policeman who had been called by the older brother immediately arrested Van. Even though he was guilty of no sex act, at the recommendation of his attorney, Van pleaded guilty to a minor charge, since the lawyer pointed out that Van had taken the boy to the apartment, was there alone with him without parental permission, and that both boys said there had been sexual misconduct.

What did Mike say to the police? At first he was defensive and protective of Van, saying nothing wrong had taken place. The interrogation then went something like this:

POLICEMAN: You knew he was queer.
MIKE: No.
POLICEMAN: Are you queer, too?
MIKE: (angrily) No.
POLICEMAN: Then why did you leave the theater with him?
MIKE: I'm not queer.
POLICEMAN: Was it because he offered you money?
MIKE: Yes. I'm not queer.
POLICEMAN: So you let him fool around with you for money? That's not very queer.
MIKE: (very emotional) Yes. I'm not queer, but he didn't do very much.
POLICEMAN: Did he screw you or have you screw him?
MIKE: (sobbing) I never did anything like that in my life.
POLICEMAN: He just blew you? You might as well tell us the truth, because he's admitted it.
MIKE: I never did anything like that. We just wrestled around on the bed.
POLICEMAN: And your clothes came unfastened?
MIKE: Sort of.

POLICEMAN: He did fool around with you sexually in your bedroom
    then. Your brother saw it.
MIKE: Yes.

So Mike signed a statement charging Van with sodomy and his
brother signed a statement that he had witnessed it. Both boys were
worried about previous minor arrests.

When asked at school about what had happened, Mike made
himself out a hero who had trapped a pervert. He had so bad a
conscience about it, however, that he hunted the streets for months
until he found Van and tired to make amends with an expensive
present he had stolen. Van befriended him and helped him as he
grew older, and found that Mike's bad conscience was keenest in that
he had lied to the police, pretending to be innocent, when in fact he
had been involved in extensive sex play with his brother, with
friends, and with other men he had solicited at the same movie
theater. Mike and his older brother had from an early age been
involved in elaborate sex rituals—which might better be called
dramas—so that he was very much afraid of his brother, who always
took from him the money he got from hustling. Mike was easily
intimidated by his brother, and also by other boys who knew of his
deviant activity. While each story is different, there is evidence to
suggest that the "innocence" of boys in such arrests may be questioned in as high as 50 per cent of the cases.

ENABLING CLIMATE: STATISTICS

Before saying more about seduction, it may be helpful to review
the current climate of adolescent sexuality, as discovered by a survey
of a representative sample of American youth.[10] Sorensen found that
teen-agers are tending today to reject religious and moral prohibitions against deviant sexual behavior. In the sample, 17 per cent of
boys aged 13 to 15 admitted that on one or more occasions they had
engaged in sexual activity, mostly to show that they "did not care
what society thinks." In the same survey 61 per cent of boys aged 13
to 15 disagreed with their parents' ideas about sex; and 77 per cent
said that teenagers should make their own moral code, and should
determine for themselves what is right and wrong on the basis of their
own experience. Though 75 per cent of adolescents said that the idea
of two men having sex together is disgusting, 41 per cent said it would

be all right for two boys to have sex together if both wanted it, and
nearly two million teen-agers were what Sorensen called sexual
adventurers who prowl around in search of varied experiences. He
found on the whole that adolescents are very tolerant of homosexual
behavior in others, because "love is so accidental that no one can
predict when or with whom it will occur." Adolescents also said that
persons should be honest in accepting themselves as they are, and
that those who indulge in homosexual play are "meeting what they
find to be a basic need."

In this climate of tolerant adventurism, where many
youngsters—less inhibited and restrained—are curiously exploring,
29 per cent of boys who admitted having homosexual experience said
they had seduced a younger boy, 56 per cent of such boys said their
first homosexual activity had been with someone their own age or
younger. These statistics do not show what percentage of the other 45
per cent had their first homosexual experience with an older boy.
Also, 51 per cent of city boys said: "You are probably a fag if you
haven't had sexual intercourse with a girl by the eighth grade," yet
only 18 per cent of them reported such coitus. Does this mean that 33
per cent of city boys were worried about being gay? Probably not, but
they may be more vulnerable to explorations since so many of today's
youngsters report their intention of trying things out for themselves.
If Sorensen's percentages are correct, then approximately 5,161,000
teen-age boys had been homosexually approached *by other boys*, and
1,558,000 of them had responded. The boys in the mass sample were
asked no question about oral sex, so Sorensen says it is quite possible
for an adolescent to have participated in such acts and still qualify as
sexually inexperienced in the survey. He also had reason to feel that
the figures are low, since young adolescents are very reluctant to
report deviant sexual activity.[11]

In some schools and neighborhoods it is now a fad to champion
the rights of sexual minorities. Many adolescent girls are caught up in
lesbianism, partly through the movement for women's liberation, but
also because it is another way to rebel against a society they feel to be
irrational on sex matters. Some young boys associate with gay activists out of curiosity, rebellion, or for political reasons. Although
some surveys suggest that young teen-agers are now becoming more
conservative on sexual and political matters, there are neighborhoods
where a significant minority of boys are related to anarchist and sex
freedom groups. The boys we found in the "underground," however,

are rarely of this type. For the most part they come from typical middle- or lower-class families representative of their neighborhoods.

ATTITUDES TOWARD ARREST

We cannot draw firm conclusions from the limited number of boys we interviewed who had been involved one way or another in arrest cases, but what they said does suggest the value of further study. When a boy is "molested" or "interfered with" against his will, he is more likely to report the incident to parents and police. Of seventeen cases we investigated, involving the arrest of men for sexual involvement with boys between the ages of 12 and 15, only one boy had reported the incident to the police himself. In that incident the boy did so in anger, to get even with a man who (out of real affection for the youngster) forced him to return to his parents when the boy kept running away. The other sixteen cases broke down as follows:

5 CASES: Parents solicited the help of police to find a missing boy who had run away or stayed out overnight without permisssion.

2 CASES: Neighbors reported a boy being at the house of a single man at unusual hours of the night.

1 CASE: A pederast reported to the police that his car had been stolen, not knowing it had been taken without his permission by a boy he was fond of.

1 CASE: Police checked a boy playing pinball machine in bus station at 2 A.M. and found he was from another city and was traveling with a man his parents didn't know.

1 CASE: Police discovered a pornographic film showing the man and boy.

1 CASE: A jealous older brother told his parents and police.

1 CASE: Police stopped a car for speeding and found a runaway boy inside.

1 CASE: Boy caught in theft and address on his forged credentials was that of his "uncle."

1 CASE: Parents tried to blackmail a pederast who was involved with their son.

1 CASE: A boy told his friends of the fun he was having, and one of his friends told parents.

1 CASE: An aunt found letter from a man in her nephew's desk.

In fifteen of these seventeen incidents the boy involved was reluctant to admit anything to the police and did so only if tricked, beaten, or threatened with a jail sentence on other charges. For the most part the boys' attitude was: "What we did is nobody else's business. Why don't they leave us alone?"

It would be useful to study the attitude of adults today to the sexual experiences they had with men when they were adolescents. Discounting the reports of pederasts themselves, we are left with only a few incidents in this study of males now over the age of nineteen who reported on their present attitudes toward the man and experience they had as youngsters. Three incidents in which the pederast was arrested are very different. In the first of these, one young man has recently purchased a car as a gift for a clergyman who was arrested as a result of an incident that happened when the young man was thirteen or fourteen years old. He did so out of bad conscience, feeling responsible for the arrest. He said: "There was absolutely nothing wrong with what we did, because we liked each other." In a second incident, after getting out of the Marines an older teen-ager beat up the man he had been involved with in earlier days, but not for the reason most persons would expect. When the pederast had been arrested, the boy had held his tongue, but then the man had confessed, thus humiliating the boy—who felt betrayed because the man had talked. In a third incident, in which a boy had sobbed for weeks after the arrest of the man he loved, a psychiatrist helped the boy resolve his emotional tension by developing strongly antihomosexual attitudes, so that as an adult the former boy now speaks of the man as "that damned fag." However, he still cherishes the pederast's photograph.

Among the pederasts who were not arrested, it was possible to meet a dozen of their ex-boys. It is obvious that they are more likely to keep in touch with those boys who continue to be friendly; in fact their statements tend to bear out the thesis of Goodman in Chapter 6 that friendship often remains after sexual interest passes. One young man said: "I'm going to name my first baby after him." Another said: "I would trust him with my own young son as soon as I would my own father." The intention in reporting such comments is not to justify the sexual relationship, but to show that these young men, along with younger boys themselves, tend to view the sex acts as relatively unimportant incidents in a friendship of larger value; or else they consider themselves not as victims but as co-conspirators in any sex play that took place.

THE ACTUAL SEDUCTION

Since this chapter is based upon interviews with three hundred boys who were either "hustlers" by choice or were happily involved in a relationship with a man, it is presenting a picture which is out of perspective. We will, therefore, conclude on a more negative point, by reporting on replies to the question: "Have you been seduced? If so, by whom?" Some of the boys gave immediate affirmative answers: "I was seduced by my uncle when I was thirteen, although that really wasn't the first time." Or "When I was fourteen my eighteen-year-old friend got a car and he wouldn't let me drive it until—well, I guess you could say I was really seduced by the car!" The ancient Greeks had a saying that a boy doesn't get caught unless some man goes fishing, and seduction doesn't begin necessarily with a verbal proposition or a sexual gesture. For this reason many boys who had a vague feeling that somehow, somewhere, along the way they had been seduced, were unable to pinpoint the precise time and situation.

Seduction, whether of a girl or boy, begins with the creation of a climate in which there can be a positive response to a proposition or gesture, which triggers nature's chemistry or a boy's emotion so as to excite him sexually. If many boys seem confused about that process, it is because they had, for the most part, been seduced by society, plus their own prowling and fantasy, in that they were already aroused and ready for the actual seduction. There are two dimensions to the seductive climate of society. On one hand there is the eroticism of advertisements, films, books, popular music, and the influence of older persons—especially the influence of boys a few years older; on the other hand there is his immediate "tribe" which influences a boy the most, with its sex talk and bragging (much of it probably untrue), along with the teasing, dirty jokes, and everything that creates a climate of sexual arousal and readiness. For example, one pederast said: "If I set out to seduce a boy, I'd use the same method boys use on each other. I'd simply start telling dirty jokes, and I'd encourage the boys to tell dirty jokes, until I could tell by the tone of their voice, their emotional reaction, their laughter, their lack of embarrassment, which boy was experienced and available. Within a half hour of watching and listening, I'd know which boy to go after. How would I then seduce him? I'd nod and signal for him to follow me as I left. The pederasts who get arrested are those who make overtures to boys who don't take such initiative themselves. This country so neglects its young, gives them so few exciting adventures, and so sexually frus-

trates them, that many an inexperienced boy will follow right after
you if you but nod."

A boy tells of his pederastic seduction—that is, his first sexual
experience with a man: "We were clowning around on the tennis
courts and I saw this man had an eye on me. I didn't know who he was,
but I saw his Mustang and figured it might be my ticket out of that dull
neighborhood; so when he smiled I walked over to his car. I was only
thirteen, but I knew what I wanted. He asked me if I'd like to go to his
place and listen to some records and when we got there I asked if I
could take a shower, because I was hot and sweaty. He said he'd take a
shower with me and I said O.K. I enjoyed it all and started going over
there to listen to records a couple of times a week or whenever I got
horny." There are, of course, city neighborhoods and small towns
where no boy has had such an experience, and others where nearly
every boy has been with such a fellator at least once.

Another pederast said: "I consider a boy to be available if he has
participated in enough sex play with boys his own age to discover that
he enjoys it, and to an extent that he is interested and willing to try it
with me or with some other man. Each such pederast has his own
game which he plays to find out which boys are interested. One asks
boys where they go to school, and then disarms them by saying: 'Oh,
that's the school where a lot of the boys have been playing around
sexually with—uh, who was it? some older boys or one of the
teachers?' Frequently he gets the reply, with a gasp: 'How did you
find that out? It's supposed to be a secret!' In any case the erotic
climate between the two of them immediately changes, since the man
has become a co-conspirator by virtue of knowing the boys' secret.
With many boys it takes no more than that. They expect adults to be
judgmental and condemnatory, and so a boy may find it highly erotic
to discover an adult who approves of the sex play. Most boys immediately jump to the conclusion, aided perhaps by the pederast's
manner, that 'this is one of those men you hear about' who gives boys
a good time." This pederast then repeated, and most of those interviewed confirmed, that boys who get sexually involved with strange
men are for the most part those who have already been seduced by
friends or relatives near their own age. The other boys—who respond
to a stare, smile, or invitation to visit a man's apartment—have
perhaps already seduced themselves in their own fantasies and imagination. The experience of seduction begins long before the first
sexual invitation by word or gesture.

Up to this point, to keep our data in perspective, it must be remembered that we have not been discussing all adolescents, but only those whom we found to be involved with the pederasts we interviewed—boys who for one reason or another are interested in sex play with an adult. There is, however, one troubling note for society. It is sounded in fact, as reported by a number of pederasts, which may be worth further study. Typically, it runs like this: "I do not get involved much in actual sexual intercourse, but I amuse myself with a game since my work keeps me on the road. I pick up' nearly every boy I see hitchhiking and I ask them all if they would like to go to bed with me, just to see what the reaction will be. Twenty years ago, many boys were frightened, angry, or indignant— demanded that I let them out of the car immediately. Nowadays those who say they wouldn't be interested are more likely to be amused than frightened, annoyed rather than angry, and few are indignant enough to refuse my offer to take them to where they are going. Twenty years ago it was only boys who had been in reform schools, young delinquents, or desperate and hungry runaways who were immediately willing to go to bed with me. The average youngster today seems much more prepared to consider the possibility. He uses such limited negatives as: 'Thanks, but not this time' or 'If I did it someone might find out' or 'I'd never do it for money, but maybe for fun.' Is there a real change of attitude or merely of tolerance? It isn't just my imagination."

No matter how consenting and pleasing the sexual experience may be, it is almost inevitable that a boy who engages in sex play with a man will at times be plagued by feelings of guilt and anxiety. If his friends find out, they may accuse him of being "sick" or "queer"; if he is religious he may have a sense of being sinful, and in most cases he is quite aware that the activity is against the law, which may lead him through an emotional crisis to deciding that he is a criminal. All of this is part of his sexual experience. A sense of furtive guilt, of chasing forbidden fruit may in some cases heighten the sexual pleasure. In other cases it may throw cold water upon the affair or at least dampen the enthusiasm in time. If a boy finds the experience so pleasurable that he continues pursuing it, or even if he does so only for money or other advantages, he begins to resolve the conflict over feelings of guilt and anxiety by adopting the life-style of a rebel or delinquent, which makes it possible for him to rationalize or discharge the accusations he has made against himself. As a "rebel" he may give up religion and define himself as someone who believes in "sex free-dom." Better educated boys seem emotionally more likely to accept the label of "gay" or to explore a bisexual or homosexual life-style.

Lower-class boys are more likely to define themselves as delinquents, freed by their sexual delinquency to turn to other types of crime also. It may well be that many criminals are created by this tendency of society to teach adolescents that they are criminals if they are sexually adventurous or deviant.

SOME CONCLUDING OBSERVATIONS

• Our data from boys correlate with similar information from men in prison for pederastic offenses,[12] confirming that a high percentage of boys who are involved sexually with men actually *were first seduced by other boys*, and boys who are sexually experienced with each other are more likely to respond to pederast overtures or to become adventurous in seeking sex play with men out of curiosity, for money, or for other reasons.

• Since boys are responsive sexually and so often take initiative in seeking sexual adventures, the Gebhard study suggests that it is unfair to depict all pederasts as aging "aunties" who prey upon and seduce the immature, for "in many instances a real and deep relationship" exists.[13] The notion that pederasts are senile or "dirty old men" is disproved by the fact that such offenders in prison are on the average thirty-two years old. Only 5 per cent of them had any record of mental or emotional illness, even those who had been arrested or imprisoned. The average age of the boys involved with them was 14.1 years, and in one case out of ten there was no sexual intercourse. One fifth of the men arrested had simply masturbated the boy, and 50 per cent of them had fellated a boy. Many of the imprisoned men had *started such activity when they were teen-agers* and had simply continued the behavior into adulthood without interruption. A high percentage of them had had sexual intercourse with boys aged 12 to 15 when they were older teen-agers.[14] Many of them had continued this sex play with younger boys because of the "naive interest in sex coupled with quick response" on the part of the youngster. who "exhibits an intensity of response matching or frequently surpassing that of an adult."[15] The Institute of Sex Research study says that this sexual attractiveness of young adolescent boys is well known to many men who "are thereby subjected to temptation." If young girls, the study concludes, had libidos as well developed as teen-age boys "our penal institutions would burst at the seams."[16]

• The young boys involved with arrested pederasts showed "a high degree of participation" and co-conspiracy—indeed, more than in other types of sex crime. Less than 6 per cent of boys involved with imprisoned pederasts had in any way resisted the man's overtures.[17] Force and threat were infrequent and untypical as also shown in Merrill's earlier study.[18]

● Boys involved with pederasts do not seem to become homosexual or pederast, unless they are preconditioned by earlier childhood experience or by young adolescent experience with other boys. Indeed, our data suggest a hypothesis for further study: that a pederast relationship with a masculine man seems to direct many boys away from confirming a homosexual identity and into normal heterosexuality. Exclusively pederast sources, of course, are not adequate for studying that thesis. One repeatedly discovers, however, that a *paiderastia* relationship frequently salvages boys from sexual and other delinquency.

● The experience that strongly influences a boy to become either gay or pederastic may most often be fantasy or imaginative experience. For this reason, the most dangerously seductive homosexual experience may be dirty jokes, or teasing gestures from other adolescents or from heterosexual men. An actual perverse act, on the other hand, is often found to be distasteful and can result in a decline of interest in the deviant sex which had seemed so fascinating when it was purely imaginative. Our study provides little evidence that young adolescent boys are swayed to the gay side by adult homosexual seduction. The most important and decisive factor may well be the preparatory imaginative experience, plus the interpretation given by adults and other adolescents to minor homosexual episodes. This suggests the need for more study of erotic fantasies.

CHAPTER 12

Response to Community Censure

How is it possible for so many pederasts to survive and in many cases even to thrive in the face of society's overwhelming disapproval? Earlier we reported how the practicing pederast receives considerable support from adolescent society, especially from subcultures which are rebellious and secretive. Even among adolescents who disapprove of deviant sex play, many keep a friend's secret because they believe sex to be a personal and private matter, and they disapprove of society's official policies and laws. In this chapter we will examine other reasons why it is not necessary for practicing pederasts to withdraw completely into a criminal underworld. For when the pederast looks into the eyes of the community—and, as with all persons, his self-interpretation is greatly dependent on what he sees there—he frequently discovers more support and encouragement than would be expected.

In principle, Western society considers itself to be in unwavering opposition to pederasty, with strict laws and firm punishment. The trend in most countries throughout the last century and up until now has been to tighten the laws against homosexual involvement of adults with youngsters, even when those laws are being relaxed to tolerate consenting homosexual activity among adults. When exposed to arrest with resultant newspaper publicity, a pederast frequently loses his job and reputation. Public opinion frequently forces him to seek a new life somewhere else, even when he is not convicted; and not infrequently the threat of arrest and publicity leads to suicide. The pederast faces the continual danger of blackmail. When he is arrested he may be beaten up by the police or placed in a jail situation where the authorities know he will be beaten up by disapproving prisoners. Younger pederasts are frequently beaten and

165

raped in jails. In the face of all this and more, one should not be surprised to find the self-view of most pederasts to be self-condemnatory, deeply troubled, or profoundly defensive, and such is true of many who are arrested. Those who have not been arrested, however,—many of whom believe that only one in a thousand ever faces arrest and trial—tend to look upon potential disaster with the same fatalistic optimism which imbues the Californians who lead tranquil lives on an earthquake fault. This is not to say that strict law enforcement does not have an effect. Many pederasts scrupulously avoid places and situations known to be dangerous, and practicing pederasts frequently move to large cities, or even to other states or foreign countries, to avoid arrest. The pederast who believes he has about a one in a thousand chance of being arrested does not rest his optimism on a growing climate of sexual permissiveness—few have any real illusions about that. The current sexual situation provides a sort of jungle in which the pederast at times can hide, or at least a jungle of ideas he can use in rationalizing; but his survival as a pederast rests upon support he receives from unexpected places: the result of a selective process of avoiding persons whom he knows in advance will be disapproving; and a tendency to relate to persons in the underground, who give him supportive interpretations of reality and events.

FEAR OF CENSURE

The Establishment's censure of pederasty is intended to be devastating. From the Church and public morality he hears himself condemned as a sinner and he responds with feelings of guilt which are at times inescapable. From the law and public opinion he finds himself condemned as a criminal and he responds with feelings of fear which at times are overwhelming. In the eyes of the medical profession he knows himself to be condemned as sick, as mentally ill perhaps, which leads him at times to seek treatment. He knows that those around him consider him a "queer" or "fag" even though gay-homosexuals themselves usually reject him, at best calling him "stupid." At worst his anxieties and fears can destroy him, and at best he finds himself split into two persons, unless he withdraws completely into an underground where he can be open and truthful with himself and others. He tends to react to the community's censure in one or more of four ways:

1. He may seek to revise his religious and moral convictions, as we will discuss in the next chapter.

2. He may struggle for a new self-understanding, also to be discussed in the chapter following.

3. He may tend to become cautious and selective in revealing himself, seeking out the minority of persons who will sympathize with him and give him support.

4. He may withdraw from time to time into the pederast underground to obtain help and support in integrating his experience.

He Looks Only Into Sympathetic Eyes

"The typical pederast does not talk about boys with persons who would disapprove," one interviewee reported. "He gets encouragement and support from conversations with others. I realize this once in a while when on a train or plane I hear an angry remark by someone who is reading about a pederast arrest in the newspaper. His angry tone of voice actually astonishes and surprises me." Many pederasts receive support from persons who are simply tolerant of eccentrics. Another pederast said: "I was surprised, after being arrested and receiving some rather sensational publicity in the press, at how many sympathetic telephone calls and letters I got from complete strangers, who said they did not feel that what I did should be considered as so serious a crime. For example, two persons, one of them prominent in the community, asked what they could do to help me, admitting that they had barely escaped a similar plight when younger." Another said: "I never hesitate to show my affection for Alexi around my business associates, when I take them hunting or fishing. Once in a while one of them will make a joke about my sleeping with the boy, since they know he isn't my son, but none have ever expressed any disapproval. I find I can talk quite frankly with some of them." Other pederasts report sympathy or tolerance from their parents, brothers or sisters, wives, and children. One reported: "My parents know all about it. They once asked me to go to a psychiatrist, and when I did and kept them posted on what happened, all they asked after that was for me not to bring boys around to their house. Actually they are even tolerant of that now, as long as I have permission of the boy's parents."

Pederasts have found some support from women—a recent newsletter of one underground group quoted supportive opinions

from many women in the left wing of the women's movement. One
pederast said: "I was frightened when I found that this social worker
suspected the sexual relationship I had with the son of her client.
However, she said: 'Better for a kid like that to be loved by you than be
frozen out of life'." Another pederast had a similar experience with a
woman schoolteacher who considers herself avant-garde on "children's liberation." Several pederasts reported friendly support from
young lesbian activists and from some European gay organizations.
Another pederast said: "I have a cabdriver friend who is tolerant of
my affairs with boys, simply because, as she says: 'Everyone has her
kink.' "

Support From Some Parents

Some parents are permissive, some tolerant of homosexuality—
such as the civil rights attorney who told a pederast: "Because my son
loves you, you can sleep with him as long as you do it only at our
house." One would least expect pederasts to find encouragement
from policemen, yet one pederast reports tolerance from a parent
who is a police officer: "Dan's parents were very permissive. They
gave him money to take trips alone when he was fourteen, and let him
hitchhike to the Coast when he was fifteen. His father said he pre-
ferred for the boy to be involved with girls, but that at that age 'a little
fooling around wouldn't harm the kid if it didn't become habitual.' I
asked him if he was worried about the men who picked up his son on
the road, and he replied: "Dan can take care of himself, but if he's
going to fool around with a man I'd rather it was someone I knew like
you."

Another pederast said: "I have hidden nothing from Alexi's
mother. She has no illusions about my relationship with her family,
unless it is a vain hope that I would divorce my wife and marry her.
She knows that I've been a better father to her boys than their own
father ever was, and that I have a great affection for her and her kids.
She is very dependent upon me emotionally since her husband died."
Another said: "Dill's mother is quite frankly glad when I take him
somewhere overnight so she can better entertain her men friends at
home." Another said: "His mother told me she knew her 14-year-old
son was sneaking girls to his room and she didn't care what he did
sexually with them or with me as long as she didn't have to know. She
said that he had been stealing money from her, and if I wanted to take
him to live with me it would be a good riddance." Another said:

"From the time I first rented a room at her house she tried to push the boy off on my by saying he needed a man's discipline. Her only reaction when she found him sleeping with me was to ask if she could move his things into my room so she could rent his room to another boarder." Another said: "She told me she was very liberal on sex matters and she was very permissive in letting me take him on trips, until it was clear that I had no intention of marrying her." Another said: "His mother told me she wasn't worried about me taking sexual advantage of the boy, since he was only eleven and wouldn't be old enought for that sort of thing for another year or two." Another pederast reported: "They weren't that sort of family, yet they took it for granted he could sleep at the motel with me whenever I was in town, which was one week end out of every five or six. They couldn't possibly have been so naive as not to know. When one week end he brought a friend along, his mother asked me if another time I wouldn't take his 12-year-old brother along for the 'fun.' When I asked his father what to get him for Christmas, he suggested I take him on a month-long summer trip, 'since he enjoys sleeping with you so much"! Such incidents could be reported for many more pages, but the main point is that nearly every pederast interviewed had at one time or another in his life encountered a parent who knew of and permitted or tolerated the sex play. Such experiences can easily become deceptive to the pederast, who tends to avoid contact with the overwhelming majority of persons who disapprove of his behavior.

THE RESPONSE TO OVERKILL

Between the persons who are tolerant or permissive, such as parents who belong to sex freedom groups, and the sympathetic persons a pederast meets in the underground, an increasing number of persons—both professionals and less well educated working people—are reacting negatively to the excessive brutality and insensitivity of many police and law-enforcement officials in dealing with sex deviants. A mother who might otherwise have cooperated with a police investigation was horrified and angered to discover that police officers—in an effort to force her 12- and 13-year-old sons to give evidence against a man they were fond of—had held the two youngsters dangling over a cliff, threatening to drop them if they did not provide the requested information. In another instance, friends, neighbors, and relatives became incensed when they learned of a situation in which police officers had harassed and threatened an entire family—including two children aged six and eight who could have known nothing—for an entire night to get them to pressure a 16-year-old boy into testifying against his will against a man the whole family loved, a man who had influenced the boy to go back to school and rebuild his life after a bad drug scene. The methods used by some police to get information from minors and their families, and their consequent humiliation in police stations and courts, is a fitting subject for another study. The point we make here is that in neighborhoods where such methods have been used, people become less willing to cooperate with the authorities. One older teen-ager said: "I'd tell on the man who is involved with my brother if I thought the police would get him help, but they would just beat him up and ruin him. It isn't worth that."

A university professor said much the same thing: "I went to the director of the camp and reported to him confidentially that a member of his staff was fooling around with my son. I told the director that after talking to my son we had decided that the incident wasn't important enough to be reported to the police, if the pederast would seek treatment. The camp director agreed not to rehire the man another year, and to make sure there were no more incidents if he stayed. None of us wanted to have a hand in destroying such a fine, sensitive, creative person, as police action was sure to do." A pederast reported: "Someone in the district attorney's office tried to send me a warning, before it was too late, about the investigators who were trailing me and the boy. He did not approve of the ruthlessness and political goals of the D.A., who was not trying to prevent crime, but to get sensational headlines to advance his political career. My family decided I should leave the country, as the publicity would be horrendous and would hurt innocent members of my family. Some of the police were themselves so disgusted at the D.A.'s abuse of youngsters in getting his headlines that they were closing their eyes and not making certain arrests." Again, the law-enforcement authorities, harassed a mother whose sons had not been involved with a pederast, to force her to make false statements against him. First they threatened to put her 9-year-old son in a reform school, and when she complained at the improper language they were using in the presence of her children, the investigators secured a court order to have her children taken from her and placed in a foster home until she agreed to cooperate with the investigation, justifying their action by saying, "Anything is justified in getting the queers." Such treatment of young children is an illustration of the sort of overkill which leads many persons to close their eyes to some illegal sexual behavior, believing that the situation would be worse if the police were involved. Many persons would persuade a relative or friend to turn himself in, if they were convinced that he would receive help and therapy without publicity to harm his family and other innocent persons. In the present situation, the excessively brutal treatment of pederasts in many police stations and prisons is therefore in some instances a prejudicial element in his favor.

UNDERWORLD EXPLOITATION

The pederast who withdraws to the *underworld*—in contrast to the *underground*—may soon find that protection has a sting to it. One pederast said: "I chose deliberately to live in a high-delinquency neighborhood where most people have something to hide. Everyone, therefore, ignores his neighbors as long as they keep their noses out of his business. For a while I had a boat at a marina, but my boys attracted too much attention there, since it was a middle-class yacht harbor, and not an upper-class one. But here in this neighborhood no one notices young boys coming and going. If there were not a drug problem here I'd face no difficulties at all, except that my apartment gets broken into all the time."

Underworld parents may also have reasons to be tolerant or permissive: "His mother was frankly a prostitute. She was always glad to have me for a baby-sitter." Another said: "When my house was burglarized, the police found my stereo at the boy's house and arrested his father, who screamed at the police that I was a fag who had molested his son. The cops said they would be glad to press charges against me if the evidence justified it, but that it was no excuse for burglary. The cops found that the father had taught his son to hustle as a means of getting into apartments for burglary." Another said: "They seemed like ordinary people, a well-knit family, and both parents had good jobs, but they offered to have their kids be used in pornographic films if the pay was good, and even gave signed releases." In another situation: "It came out later that their father had trained his sons in homosexual techniques in order to seduce me for purposes of blackmail. They were very nice people, and I had done so much to help him when he was unemployed that I couldn't believe him capable of a trick like that." Another pederast said: "The boy threatened to run away if I didn't take him with me when I moved to another state, so his parents said they would give their legal permission for me to take him. The father didn't come right out and say so, but he was glad to get the boy out of his hair, especially since the boy kept getting in trouble, which risked calling police attention to the fact that the father was a dealer in narcotics."

Police corruption and underworld dealings also often provide assistance to the pederast: "The cop told me of my rights before completing the arrest, then hinted that a hundred dollars would fix things up. I paid it gladly to avoid arrest since I was from out of state."[1] Another reported: "The best collection of man-boy pornography in this city belongs to a policeman who has taken much of it himself." Another pederast reported this experience: "I was clearly in serious trouble. They caught me parked on a country road, in a rented car not in my name, with a young boy, half undressed, whose family didn't know where he was and didn't know me. When we got to the police station about 2:00 A.M. it was largely deserted, and the officer in charge asked if I knew anyone I could call. I telephoned a friend in the syndicate and asked him to bring all the money he could. After we paid them off, all the police did was follow us to make sure we let the boy off at his house. Then they stopped my car again and suggested I stay out of their county. I had to pay my syndicate friend back at the rate of 200 per cent." Another reported an incident from the early 1960's: "It seemed like a very nice place, a nonalcoholic soda bar where boys came after school and early evenings, with no sexual hanky-panky allowed on the premises—the mangement assuming no responsibility for what a man and boy who met there might do later. I discovered, however, that the place was corrupting in an entirely different way than I would have thought. One boy had received a thousand dollars for allowing himself to be planted in the bed of a civil rights militant as a means for white racists to destroy the man, who presumably was not a pederast at all. Another boy got five thousand dollars for a similar episode with a prominent Southern politician, who I presume was also innocent. Evidently a ring of gangsters who operated the bar were not blackmailing pederasts, but were involved in many incidents of framing nonpederasts in cases that for the most part were never known. I thought of this when I saw that scene in the movie *Godfather II*, where the Senator was framed by the placing of a dead prostitute in his bed when he was drunk."

Our concern here, however, is not with the blackmail of politicians—pederast or not—but with the shield to deviant practices that is possible in a climate of general corruption, when police and other officials do not or cannot deal with the large and frequently powerful criminal underworld, which unintentionally or deliberately provides support for pederasts.

UNDERGROUND SUPPORT

In contrast to this criminal *underworld*, what does the pederast find when he turns to the *underground* for friendship and support? There are a few militant organizations such as the "Gay Pederast Liberation Front,"[2] but for the most part the underground consists of a silent fraternity of men, many of whom know only a few of the others. The persons a pederast meets in the underground, however, are for the most part far different from those in the criminal underworld:

Lawyers. "I discovered he was a corporation attorney whose annual salary runs to six figures. I met him in a bar in Acapulco, when our tongues loosened a bit late one night, far from home, and we discovered we were both attracted to the same boy waiter." Another reports: "I received a telephone call from a stranger I had never met—a pederast in the district attorney's office—warning me of steps I should take to avoid arrest and to dispose of evidence, since authorization for a search warrant against me was in the works. Actually no one ever came." Said another: "Many lawyers believe such anti-sex laws are wrong and will be changed."

Doctors. One pederast reported: "There is a whole coterie of pederast physicians in this town." Another said: "I know a doctor who is most generous in contributing his services to a social settlement and charity camp, because he has had across the years as a result a series of lovely relationships with boys." Another pederast writes: "A well-known physician here has just been arrested after thirty years of sexual involvements with members of a boys' choir which he has served as physician." Another said: "Whenever I come home from a vacation overseas my doctor insists on VD tests. He's been a pederast himself since he was a teen-ager, although I don't think he has ever been involved with boys in our own community." There is no reason to extend such quotations, for the point is that many pederasts find sympathetic counsel and support from selected members of the medical profession. In Western Europe there are at least two underground groups of physicians who advocate for themselves and for others "pedofilie as healthy and good for youngsters."

Clergy. Two separate studies have shown that a higher percentage of clergy are arrested for pederastic offenses than are any other vocational group.[3] It may be that a higher percentage of pederast clergy are arrested because they may tend to be more naive and innocent in unintended offenses. A recent study of theological students—both Catholic and Protestant—revealed, however, that (1) a large percentage had been involved sexually with an older boy or man, at least occasionally, when they were young teen-agers, and (2) those who were so involved—as in a similar study of younger schoolteachers—tended to be tolerant of pederasty. The pederast who seeks supportive counsel can usually find a clergyman who will be more than helpful if he shops around. One pederast said: "I've talked to many pastors, sometimes admitting I had a problem, sometimes asking advice for a 'friend.' I find they are for the most part sympathetic and helpful when it comes to arranging therapy. Many of them are reluctant to involve the police—for the sake of the youngster involved—and are unwilling to condemn a kid who gets involved in homosexual acts. They tend to feel that arrest is no way to solve the problem, especially for a person who is willing to undergo therapy. When I point out that therapy doesn't seem to work in many cases or when I ask what is wrong with sex play, anyway—especially among the unmarried—the clergy are usually unable or unwilling to help. They do not know how to handle pederasty—and this goes even for those who are now trying to be helpful to gays—because of the range of taboos and their uncertainty about age of consent. I have, however, found several pastors who were pederasts, at least to the extent of being aware of desires and temptations, who were willing to give counsel to or meet with pederast groups."

Another said: "I have collected information on over one hundred arrested clergy. For example, a parish priest in New England was so popular with the men of his parish that he was protected and defended by them. There is a Catholic priest in Pittsburgh who, after his arrest and conviction on dozens of counts of sexual involvement with boys in his parish, continues to serve as a parish pastor. I suppose he was put on probation in care of his bishop if he would undergo continuing therapy. The number of pederast clergy must be large, including even bishops, if one judges by their names on mailing lists. One group of pederasts in Europe consists of clergy who meet informally once in a while. Another clergy pederastic group consists of militant-on-sex-reform types who get together to discuss theological issues on sex. A group of priests in America, older men now, many

years ago banded together with a pledge to limit their pederasty to
fantasy and photography. They have on occasion reached out to help
and warn younger priests who, they felt, were not aware of the extent
to which they were walking on ice." Another pederast said: "There
are in the 'church'—a common word among pederasts for the
underground—many pastors who, like Horatio Alger in his day, had
to move into other kinds of work because of pederasty. More often,
like Henry Ward Beecher, they try to be helpful while keeping their
own proclivities secret."

Teachers. A noted educator has written candidly about the
pederasty of teachers, including his own, in his autobiography,[4]
seeming to agree with a frank pederast who said: "If they cleaned the
pederasts out of the schools all the best teachers would have to go."
Another said: "My own school, when I was there, had to develop a
rather strict policy that no teacher and boy could be in a room alone
with the door closed. Today that school handles the problem by
enlarging the co-educational direction of its programs. From talking
to boys who attend my school now I'd say it definitely is helping, in
that there is less sex play now among the boys. At the same time the
boys are freer to do what they wish sexually. The big thing is still to do
whatever is forbidden. Most fourteen-year-olds therefore try at least
once to smuggle a girl into their rooms. They are all frank to say that
what gay boys do is nobody else's business." Another wrote: "The
very sexually permissive schools that grew up in the middle of the
century were never tolerant of pederasty. Teachers and pupils were
encouraged to hug, touch, and express natural affection, but only in
Germany[5] perhaps did any prominent educational philosophers
suggest that eroticism between teachers and pupils might be put to
educational use. Privately many educators have admitted to me that
eroticism in education is going to become an explosive issue, as
illustrated by new sex education materials in Europe which take the
position that adults should be tolerant of adolescent sex play—even
pupil-teacher, man-boy activity—as long as it is affectionate and
nonexploitive. A far more conservative booklet was confiscated in
France, and the author was suspended from his teaching post. There
are, however, a growing number of books in the children's liberation
field which advocate self-determination for youngsters in sexual matters, some of them written by responsible educators.[6] While these
materials—and the increasing number of novels[7] about man-boy
sexual involvement written for young adolescents and published by

responsible publishers—do not intend any endorsement of pederasty, this literature does remove some of the sting of society's disapproval for many pederasts, and provides ideas for others to use in rationalizing and justifying their sex play."

Police. One pederast said: "This very nice pederast cop came to my house to warn me I was going to be arrested. He explained who was making charges and said he had been mixed up in the same sort of thing as teen-ager. He advised me to leave town immediately to avoid arrest." Another said: "If I had stayed there on the corner any longer I might have gotten into trouble, but this cop walked by, winking his eye and shaking his head to suggest that I move on. When he came back by, I realized he was warning me that I was under surveillance." Another pederast said: "When I got acquainted with him on this holiday abroad, I didn't realize he was a police chief. He probably hadn't intended to tell me, but later he introduced me to a local officer, also a pederast, who advised us where to go to find boys who would like to sleep with us." Another wrote: "I am in close touch with a police officer I got well acquainted with through my playground job. He will let me know when it is safe for me to return home." Another pederast reported: "A boy from my neighborhood said that he had regular sex relations with a night guard while in reform school, and when he was released from the institution that guard introduced him to a policeman at home, with whom he lived for a year." Another said: "A policewoman I know pointed out to me a shivering, hungry, runaway kid and suggested I buy him something to eat. 'I know you'll try to help him,' she said. 'And otherwise they'll return him to the detention center where older boys keep raping him.'" In another situation an officer said of an arrested pederast: "What he did didn't sound so awful to me. Sex laws divert police energies from solving important crimes, and from protecting people who want help." In a European court the arresting policeman asked the judge to return a 14-year-old boy to the pederast's care, saying: "I don't care whether or not they've been sexually involved. The boy has been sleeping with various men for two years without any affection, and it would be much better for him, no longer virgin in any case, if he had the love of this man who would protect him and care for him. To separate them, and punish this man, would simply inspire this youngster to hate society and the police to such an extent as to make him a criminal."[8] In another case: "When we were arrested, jail officials arranged for my boy and me to have time alone almost every day, although we were incarcerated on separate floors."

BUSINESSMEN, POLITICIANS, PUBLIC FIGURES QUA PEDERASTS

Pederasts frequently justify their own behavior by referring to prominent men who are pederasts. For example: "The truth is learned about some of us only after death, such as the founding president of Turkey or General Gordon. For most well-known people succeed in hiding such episodes in their lives. There is more likely to be published gossip about a recent Pope,[9] than about Z, who was high in the Eisenhower Administration; or about Y and X, who bear the names of major American industrial families; or of ex-Senator W, sports hero V, or certain stars of TV, films, or rock music, or the heir to one of the country's leading oil fortunes." Since that statement was made to us, the oil heir has been indicted for making pederast films. His identity was perhaps not so secret in any case as the above quotation suggests, since his picture appeared in a 1972 film magazine,[10] along with scenes from the film he called "a nude ballet" in the magazine interview. The average person hardly notices the notes about the pederasty of well-known people, since they frequently appear only as footnotes to scholarly books, or in back-page reviews of films, opera, ballet, novels, and so forth. But pederasts who seek support from such sources can find a new item nearly every day—a note saying, for example, that Shakespeare was a pederast, or Kafka or Walt Whitman, or one of the Krupps from the German industrial family. Perhaps, even more important, the pederast who travels and seeks out such persons for conversation can meet them in one or another of the overseas resorts where pederasts congregate. If not, his ears are quickly filled to overflowing with gossip about what such-and-such a well-known person did or said when he was there earlier in the season. For example, the European film producer's girl friend who said she didn't dare refuse to sleep with him during her monthly period, because whenever she wasn't in his bed she could be sure some newsboy or delivery boy would be.

A publisher said: "It is too easy to forget the law and public opinion at home, when one spends much time overseas associating with persons who find my pederasty merely amusing. I don't associate with pederasts very much. However, I have prominent friends who are strictly heterosexual themselves, but who are always introducing me to boys they think I would like. In Sri-Lanka, for example, I often visit a home where my host is scandalized if I sleep with low-class or servant boys. Why should I so lower myself, he says, when he can introduce me to so many young boys from good families who are eager to have a bit of fun in bed?" Similarly, Michael Davidson tells how Indonesian Government officials provided him, at public expense, with boys to sleep with while he was employed there on a special project. Because they keep their proclivities secret, except in such situations, many pederasts experience more incidents of support than they do of disapproval and condemnation. One said: "The law intends to make it difficult, but nearly everywhere one meets people who ignore and circumvent the law—the hotel keeper in Spain who deliberately employs the most handsome 13-year-old bellboys he can find, 'because it helps business'; the cabdriver who offers to bring along either a 'niece' or a 'nephew' if one will employ him for an all-day expedition; or the businessman who is glad to encourage and abet bizarre sexual encounters if a large-enough contract is in the offing." More than one orphanage has solicited large gifts from pederasts, who have then been allowed to "adopt" a boy, taking him on week-end trips and so on.

The pederast's emotions of guilt, fear, or anxiety are therefore tempered by experiences which continually tempt and reassure him, alongside the condemnation which society intends. On the forge of the human dialectic, social forces tug a pederast apart, forcing him to absorb and integrate widely divergent attitudes and experiences. Torn between his own desires and self-justification one one hand, and the censure of society on the other, the pederast enters the underground as a place for rethinking his religious and moral point of view, and for help in finding an identity and self-understanding that will make it possible for him to integrate, and thus come to terms with, the deep conflicts that are present in his experience.

SOME CONCLUDING OBSERVATIONS

• Although the pederast underground rarely seems to exist so concretely that one may point to specific places or organizations, it is nevertheless real as seen in the selective behavior of pederasts in tending to associate with, and listen to, those persons who are supportive of their behavior and attitudes. Such supporting persons may be only a small percentage of professional persons, for example, but they also may constitute the total conscious world of a pederast.

• The number of parents who tolerate man-boy sex play may be very small, but nearly every practicing pederast interviewed had experienced at least one such parent.[11] This not only provided him with support for his pederasty in that instance, but fed his dreams of finding other parents like that—which the French novelist Montherlant[12] said is the "dream of every pederast."

● Not much has been said in this chapter about society's most visible disapproval of pederasts, as seen in the arrests, trials, newspaper stories, and imprisonment, because this study centers for the most part on pederasts who have not yet faced such experiences. Even when they seek to help a pederast friend in jail, the pederasts we interviewed tended to view the incident as an accident that happened to someone else, with little bearing upon their own actions. Insofar as society is successful in jailing pederasts, and withdrawing them from such activity after incarceration, the pederast underground does not much feel the continuing impact of arrest and imprisonment, as those persons are absent and therefore are invisible.

CHAPTER 13

Impact of Conscience:
Morals and Religion

Most pederasts sooner or later talk about religion and its impact upon sex attitudes and practice. If it be true that eight of each ten men who have pederastic desires, temptations, and opportunities restrain themselves from illegal sex play, or lapse only once or so in a lifetime, what are the effective restraints which make possible this self-control? Our evidence suggests that in such sexual activity, effective restraints are ultimately dependent upon the conscience of the individual and community, rather than on exterior controls which in any case are today eroded by confusion in society and its institutions. Most pederasts say that their own experiences early led them to question what they had been taught about sexual morality. Those pederasts who refrain from illegal sex play generally give credit to several factors: a) respect for the law and structures of society even when one disagrees with them, b) respect for the feelings of friends and family, not wishing to hurt them, c) the wish not to wreck one's life. Generally, these restraints are effective only if professional goals are being successfully attained and the commitments are expressed in terms of religion, ethics, and conscience. The pull of conscience is less effective in the lives of: a) those pederasts who do not have good jobs or very much to lose, b) those whose lives have already been wrecked by arrest, or c) those who already consider themselves to be failures in their professions.

In this chapter we will report on how practicing pederasts see religion and morals functioning in their lives, especially in limiting and controlling their sex play with boys. The interviewed pederasts represent such a wide spectrum of religious affiliation and interest that it is difficult to determine what may be meaningful in their fragmentary comments on religion or what has effective impact.

Some pederasts believe that organized religion is their enemy, and express anger at other pederasts who have religious faith and who support religious institutions. Nor is it possible to determine on the basis of our limited evidence whether or not some pederasts are more responsible because of their experience in the Church—that is, strive hard to avoid any sexual contact with youngsters, often by avoiding boys completely, or by commitment to a position which enables and supports self-control.

WIDE RANGE OF VIEWS

Roman Catholic. Said a priest: "My religious faith and nothing else has kept me from sexual encounters with boys whom I have so desired. I have taken shelter in the Church to escape from the promiscuous existence which well might otherwise have been mine."
A well-educated layman: "I consider myself to be a good Irish Catholic. My children attended parochial school, my wife always goes to mass, I contribute generously to the parish, and I have confessed all my sins to the monseigneur. If he isn't as helpful to me as I might wish, I have to ask myself what else can he do, dealing as he does with a parish of five thousand sexually frail persons. He says that I can be understood and forgiven so long as I am penitent and struggle to lift my life to a higher level. He and I compromise on how we understand that. Because he is gracious to me I faithfully keep my promise never to touch a boy in this parish, in this country, or a Catholic boy anywhere in the world. That leaves me room to enjoy myself a bit when on vacation." Said a less-well-educated pederast: "I go to mass with my boy every Sunday. He's sixteen now and we're more like brothers. He's quite happy that having confessed his venal sins he is in good standing as a Catholic. What's O.K. with him is O.K. with me. I'll not bother to tell you what the priest said when I finally leveled with him. He tried to judge me strictly, but in the end all he said that I heard was that he and I are both sinners."

A theologically well-read pederast said: "I was a religiously sensitive youngster, so I am aware how many kids suffer because of the confusion and conflict in sex attitudes and behavior. The most sensitive and intelligent of them may suffer the most because of the inadequacy of the moral and religious answers to their questions about what they do and believe sexually. Mostly we have been educated in school to believe that society gives us our values and determines our behavior, and a perceptive kid may lose faith when he sees how impersonal and unrealistic the system really is. On the one hand they are punished for self-expression or sexual self-assertion hand they are punished for self-expression of sexual self-assertion when they violate the legal and conventional behavior which society has failed to condition them to accept. The moral person, I think, is the one who has high hopes, dreams, and desires for the rich fulfillment of human life, for a more humane and reasonable community which will stimulate the creative imagination to solve all human problems, and which will despise simple and legalistic answers to complex questions and issues. I aim to be ethical—that is, to raise the sights of human morality so as to help it to be guided by love. Christians give lip service to the notion of 'transforming evil into good,' but I do not see much of that going on in the sexual realm, except perhaps in some marriages. My pastor told me I was expected to sublimate my sexual temptations and desires, but he was never able to provide me with the power to do so, even though I did everything he suggested. Such powerless religion can mean nothing to the young. The news media are sex-oriented and the Church merely wags a disapproving finger, obscuring the crime involved in the Church's failure to provide power or exciting new alternatives. In a time of plurality of options, the Church offers no options at all, in the view of Catholic kids I talk with—at least not on sexual questions. Who are the dirty-minded? Not such kids as yet. They have failed to learn that what they enjoy and find good is supposed to be seen as ugly and dirty, that their sense aren't to be trusted because they are 'flesh,' that the body is shameful, that pleasure is sinful, that 'anything you enjoy doing is wrong.' True Catholicism, I think, will rather suggest that they pray honestly, accepting the body God has created as good, and ask for His vision of beauty and truth in their sexual lives." A less committed pederast said: "I haven't attended mass regularly since I was a teen-ager, but I read a lot of Catholic theology and psychology, and I find a good deal to encourage me. I often talk religion with boys I'm involved with. Some of them are very religious, but do not seem to have a bad conscience about sex. Many of them, like me, have worked out their own philosophy of religion which they never discuss with anyone else." Said another: "I attend the gay church because its style suits my taste, not because I find more support there than anywhere else. Even there I keep my mouth shut. I agree with the gay pastor who said: 'Any kind of sex act can be holy if you love God and your sex partner.' Each time I meet a new boy I like I pray for him, and then, with confidence in God, I ask him if he would like to make love. I no longer have a bad conscience at all."

High Church Protestant. "Perhaps my faith is in my parents," one pederast reported. "They are very religious, so I cause them problems. We go to church and hear talk about being loving and forgiving, and my mother tries hard to be accepting and understanding. I have to be careful as long as she lives. My father exists in a more realistic world, and perhaps I inherit some fatalism from him. The Church, however, was very helpful and understanding for them, and me, when I got into trouble." Said another: "My own pastor was as helpful as he could be until he died. He admitted to me privately that he had himself almost gotten into similar difficulties once and he certainly knew what could happen. With his encouragement I was very careful, but now I do not find anyone of equal help." A less responsible pederast said: "I continue to be a member in good standing of the Church, and among my friends are clergymen who are prepared to support my eccentricities as long as I am loving. One of them, active in encounter groups, sleeps around some himself." Said another: "My church attendance is impeccable, as long as I can find a church with a boy choir. I've been singing in choirs since I was eight years old and I love church music. I do not abuse the church deliberately, but I do not consider myself as having the sort of religion which cramps my style. I do not need to give much thought to conflicts that might exist between my church membership and my sexual life."

The author of a study of pederast books, seeking to define their role in freedom from guilt[1] has noted that many clergymen have been pederasts, and that in England a number of them have written poetry about boys; for example, the Rev. E. E. Bradford: "Our yearning tenderness for boys like these/has more in it of Christ than Socrates." Considering himself attracted to boys by no choice of his own, he decided it was a God-given gift to make him especially concerned for youngsters; in a similar way J. G. Nicholson considered pederast love as a path to God. Another Anglican, Henry Somerset, spoke of sexual delight with a boy as "both of our lives are bathed in love divine." George Gillet "sought to justify his pederast passion on aesthetic as well as religious grounds, saying: '. . . beauty gains a glimpse of God.'" Ralph Chubb, who was almost mystical in his pederast writings, spoke of boys as "heavenly cupids," or angels, who were the unblemished advent of the Holy Ghost. Cuthbert Wright maintained that Jesus himself was a pederast, and John Francis Bloxam wrote the

story of a priest and an acolyte who committed suicide together after
taking the eucharist, when it appeared they would be separated,
affirming pederasty as a God-given love and that "death was preferable to its public defilement." Alphonse Montague Summers wrote a
poem also about the glimpse of God given to him by the boy who was
his lover. The aforementioned Rev. E. E. Bradford, who said ". . . 'tis
strange if nature left alone becomes unnatural" was curate of High
Ongar and St. Swithins in England, and he published twelve books
about the beauty of male friendships, including one titled *Romantic
Friendship*. His writings continue to be widely quoted among religious pederasts.

   Low Church Protestant. "I find liberal, well-educated clergymen to be of the least help. They become embarrassed when one talks
about something like pederasty. I therefore dropped out of the
church I grew up in and have joined a small evangelical fellowship.
The members know about my pederast temptations, and I get lots of
encouragement and support to toe the narrow line. They keep an eye
on me, and keep me happy and busy. Most of all they trust me to work
with kids, which is what I enjoy more than anything. I wouldn't let
them down." Another pederast: "I'm afraid I find it easy to live two
lives. Outside of the closet I'm conservative, Republican,
evangelical—and truly so. In my sexual underlife, which sometimes
seems to get out of control, I know myself to be a sinner, badly in need
of God's help in getting the two parts of my life together." Another,
less responsible, pederast said: "After being a Presbyterian Church
officer most of my life, I have now—my friends say I've become a
hippie late in life—become a Buddhist, joining a sect here on the
West Coast which is very small. Its philosophy is *sympatico* to my
taste for boys. I'm about to move in with a woman who is a fellow
member, who has two boys I'm crazy about." Still another said: "I
now attend church regularly with my mother, and I note what is said
and how it applies to me. I do not feel condemned more than the
others, although it is sometimes depressing to feel that I am not
finding the spiritual strength I need. I've never asked to hold church
office, but I don't refuse when I'm pressed to do so. I can't well refuse
on the grounds that I have a relationship with a boy who comes to
work in my garden."

   Jewish. "I am a religious Jew who thinks that religion, including
the Christian religion, has the solution to our problem in its pocket,
like a new miracle drug which might cure cancer but which has not
yet been proven out as safe," was one pederast's comment. Another

said: "You might call me a Jew, although my father was Christian. I participate actively in both Protestant and Jewish religious activities, especially working with church athletic teams. Since I intend never to touch a boy sexually, I prefer to hang around nice religious boys whose innocence protects both them and me."

A good many pederasts said they had never thought much about religion one way or the other. Some took a strong antireligious, anti-Christian line: "The Church has burned us alive, drawn and quartered us, hung us, tortured us, abused us—all in the name of religious love. There can be no healthy sex until the young are freed from that oppressive tradition which says that all sex is dirty and sinful." One pederast who took such a line said that he was cynical about the Church; for, like Edward Alexander Crowley who was introduced to pederasty by a missionary, he had been seduced by the president of his church youth group.

Some pederasts affirm that they root their conscience in a sort of secular religion based on the pederastic philosophy of the ancient Greeks. One said: "Love is always beneficial. I do not seek to evade responsibility, but accept the consequences of loving acts with boys, since in my own heart I know that I never harm a youngster, and that our relationship is always beneficial." "What harms boys is the guilt-ridden, morbid views of so many religious persons," said another. Such views are contrasted with the agonizing of novelist T. H. White, author of *Sword in the Stone*, who said that he did not believe that sexual relations with the boy he loved could hurt him or that any law of God would be violated, but on the grounds of expediency, because of what others could say that might hurt the boy, he would do nothing illegal.[2] "My effective morality," a pederast of high principles said, "is based on the love I have for boys. In my judgment, prohibitions against sex play rest on grounds similar to those which forbade work on the Sabbath or eating meat on Friday. Morality must be positive, not based on negative rules and prohibitions. I have a secret friendship with a lovely boy, but I'm not going to lead him down a path that might cause him grief, even though my heart aches because so much of what is beautiful is denied to him by foolish prohibitions. I used to be a Presbyterian elder, and I've given up on all that, although I believe my moral position is essentially that of Jesus, who nowhere condemned prostitutes, homosexuals, or deviants but only commanded his followers to love one another."

So many quotations are not essential for demonstrating the

diversity of religious opinion and practice among pederasts, but these and other comments suggest that religion is not an effective inhibitor of illegal sexual behavior—nor does it support a high level of pederast conscience—unless *a*) religious faith and values are experienced as commitments to and are embodied in relationships with valued and supportive persons, such as relatives and friends, and *b*) unless a pederast is an active participant in a warm, enfolding, supportive religious community *which knows of his desires and temptations*. To illustrate from another type of sexual experience, a young couple who live together out of wedlock are likely not to attend church services because they assume they will be rejected for "living in sin." As a result they tend to associate with other unmarried couples, who thus support each other in the rightness of their extramarital sex relationships. They will find it easier in such associations to become involved in other irregular sexual activities, such as "swinging" or "wife swapping." On the other hand if they were involved in a religious community of young couples they would be more likely to get married to affirm the values they found there. Similarly, pederasts of good conscience who exclude themselves from religious groups which they know to disapprove of their penchant are then likely to spend more time with other pederasts, or at least with persons who will be tolerant of sexual eccentricities. The more time a pederast spends in the underground, the more his point of view and conscience will be modified. The underground is not so much a place for illegal activity, as it is a substitute community for those who exclude themselves from conventional religious groups. More accurately it consists of persons searching for a community of people who will provide understanding, support, and help in the pederast's quest for self-understanding and struggle with conscience.

A French author[3] suggests that pederasty is, for some persons at least, a part of the struggle for self-understanding, that not only does the pederast seek out other men with similar desires in order to discuss with them the nature, cause, and meaning of their common experience, but there is also a sense in which the involvement of the pederast with young boys is a continuing search for an understanding of himself and his sexuality at that same young age. In the effort to understand his own sexuality, it is only natural that a boy will first turn to those who are similar to him, *i.e.*, other males, and if this curiosity is not satisfied, if the questions he asked did not receive adequate answers, the search for sexual identity may last a lifetime—especially if he has deviant inclinations not resolved with heterosexual intercourse. In any case, religious institutions tend to give what one pederast called "assembly-line answers, packaged for the masses," by which he meant that persons with untypical sexual desires received generalizations which did not seem to fit his peculiar situation. This same pederast went on to say: "I am a man of conscience, high principles, and strict morality, who agrees with the puritan attitudes of the Church—until once in a great while I chance to meet a seductive, sexually experienced boy. Then I grow faint, physically and morally, to such an overpowering extent that the moral and religious pabulum passed out by the Church is insufficient to help. Society treats me like a four-year-old, whose questions are ignored and not taken seriously. When I was that age or perhaps a little older I learned that I would be punished for the masturbation I enjoyed, so I withdrew into my own little world where I could nurture my conscience on what seemed good and right to me. I have continued to do so to the present, keeping my forbidden joys secret and struggling in private to maintain the ingegrity of my own conscience." What he and others seem to be saying is that restraints are eroded in a situation which calls forth dishonesty and secrecy, and which does not provide adequate opportunity for honest dialogue with sympathetic nonpederasts.

MORAL ISSUES

It may well be that if the pederast frequently has an immature point of view it is because his moral philosophy—as bearing on sex play with boys—was formed in his adolescence and without much guidance and help then or since. The British novel *Sandel*[4] reports the moral struggle of an older teen-ager whose awareness that he is a pederast is coincident with his involvement with a sexually aggressive 13-year-old boy. "Murder and killing hurt someone," he says to a religious friend. "But who is harmed if I make love to the boy who finds it beneficial?"

One pederast said: "As I see it, the basic moral question is—'Am I hurting anyone?' It is tempting to say that something is good and not hurtful if I enjoy it. But I happen to enjoy driving down the highway at a hundred miles an hour and I know that is not good. It is likely to hurt me and others. I happen to be a very sensitive person who believes that it is a crime to hurt anyone. Ironically, I would be more seriously punished by society for giving a moment of sexual pleasure to a boy than for beating him savagely or for breaking his heart. I consider myself to be a very moral person, resolutely opposed to graft, killing, or anything that hurts society or any one person. I also happen to believe that the only sure way to find out whether someone is hurt is to examine that person. Certainly, if a boy says a pederast has hurt him, or if there is evidence of damage, then the pederast should be punished. The moral issue is whether—or at what age—a boy is competent to judge whether or not an act of lovemaking has hurt him. Of course a boy knows if he has been physically hurt, but can he or anyone else know when he is hurt psychologically? Society assumes that the pederastic experience will make a boy homosexual. Where is the evidence? It makes no sense at all for society to ignore the fact that once a boy has had a great deal of adult-type sexual experience he is sexually an adult, no matter how young he is. Why should the law consider him innocent if since he was thirteen he has slept with boys and girls and has fathered a baby? One of my friends is in prison for a playful sexual act with a boy of fifteen who had been a prostitute for two years. How does society judge the hurt he did to that boy? The boy initiated the sex act, enjoyed it, and did it for fun rather than money. What kind of morality destroys a good citizen for this?"

A European pederast said: "I've reviewed the literature for any possible psychological harm that could befall a teen-age boy as a result of playful sex with a man, and I can't find corroborated evidence of any damage whatsoever. There are studies which show that even young children are not negatively affected by consenting sexual intercourse with adults,[5] unless adults tell the children they have been damaged. It would seem that psychological damage can result from the way sexual experience is interpreted to youngsters, and such damage may be more frequent when there is no sexual intercourse at all. For example, a boy was traumatically affected by his sexual experience in one of the correctional institutions that is called a 'junior republic.' The staff of the institution, by close supervision, was for the most part able to prevent sex play and abuse, but there was continual talk and teasing by the older boys which scared this younger boy, with traumatic results on his later sexual attitudes. It might actually have been easier for him to recover healthily after a real rape than it was to suffer from the fantasies and worries which grew out of teasing and threats. In other words, the law and supervision can protect boys from physical hurt, but there is no way to protect boys from the psychic sexual experience which is shaped in their own imaginations. Jean Genet has described the intense psychological damage of such a psychic process in a school where older teen-agers, as a game, sexually caressed every younger boy they met. Even that experience, however, may have been actually less damaging than the curious fantasies a boy can have after seeing or hearing of such a thing. It may well be more moral to give a boy an orgasm than to build up his sexual tensions and stimulate his imagination with teasing, dirty jokes, horseplay and psychic games. Yet adults and older boys who tease youngsters are not arrested. Some of them enjoy a peace of mind in their moral conscience because they 'never touch a boy' sexually. Pederasty may disappear or become essentially unimportant in a society which provides adolescents with a healthy, happy environment for growth instead of the stimulus of imaginary deviancies. The fundamental moral issue is not what is bad for boys, but how can society provide them sexually with what is healthy and good."

A young pederast seems first to ask himself if he is unique, different, queer, in an effort to determine if something is "wrong" with him. If he withdraws into his own private world or even into the pederast underground to test and validate the authenticity of his deviant experience, he then tends to decide that something is wrong with society rather than with himself. One such deviate said: "How moral would it be for the government to spend its cancer research money to arrest every hundreth cancer victim? Or perhaps society should shoot one out of every hundred drunken drivers? I guess society views me as 50 per cent sick and 50 per cent irresponsible. But the only thing done to prevent me from working damage on the innocent—by those who consider man-boy sex play as damaging—is more or less comparable to such random and senseless arrest and shooting. Society doesn't know how to deal with me, I suppose, because I do not fit into the categories. The moral issue is this: Is pleasure good? If so, then shouldn't kids be allowed to enjoy themselves sexually? I don't know why I so enjoy giving sex pleasure to boys, but I don't see sex as belonging to the same category of damage as alcohol and drugs. They say a healthy kid doesn't get addicted to anything and the moral issue revolves around what is healthy and who is to decide. I agree that a line has to be drawn somewhere. I personally disapprove of anal intercourse, for example. But when I was a teen-ager—and I think it is true today also—we couldn't have a healthy discussion of such things because all sex was wrong and forbidden to us. Parents who know the power of alcohol often teach their kids to drink moderately, to save them from the perils of alcohol in the alley, but they let their kids go to strange men for sexual experience because one isn't allowed to admit to kids that the sexual alley exists. I am sure I would not be a pederast today if society had permitted me to follow my natural inclinations when I was a young teen-ager."

Another pederast wrote: "A British psychiatrist has been seriously flirting with the idea that some types of mental illness are really signs of health, reflecting the fact that society is ill. A sensitive person naturally becomes neurotic if he has to adjust to a sick situation. People become twisted by a sick society—and ours is sexually sick—so that 'normal' perspectives are really abnormal. How do I see myself in this perspective? I love women, boys, life, and I know myself to be an essentially good person in all my relationships. I am kindly, supportive, and loving. Sexually I'm free from the hang-ups which drive some of my friends to the wall. I have a happy sex life which I consider to be more well-rounded than that of many of my 'straight' friends. If I seem to be out of step with society, it may well be that I'm out in front, leading the pack. And if I'm ill it is because the pack keeps nipping at my heels."

A similar moral point of view was stated by another European pederast substantially as follows: "Can we begin the discussion of morality from where we are, rather than from where society says we ought to be? As I see it, society's moral efforts should be directed at moving us, and all persons, up the ladder,[6] out of the underground, rather than merely condemning us for wandering around lost in the pit at the foot of the ladder. If pederasts are sinful or sick, then the question is: How can we be healed? Not by our own efforts, except in certain heroic instances. If we are tempted, how can we be strengthened, and who will help us? It certainly is no help to be kicked back into the pit, which is what usually happens now. Don't apologize for referring to me as a 'case,' for it suggests to me—and I assure you that it is true—that I am unique and different from all other persons, including all other pederasts. A 'case' in our hospital is not a faceless person to be disposed of, but is a challenging demand for unique diagnosis and treatment—not that we ever cure anybody. Society forgets that! Cures happen only when society creates a healing environment and lets natural forces take over, which is very moral. Law and police can never cure. It is highly immoral to assume that they can supervise what happens in people's beds or can prevent sexual deviance. How moral is a society that can't forgive a first mistake, which over and over again kicks a young man down into the pit, instead of first trying to love and help him, and accepting some share of blame for his sexual misbehavior?"

A PEDERAST STATEMENT OF PRINCIPLES

It would be absurd to assume that such statements are typical of all pederasts. When we express a willingness to listen, however; when we try to understand what they feel and experience, they naturally try to put their best foot forward to make a positive impression. Our exploration of the pederast underground revealed that even such furtive dialogue begins to raise moral concerns. Asking questions they have not previously faced begins to affect their attitudes and behaviors. One pederast who had been rather promiscuous, usually seeking hasty sexual encounters with boys in movie theaters, having thought through his point of view in order to answer our questionnaire, said: "I always knew that my concern was not for conventional morality, but for a higher ethic. Some of my promiscuous behavior has been thoughtless, but some of it also has been a rebellion against a hypocritical society, in which I defied the police and law as a kind of personal protest. I'm putting all that behind me now, however, because my goal is to see that youngsters become healthy, happy, whole, loving, creative. Somewhere along the line the Establishment decided that conventional repressive goodness is better than free creativity, even if it meant the sexual unhappiness and torture—I think that word is well advised—of young adolescents. My aim now is to help create a healing rather than a destructive sexual environment for the young, who are already operating on different sexual values than is the Establishment. In a sense many adolescents live in a sexual underground, at least part of the time, because they actually live by a different sex ethic than they publicly affirm. Their real values and behavior are not open to searching public discussion. Those who should be asking the value questions are too disapproving of us—I feel I can still speak for older teen-agers since I'm barely twenty myself—for us to be really able to trust them." This young pederast further said he felt it is the responsibility of pederasts to examine their own behavior, and together seek to propose ethical standards which might be based upon a "more creative approach to sexual morality." The term *Better Life,* he said, which is used by one pederast association and publication, suggests a continuing of the efforts of the ancient Greeks to find and to enhance the beautiful in all relationships. "Those of us who love boys should encourage and help each other to put their welfare above everything else. An ethical code must give us a positive image for the future. Rather than living *in* and *for* gratification in the present, we want to assume responsibility and make commitments which can lead us to a 'better life' for all. A pederast ethic should seek to enrich and ennoble the lives of boys. First, however, we must deal with our own questionable behavior."

Within the pederast underground several ethical statements or "bills of rights" have been drafted and discussed, the first effort taking place in the late 1960's.[7] Some of these statements contain elaborate theories and philosophies, with proposals for law reform. Others are more self-serving, such as one that begins with the statement: "I'll give up boys when there are no more who need me and want me," and ends with the gay slogan: "Any love is better than no love at all." This statement asserts that the "quality of relationship" between two persons is the basic ethical issue, and opposes "all dishonesty, force, prostitution, and abuse." Three of the documents are addressed largely to pederasts themselves, urging them to avoid and to correct disapproved types of behavior, which might be summarized as follows:

1. Boys should not be treated as sexual objects to be enjoyed at the whim of a pederast.

2. A pederast should not seek intimate contact with a boy, without knowing and understanding the boy's interests and feelings.

3. A pederast should not "cruise" to pick up strange boys for sexual encounters, because that encourages boys to "hustle" or prostitute themselves.

4. A pederast should protect his own reputation, so that his young friends will not be hurt or suffer as a result of association with him.

5. A pederast must always be truthful and honest, and never lie to his young friends.

6. A pederast who takes pictures of his young friends must not sell them to commercial dealers or pass them on indiscriminately to others, without permission of the boy and his parents.

7. Friendship with a boy should never develop into sexual intimacy without the boy fully understanding and consenting to any sex play, including the social and legal implications of the relationship.

8. A pederast should not provide his young friends with alcohol

or drugs, and certainly will never use drugs to weaken a boy's sexual inhibitions or "to get him into the mood" for sexual intimacy.

9. A pederast has the responsibility of encouraging and helping a boy to develop his normal heterosexual tendencies, unless the boy's family confirms that he has an innate homosexual orientation.

10. A pederast should guide and encourage his young friends to stay in school, avoid crime, and do all he can to help them to develop a successful career.

11. A pederast should strive to guide and discipline his young friends by a code of behavior which will be compatible with reasonable standards of his family and society, with the sort of direction a boy should receive from father or teacher.

12. A pederast should never offer his young friend to another pederast for sexual purposes, even if the boy expressed an interest in his doing so.

13. A pederast should do everything possible to protect his young friends from any harm, including exposure or embarrassment from arrest.

The above list has been included here not only as an illustration of some beginning efforts of pederasts to be morally responsible but also because it presents more evidence of pederast behavior which has not been adequately described in their portrayals of their own behavior as presented in this book.

Perhaps the most widely distributed and discussed sexual bill of rights for adolescents is an adaptation of a statement prepared by the Child Sexuality Circle of the Sex Freedom League, which begins by asserting:

—a child's sexuality is a part of his whole person from birth, making his sexual rights inherent and inalienable,
—the child's sexual rights should be encompassed in the United Nations Declaration of Human Rights,
—a child not allowed to express all instinctive desires becomes unhappy, frustrated, antisocial and potentially criminal.

A pederast study group has adapted the statement[8] as follows:

1. Every adolescent is entitled to legal protection of his sexual rights, which includes the right to privacy for his own personal thoughts, ideas, dreams, and explorations of his body, without interference.

2. Every adolescent has the right to accurate sex information, and to be protected from sexual misinformation and prejudices, including the right to debate and disagree with majority opinion and law.

3. Every adolescent has the right to enjoy fully whatever sensual pleasures he may feel, without shame or guilt, with any partners he may choose. He has the right to be protected and aided in doing so with contraceptives and aids to prevent venereal disease.

4. Every adolescent has the right to learn the art of lovemaking, as any other art or skill, whenever he is ready to do so, and not merely from books and lectures, but from adequately interpreted experiences of his own choosing.

5. Every adolescent has the right to affirmative, affectionate relationships with adults of his own choosing, and to a full understanding of any implications or dangers that may be present in such relationships.

Many pederasts, in contrast to those just quoted, would instead agreed with the pederast who said: "I find talk of a pederast ethic as amusing as I do the idea of a just war. Society is becoming tolerant of gay-homosexuals because they are seen as 'poor sick things' who are unable to help themselves. However, society isn't tolerant of the Weathermen or other revolutionary groups, sick or not. And the taboos I violate are more hate-arousing than anything the bomb-throwers stand for. Society is at war with me, and in war anything goes. No one has time to stop and talk about just wars or the most decent ways to bomb Vietnamese children in the midst of battle. Society hates me because I love kids and they love me in return. The kids I love come from such lousy sick homes and schools that they need alcohol and drugs to deaden their pain. I've had so much pain in my life, too, that I'll not be bound by any code of ethics which would prevent me from doing all I can to give a moment of peace and joy to a kid in the midst of his pain and fury at life."

SOME CONCLUDING OBSERVATIONS

• Lowen[9] says that the fun culture's view of "experience as the only true value in life" cannot be shown to contribute to sexual health within a disapproving society. Sex without love, Lowen says, provides no possibility for creative development, and sex play of the type reported in this book cannot be creatively assimilated and integrated into the personality, he suggests, at least until society itself changes.

This is a challenge which some responsible pederasts find difficult to answer.

● On the other hand, when religious traditions interpret sexual acts and experiences, they appear to be more successful in creating emotions of guilt or rebellion than in effectively inhibiting or preventing sexual deviance, as judged from the evidence of pederasts interviewed. Bernard (1975) found that pederasts suffering from feelings of guilt did not think that repeal of laws against man-boy sex play would relieve their moral anxiety.

● It is not possible to derive conclusive opinions from the data in this chapter—which is fragmentary because of being limited to whatever the pederasts being interviewed said about religion—often nothing. Their life stories and church involvements do strongly suggest, however, that personal face-to-face relations—and not abstract church teachings—provide moral strength, self-control, and an effective conscience. Even more important, these interviews provide evidence that moral standards and religion have an inhibiting effect in deviant sexual situations only on those persons who have a chance to assume responsibility for establishing ethical guidelines which seem to make sense in their own lives. That is to say, imposed ethical and moral standards prove to be weak and ineffective when they come into conflict with the values which have been tested in a person's own sexual experience.

● The number of non-Christians interviewed was limited, but it would appear that these same findings are true within other religious traditions. Whenever anti-sex attitudes become repressive and dogmatic, an underground develops. There are underground religious traditions which view deviant sexual practices as "energizing the artistic, poetic and mystical faculties," and as being sources of spiritual power or even types of worship and meditation.[10] A number of unpublished philosophical papers by pederasts—combined with ideas from Plato and others, including some of the pederast clergy quoted in this chapter—describe pederasty as a God-given mystical experience. In this context, taboos against sex play and recreational sex are frequently viewed as being outmoded like the old prohibitions against eating pork.

CHAPTER 14

Identity and Self-Understanding

A sense of identity as a pederast may begin diffusely with a growing awareness that one is erotically attracted to boys, but it starts to consolidate with the demanding emotion, so powerful it cannot be ignored, of being enamored with a specific boy. For the majority this experience first happens in adolescence, at an age when most youngsters are plagued with self-doubt and emotional growing pains, and when few boys are prepared to cope alone with such a crisis. Yet few of these budding pederasts dare admit the crisis to anyone, for most are keenly aware of the penalties of being different, or "queer," in our society. It may well be that those whose first experience of being enamored of a boy happens very young grow up to accept and accommodate to the fact much as they would a crippled leg. Those who live with the fact the longest may find it easier to accept the identity and label, and to integrate the accompanying sexual behavior and preferences into their total personality structure, step by step, incident by incident, as they grow and develop. The opposite seems clearly to be true, on the basis of our interviews, that those who were adults or older teen-agers when they were struck with the first overwhelming powerful infatuation have a more serious crisis in self-understanding.

WHO AM I?

In the general adolescent and young adult quest for a sense of identity, a person at times may seek to affirm his uniqueness, and at other time to prove that he is the same as everyone else. If he is unique in being more intelligent, better-looking, or a better athlete, he will take more pride in his uniqueness, and he may organize his personality around these special characteristics. A person's identity consists of more than his own self-view of his physical, mental, emotional and character-personality traits, however. The view of himself which an adolescent constructs must take account of, and be reshaped by, what he sees in the eyes of others. A crisis in identity can result from many types of rejection or self-rejection, but none is so severe as the self-awareness of society's fundamental disapproval. The adolescent is caught up in questions: why am I different? why did this happen to me? Some pederasts report that they later had successfully repressed or ignored a second enamoring, since it was something one was not allowed to consider as a possibility. In one way or another, many pederasts as adolescents were plagued emotionally by the word *queer*, which was frequently on the lips of their contemporaries. To this question—Am I a queer?—was often added the question: Am I wicked or sick?

PROFILE OF THE PEDERAST

If one can speak of a "typical" pederast by listing the characteristics of the majority as shown by questionnaires and psychological tests,[1] he may be described as follows. He is in young to middle adulthood. He has an above-the-average education, a good job, and is not yet married. He became aware in his young adolescence that he was erotically attracted to boys thirteen or fourteen years old. As he has grown older he has continued to be smitten with boys of that age, one after another. When he had the chance to carry on mutual masturbation with one of these boys, his infatuation and fantasies increased the pleasure and power of the experience over what it would have been for another boy. If he had other adolescent sex play or experience it was with relatives or very close friends. In mid-adolescence he began to date girls, perhaps a bit more than other boys his age, because he was anxious to prove to himself as well as to others that he was normal. At that time he still hoped that his crushes on boys were a temporary phenomenon and that he would grow out of it. He had the supporting conviction that he had never done anything very bad—a bit of oral and anal experimentation, perhaps but mainly just mutual masturbation. In mid- and late-adolescence he developed a generalized fondness for the company of boys which led him to concentrate his activities in areas of interest to younger boys. For example, he stayed in the Boy Scouts longer and became a patrol leader or else his athletic interests turned to coaching. He intended to put his sex play with boys behind him, but every now and then a younger boy he was enamored of would respond with affection and sexual gestures. One or more of these relationships—each lasting a year or more with increasing sexual involvement—would be so happy and emotionally rewarding as to set a pattern for future such relationships. When he consciously came to terms with this fact, usually in his early twenties, he had also chanced to meet other pederasts. His accepting of the pederast identity involved his decision that this aspect of his nature was the core of his experience around which he would define himself. The underground then became important to him, not as a place for illegal behavior but as a place of self-definition, where he could assess himself in comparison and in contrast with other pederasts. For many pederasts the underground therefore, as a place for testing, validating and interpreting experience through conversations and sharing of experiences, has become a substitute for actual sex acts, at least of the promiscuous sort which are provoked by a continuing quest for self-affirming experiences.

ARE PEDERASTS HOMOSEXUALS?

This process of self-definition frequently goes through two phases. First, there is an effort to answer negative questions and deal with the brutal opposition of society; then, second, there is a positive effort to develop a pederast identity, along with self-acceptance and even pride. The first of the negative challenges, which some pederasts struggled with even before puberty, is "Am I a homosexual?" As the growing child discovers what it means to be male or female, sexual identity includes knowing what he can do and what he is forbidden to do. To be "gay" usually means accepting, and being committed to, a homosexual life-style which is more or less exclusive, rejecting sexual relations with the opposite sex, and therefore ruling out conventional marriage and life. It comes to mean far more than defining oneself as "different" or "queer." There are three typical answers that pederasts tend to give when confronted with this question.

I'm Not Gay

One pederast said: "I'm happily married, with fine children. I don't know what to call the secret identity I have which is known only to a few intimate friends. Pederasty is a minor aspect of my life which

I refuse to let overweigh more important things. I have two friends who gamble. One of them deserves the label of *gambler* because he is a compulsive gambler, continually losing his wages. No one thinks of the other as a gambler, although he enjoys himself at the races. He keeps his life in balance, and his gambling—like my pederasty—is not compulsive but is something he enjoys. Certainly my pederasty is as much a part of me as a mole on my face. If that mole becomes cancerous my identity would become 'cancer patient.' My whole life would then be altered and I would no longer be the 'sex freedom' advocate whose wife also has her little sex diversions on the side, by mutual agreement. I'm pleased that my 16-year-old son sleeps with his girls, and if my younger son has sex fun with a boy friend, that is fine with me. I want my boys to have happy lives in every way, in contrast to my own childhood, which was sexually miserable. Is it only the poor child who secretly dreams of being a prince, entitled to wealth and pleasures presently denied him? When I was fourteen I had my eye on certain very sexually attractive boys that I planned to reward by making them pages in my palace when I became king. I had no guilt about my sex play with them, because as a prince I was entitled to special favors. As I grew older I had to divest myself of the notion I was a prince, but the conviction remained that I was unique, a special sort of person, with sex tastes that were different, more varied, perhaps more enjoyable. I was never a homosexual. I was crazy about girls ever since I can remember. I knew it was wrong to have sex with little girls, for they were going to be wives and mothers and should be protected, not abused. It never occurred to me as a youngster that sex with a boy was wrong or against the law. I knew that 'hustling' was bad, but I thought that was because one sold oneself for money. When I was in the navy I took a violent dislike to gays, and after observing their life-style I knew I wanted marriage and a family. My decision was that I was a pederast and that I was not gay, but was simply a normal man who happens to enjoy sex horseplay with boys of thirteen or so. To be honest, I suppose I do consider myself to be a 'fag,' as defined by boys on my street in Brooklyn when I was a kid. They thought that except for priests all kindly, warm, sympathetic and educated men were 'fags.' "

Another pederast said: "I'm definitely not gay, for I have strongly resisted situations where boys wanted to make love or to become emotionally involved. I didn't know the word *gay* at fifteen, but I knew that lovemaking was with girls and my daydreams were about romantic honeymoon trips to gardens of love, something quite different from the hilarious and delightful sex games that I've played with boys." Said another: "A gay is a sort of feminine type, and there's nothing of that in me, even if I do love boys." Another said: "I'm engaged, and I've made it with many girls even though I'm younger than I look. One thing I'll never do is tell a boy that any kind of sex is wrong. What I love about young adolescents is the gleam in their eyes and the expression on their faces when they have had some good sex. The boys I find erotic are those who are first coming into adolescence, that wonderful shy and secretive age of first sexual experience. If I were gay I couldn't so much enjoy and share that marvelous time." Said another: "I'm absolutely not gay, nor did I think of myself as a pederast until recently when, after a string of losing games, I got bumped down to junior-high-school coaching when I was over forty. Not all the boys are erotically attractive to me, but I have to admit that some are, especially the ones who are both good-looking and athletically promising. I never touch one of my boys, except as necessary as a coach, but they got me so aroused that recently, on vacation, I went to a place where I could sleep with a boy prostitute to see if it was true—and it was. My pleasure in working with boys is now greatly enhanced by the glow and memory of that sexual experience, which fills my fantasies. One nice thing about limiting sex play to fantasy is that one can do whatever one wants."

I'm Gay

A pederast who accepts the gay label says: "Society obviously thinks that I am homosexual, since I am now homosexually involved with a young male. I try always to obey the law, except when I'm overseas, which means that I've tried to transfer my pederast activity to boys of legal age—one can find some very nice boys who are eighteen, or who at least have papers affirming they are that old." Another said: "I'm definitely gay in that I enjoy sex with males my age and older, as well as with the younger boys I prefer. I discovered that preference when I was in the university, and discovered how sexually hungry and desirous some boys are, and that's what attracts me. I find some women sexually attractive, too, but I'm satisfied with my life as it is, and I've made my friends in the gay organizations." Another said: "Yes, I'm gay in that I simply don't like women, because they are always trying to trap me into marriage, especially the mothers of boys I grow fond of. One even wanted to leave her husband for me, and I see now she was using her son as bait. I suppose you would say I've had bad experiences with women, compared to the fun I have had with boys. However I'm not gay in that I'm not attracted to males over sixteen. Perhaps I'm not really a pederast either, in that I never do the things that are proscribed under the sodomy act. I'm too fond of kids to get them into trouble. I'm a pederast in that I enjoy picturing boys as I masturbate, and I enjoy taking pictures of boys playing with each other, which will be the solace of my old age, although if I had sexual intercourse with a boy I probably would think of a woman as I did it."

The ambiguity of definition is illustrated by this statement: "Yes, I'm gay, but to me the word means someone who admits to himself that he isn't bound exclusively to women, but can enjoy sex with males as well as females—and that sex is for pleasure and not just making babies. How can I deny being gay when I so enjoy sex with young males? I do not consider myself queer. A 'queer' is someone who can't stand women, a 'queer' is someone who denies himself some of the natural pleasures which God gives. In my early teens I discovered the fountain of pleasure which many people search for all their lives, and having found it I decided to bask in it and enjoy it. I think some of the people who call me 'queer' are simply jealous. *Gay* means 'enjoying.' " Another said: "In the tough, lower-class neighborhood where I grew up it was taken for granted that boys, at any age, would spend their spare energies trying to take advantage of girls. If you masturbated, it meant you were either a 'queer' or admitting failure. When my friend and I discovered that we enjoyed playing with each other, we decided we were criminal." This pederast then reported how he and his friend joined a "gay group" at their school and the friend became gay-homosexual in life-style, continuing to have sexual involvements with persons his own age as he grew up: "As we grew apart, he said I was 'queer,' for continuing to be interested in younger boys."

Ambiguous

The third and perhaps most typical response of pederasts is ambiguity: "I don't know if I'm gay or not, for the word is puzzling. My girl friend says I'm certainly not gay and she ought to know, although she is aware that I play around with boys. She tolerates that because she doesn't want to sleep with me any more until we're married. Also, she accepts my word that I'm an honest person who admits the truth about himself and about the boys, who are irrepressibly sexed young animals who enjoy it with me. Do I seduce kids? Never! I have to fight them off. This whole antihomosexual taboo is a fraud and myth, as is most sex education. I'm not gay in that I don't care for kids that are queer, just the sexy little buggers."

Said another: "I don't know if I'm gay, but I'm definitely pederast in that I enjoy all types of play with young boys—wrestling, boxing, basketball, tennis, and sex play, too, but only if a boy wants it. If I were gay I'd be interested in the gay kids, in a possessive, emotional relationship, instead of doing all I can to help boys relate to girls. If sometime I get caught, the newspapers will probably say that I abused my position at the boy's club, but it isn't as they would think. I've never solicited a boy. It all began when a scared kid crawled in bed with me on a camping trip, and the next thing I knew he was playfully rubbing himself against me. We spent half the night talking about sex, not saying a thing his father wouldn't have approved of. Now, whenever a boy shows up at my house at night, saying he's got a problem to talk over, I wonder if he has learned something about me from other boys. Whatever my pederast friends say, however, it isn't my intention to solve boys' problems by talking things over with them in bed. I'm always genuinely sorry when that happens, and I do all I can to help them make it with a girl."

ARE PEDERASTS CRIMINALS?

One problem with any label is that it tends to freeze a person into a life-style or sex role which otherwise might change as the young person develops. Some young gay persons marry as they grow older, and some pederasts give up such activity altogether as they grow older. A European legislator[2] is of the opinion that many young persons come to accept a criminal identity through the discovery that their sex activity is against the law. Such a relationship between pederasty and delinquency is evidenced in this statement: "Of course we didn't realize at first that our sex play was so wrong, for we were just clowning around even when we sodomized each other. My hair really stood on end when I learned I was guilty of an act that could send me to prison for many years. We were criminals, therefore, who enjoyed doing things good people weren't supposed to do. As partners in crime we were bound together in a close friendship as closely as committing a crime together. So we discovered that breaking into a house or a store was as exciting as sex, exploring forbidden territory to find treasures we could keep. Even today, when a boy consents to go to bed with me, I have the same thrill of excitement I felt when I was a kid and we broke into a store and found boxes of candy, cartons of cigarettes, and money in the cash register. Sex play then and now is all the more exciting because it is exploring forbidden territory like that. The body of another person is a fascinating world to explore, for each boy is sexually so different in how he responds and what he likes. I find it highly arousing when a boy decides he is criminal because he enjoys illicit sex. I think my current boy is much more uninhibited in bed because he knows that somehow he and I are outcasts, secretly bound together by the scorn and disapproval of good people if they knew. If it were legal neither of us would enjoy it so much. Already when I was seventeen and eighteen, since I knew I was a criminal anyway, I had no hesitancy in seducing innocent boys, exploring virgin territory, and the easiest way was to take him stealing first. Then when he was elated with a successful breaking and entering expedition, and had wicked money in his pocket, it was easy to get him to consent to celebrating in bed."

For every pederast who accepts a criminal identity, however, there are a hundred who deny any criminal intent, asserting that the laws should be changed, that the "age of consent" should be lowered, and that their relationships with boys can be wholesome and good.

ARE PEDERASTS SICK?

Pederasts take varying positions in answering to their own satisfaction the question: Am I sick? Some of them say that everyone is sick in our culture! We have previously quoted those who affirm that the pederast considers himself to be a healthy person in a sexually sick society. For example: "As far as I am concerned our whole sex system is mad. I think it hilarious that some people think me mentally ill because I can enjoy myself sexually with anyone I like. I think I'm one of the few healthy people I know, and it is equally crazy that some people think I would make a boy gay by having sex with him. I bring boys alive sexually so that they are crazy for girls and are much freer to enjoy them, instead of being all tied-up and repressed sexually. It is our sexually repressive culture that twists kids, and I help them un-twist themselves. I was so girl-oriented myself that I might never have found out how enjoyable boys can be if I hadn't gotten in some trouble that led to my confinement in an all-boy institution for a time. There were a lot of sick boys there, and some of the staff seemed to me just as sick, and I was helped to see what was sick and what was not.

The psychiatrist himself said I didn't belong there and got me out because he said I was a very healthy boy."

A European psychologist[3] has administered tests to pederasts, homosexuals, and nonpederast adult males in order to determine how pederasts differ from the normal heterosexual men. On the Amsterdam Biographical Questionnaire (ABV), a group of pederasts recorded more psychological and physical complaints than is common for the test—at least in part because pederasts were much more openly self-critical and undefensive in answering. The extent to which their complaints resulted from neurosis, from a tell-and-be-damned attitude toward the test, or from the stress of keeping illegal activity secret, is difficult to determine. The psychologist concluded that the test indicated that pederasts are not necessarily (by nature) more unstable than the average person, indeed that many are above average. On another test, the Scale of Interpersonal Values (SIV), which measures the person's need for support, recognition, conformity, independence, and so forth, pederasts showed a greater-than-average need for support and recognition, less-than-average need for leadership roles or for conformity. Their felt need for support and admiration seems understandable in view of a common lack of these, as does their low valuing of conformity. Perhaps their lesser need for leadership activity arises from the necessity for keeping a low profile. On the other values on the scale, independence and altruism, the pederasts resembled men in general. The European psychologist is administering these tests and others to persons in other countries in order to expand the results, but the tests have not thus far convincingly shown pederasts to be intrinsically sick any more than the general population—although the pederasts have more problems which might be expected to make them so. Of the pederasts who took the test, 50 per cent had been arrested at one time or another.

One pederast reported for our study: "My psychiatrist has simply helped me to confine my activities to boys over sixteen, legal in this state." Said another: "Perhaps you can say I was sick at the time I was struggling to deal with the problems society caused for me as a result of accusations and disapproval. It was good that I went to a psychiatrist; for, while he did not 'cure my pederasty' in any sense, he helped me to accept it and to build up my self-control so that I can stay out of difficulty with the law. I think I am now healthier than most persons because I know my weakness and how to handle it, whereas most persons lack that much insight."

POSITIVE SELF-IMAGE

For some pederasts the underground is a source of similar self-acceptance and self-control as the result of psychiatric therapy. The underground is a place where pederasts examine together their behavior statements, verbal statements, and emotional statements, defining themselves in response to each other, and to the challenges of society which lead them to emotions of guilt, anxiety, fatalism. In the underground they tend to develop an awareness of their pederast identity by comparing themselves to other pederasts rather than to nonpederasts, ranking or scaling themselves in terms of behavior and attitudes with which they agree or disagree.

Am I a Sinner?

Says a pederast: "I'm not one of those promiscuous playboy types who are chasing after every boy on the street. I'm involved with only one boy at a time, over a period of months or years, and I judge everything we do in terms of his welfare." Said another: "I wouldn't do anything to hurt a boy's ego or feelings, and I won't have anything to do with those pederasts who simply want to use boys for their own erotic pleasure." Said another: "I wasn't the only service man who felt entitled to a bit of sex fun before going into combat. I saw myself as being foolhardy in the air and also with boys, since I might be killed the next day. I doubt if I would have become actively involved with boys if I hadn't decided that society owed me some pleasure in return for the sacrifice I was making. The little sinning I did in bed must seem trivial in contrast to the persons who suffered as a result of the bombs I dropped. I feel like the pederast in the movie, *The Conformist,* felt when the priest in the confessional was less interested in a murder he had committed than in the sodomy he had been involved in at the age of thirteen. I'm not going to organize my life around guilt over a few such acts when I was a kid, or things of lesser import that I do now."

Am I a Criminal?

One pederast said: "I'm not chasing babies who are barely pubescent. The ancient Greeks didn't approve of cradle robbers, either." He and many others made a strong point out of distinguishing themselves as different from pederasts who seduce boys. "That's criminal," this pederast said. Said another: "I try to be responsible and avoid illegal acts, whereas those who relish forbidden fruit are frequently selfish and exploitive." Said another: "When I compare myself to pederasts who have been arrested, I see in them certain unfortunate tendencies. Their judgment is poor, they are impulsive, they have been conspicuous, often even in their own neighborhoods. They have engaged in criminal use of alcohol and drugs, and frequently indulged in other types of criminal behavior. They are likely to be loners who seek out maladjusted boys. Those of us who have not been arrested are, I think, more realistic about what is possible. We are more successful in our family relationships, our careers, and so on. We are more successful in all our endeavors, including our relationships with boys and their parents. Maybe when I was young I was foolhardy at times, rushing a boy fast and acting impulsively, and I take it upon myself to point out to others the possible consequences of abusing relationships."

Am I Queer?

One pederast said: "The members of my midget football team are crazy about me because I'm really tough. I'm not one of those boy-lovers who make 'queers' out of kids, and I'm roughest on the boy I really go for. I really make him toe the line and act like a man." Said another: "I think it is despicable to manipulate a boy into playing a female role. In any healthy man-boy relationship the two males are equal and the man's aim should be to help the boy become more masculine and heterosexual." Said another: "My friend is queer over pretty blond boys with long slim legs, but I don't care for pretty boys. If they are really masculine they can be cute, but I prefer dark-complexioned Latin or Indian toughs." Said another: "I'm not interested in nice, well-behaved boys, but a whiff of delinquency really turns me on, because that indicates a boy is fighting back with his balls." Said another: "In theory I love a kid who hasn't a father, because I see myself as paternal and brotherly, there's nothing queer in that."

Am I Anxious?

Through this process of contrasting himself with others many pederasts seem to talk themselves through their guilt feelings, but anxiety remains until the pederast withdraws from the underground and gives up his illegal activity, or until he establishes an identity which is able to transform the anxiety into heroism or in some other way begins to discharge it. The anxiety of the young pederast portrayed in a recent novel[4] led him once to run away and another time to crash his car deliberately so he would not be able to go to bed with a boy as he wished. This "heroism" may take the form of solving his problem by provoking arrest; one psychiatrist concluded, for example, that a client had performed an act where he was sure to be caught because his anxiety over furtive activity had become unbearably acute. It appeared in our interviews that anxiety was greatest among those pederasts who actually had done very little that was illegal, or who had put their illegal activity behind them and now had much more to lose by exposure. Among others, anxiety frequently seemed to provide motivation for an identity quest, rather than serving as an inhibitor of illegal behavior. Through the process of comparing himself with other pederasts, and rationalizing or in some other way centering upon what he considers to be his own positive self-image, many a pederast seems to come to a sense of identity as (1) adventurer, (2) rebel, or (3) advocate of sexual freedom, or some combination of these.

(1) The Adventurer

"My, how he has changed," one pederast said of another, whom he had previously known as very guilt-ridden and anxious. "He even looks different. As a pederast he now has a positive *style.*" The pederast of whom this was said, replied: "I suspect my sense of pederast identity has developed as a continuing process, shaped in the heat of my imagination, in response to other persons and their attitudes, to sexual incidents, and to the emotions which I have felt in such experience. More recently, however, my identity seems to have jelled in the conscious emergence of three convictions, *i.e.*, that *a*) I am somehow different sexually from others; *b*) having affirmed my pleasure in sexual experience with boys, I do not intend to give up my nature, and *c*) I can affirm myself as loving, not evil or sinful. As a physician who has sought various types of counseling and treatment, I am now convinced that I could escape my pederasty only by suicide or through surrendering myself to some sort of brain operation or aversion therapy which might not work, anyway. So I have decided, instead, to adopt a life-style as explorer and adventurer, which is in keeping with my professional interests in any case. All at once I seem to have recovered—not so much wholeness of personality, as the ability to do what most people have to do in one way or another—that is, live in two worlds at once. My life is not devoted to exploring the world and anything within it that interests me, and my sexual adventurism with boys—especially overseas—fits into my self-understanding of myself as mountain climber, deep-sea diver, and one who is prepared to take on many other dangers."

Another pederast said: "I was not strong as a child, and perhaps my fantasy life was more important to me, as a way to keep up with the larger boys. I loved stories about heroic men, and I had a crush on first one and then another. I dreamed that some hero would come to invite me on a Batman-Robin type of adventure. I determined to be healthy and strong so I could become a pilot, and when the war came I much enjoyed the adulation I received from boys, because I could see myself in them at their age. It is perhaps foolish of me to keep that self-image in my present flabby condition, but when I was shot down—as I was falling—I said to myself: To hell with those who disapprove of what I do. All the time I was in prison camp I thought about little else than my determination to be true to my nature, and to enjoy myself when I got home. I did not die there, I came home, and so I now feel free to be heroic in my own way, and it takes a lot of guts to pursue my hobby!"

(2) The Rebel

"Who am I?" another pederast said. "It dawned on me one day that the labels society wanted to pin on me—sick, sinner, or whatever—were really clubs used to try to knock me down, because essentially I'm a rebel. It happened at the time of the Kent State shooting when I listened to kids I liked talk about radical politics and sexual rebellion. I'm not so sure I'm different from other males, except that I am more of a rebel against the sexual establishment."

An artist spoke of his efforts to express a similar rebellion in his painting: "It always seemed dangerously wicked to enjoy myself, and my pleasures are still more those of the mind and spirit. Partly because the sex I crave is against the law, I allow myself to enjoy it only in imagination and art. Every picture of a boy I paint is not only an emotional, sexual experience but it is also one of rebellion. Sometimes my imagination is so possessed and transformed by sexual desires that I paint a boy who is not recognizable as such, but I refuse to see myself as possessed of a devil. Why should the devil have a monopoly on beauty and joy? I was raised to the view that the devil was always close when one found joy in sex, then something slipped up on me from behind, and I discovered that I am simply a person who is sexually out of step with the majority. Call me a *pederast*, since that word seems to describe my inclinations, but don't look for deep, dark psychological processes behind my discovery that sex can be fun with a friend of a very fun-loving age; call me a *narcissist* if you wish—but my ultimate identity, as I become only half aware of it as yet, consists of more than a total of my own fantasies, ideas, and experiences. When I paint I sometimes seem to be swept along by a current of human history which I call rebellious. Deep in myself the whole of human experience, the experience of all mankind, moves restlessly. Our sexual culture and establishment is but a fragile boat floating on a stormy sea, and our human exploration of those depths hasn't yet proceeded far enough for us to understand how fragile our situation in that boat really is. It was perhaps foolish of me to rebel, and jump off that perilous, leaky boat, but that is who I am, one who *swims!*"

Advocate of Sexual Freedom

One pederast said: "I have recently affirmed my pederasty, not quite publicly but by joining a group of militant pederasts who plan to join with the other sex-freedom people in a campaign to redirect public opinion. My life seemed to fall apart when I was younger, and now I am able to put it together again by seeing myself as avant-garde, rather than gay. The wave of the future is sex freedom. The human quest for political and social freedom will never be complete until sexual freedom is also guaranteed by law. I'm a very loving person who hugs and kisses everyone, and when boys ask why I'm not married, I say because I like both boys and girls and the law won't let me marry one of each. That really shakes them up because in their liberal sex education courses they are taught about homosexuality always being either/or, never both/and. When I see a boy who is stunned by this, I may say: 'I'm going to bed tonight with a girl who'd just love to have you join us. You want to make it a threesome?' That's an invitation that is rarely refused. Almost any boy of fourteen to sixteen is likely to go wild at that suggestion, no matter what his moral or sex education has been. People who say that one could never persuade a really masculine boy to do this or that have obviously never tried giving him a cute girl to enjoy while doing it."

Another said: "I define a pederast as a free spirit, more so than a gay who is locked into a limited life-style. When I was in the reformatory, a place designed to keep me miserable and unhappy, the best way to frustrate the system was to have an orgasm—there weren't any drugs or alcohol, but we could have orgasm after orgasm with each other. Some inmates used gay or sissy kids as women, but that seemed wrong to me. When I was in bed with a friend, we were two men having fun together, which is how I define my pederasty. We would whisper: 'Man, this is really living!' Now, outside of jail, I find society to be almost as dull and sexually repressive as the reformatory was. I guess that through the same orgasm route I learned in the reformatory I'm still trying to escape from an oppressive system that locks a lot of poor kids out of a good life. I like to take to bed a youngster whose life is really miserable and hear him say: 'Man, this is really living!' "

Another member of a sexual freedom group said: "Making films as I do, I'm always meeting attractive kids of all ages and sexes, and I suppose it is inevitable that at least once in a while one will take advantage of the many opportunities that present themselves; although nothing turns me off more than a gay boy who thinks he can seduce me into hiring him, unless it is a mother with the same idea. I only go to bed with a young boy once a year or so, but when I do I have such a lovely time that I admit to being a pederast in principle. One of my friends, who chases boys all over the state, says that girls are his meat and boys are his dessert. I'd say it differently: Girls are like the sunshine that warms my days, whereas a boy to me is like an occasional bolt of lightning—illuminating my sky for a delightful moment and then gone forever. I do get struck once in a while, enough to understand the pederast who becomes enamored of boys more often, or so unforgettably that he never quite recovers enough to come in out of the rain." Said another, a member of the medical profession: "I have a healthy body which I enjoy in many ways, and in sexually free ways I recommend to others. In my view pederasty is not a sickness, but our society forces most acknowledged pederasts to become sick, by not allowing them to be free and natural. I had a love affair with Freud for a time, but my enlightened parents raised me well, so I find it difficult to be Freudian, although I consider it unhealthy not to enjoy women, or to have sadist or masochist fantasies, or to be unable to enjoy boys, or to be frozen into any sort of rigid sexual position which says that other persons' sexual tastes are wrong. Our personalities should flower, changing at different times of life, by grow-ing naturally. I also consider it unhealthy to exploit anyone, certainly to indulge in pederast experiences just for kicks, as a sort of treat for the rich or privileged who can try something new and then toss a human being aside—like a wealthy friend of mine who enjoys shock-ing people with a new sensation each week, such as making love to a black boy with one leg. I'm sure I'm not a typical pederast. Who is a typical heterosexual? the rapist or celibate priest? There are all kinds of pederasts—criminal, compulsive, neurotic, intellectual, romantic, artistic, puritan, confused, repressed, and, like me, permissive." In a conversation with a friend he agreed: "Somewhere along the way I got freed up a bit, so that in private I can be natural and playful with boys—perhaps I have now affirmed the boyish in me which enjoyed that sort of play when I was their age. When I say I am a pederast now, I mean to live as free as I was when I was thirteen, and as innocent, open, curious and playful. I no longer consider myself an outcast, as I once did, but as a free person who chooses to be and act in free ways. A healthy identity requires me to decide for myself what is good and bad, right and wrong for me, on the basis of my own convictions and values. Once my radar was always out to make sure I did what society approved, and I was caught in a real dilemma between resistance to what was oppressive, or dying inside a little bit each day. Like the black person who refuses any longer to act white in order to adjust to a white majority in society, I have decided to give up the pretense of being something I am not. I have decided to be free."

SOME CONCLUDING OBSERVATIONS

• At the beginning we warned that evidence can be misleading when it is twisted to fit categories, and this chapter in its effort to describe some styles of pederastic identity tends to gloss over the extent of guilt feelings, anxiety and confusion, by concentrating on a minority who have clarified their sense of identity.

• In addition to the life-style identities listed in this chapter for pederasts—adventurer, advocate of sexual freedom, and rebel—there are several others, of course, such as "persecuted person."

• This chapter—and perhaps this entire book—tends uninten-tionally to lose sight of the extent to which a significant minority of pederasts identify with the militant gay movement. A gay identity seems least acceptable to some married pederasts, who are also frequently handicapped in accepting a "pederast identity" if it seems to be defined as an exclusive life-style. Many pederasts live in two worlds, with two identities and life-styles.

• This study tends to quote the more articulate and better educated pederasts, for they are the ones whose self-examination is more insightful. Unfortunately the typical pederast is portrayed here as less timid and more self-confident than is true of the majority. Shy and less adventurous pederasts have less to say, and their voices have therefore not been adequately heard in these pages—as the development of a true "profile" would require.

CHAPTER 15

Are There Solutions?

Western society considers pederasty to be sinful, sick, and a serious crime. Pederasty would therefore have been eliminated long ago if anyone really knew what to do about it. As with most social problems there is an unfortunate tendency to assume that the solution is to work harder at present ineffective methods, rather than to examine present and past efforts in the light of new evidence and new possibilities. This book began by specifying more precisely what pederasty is, and by presenting more accurate information about a situation in which perhaps only one out of a hundred, or even a thousand, offenders is apprehended, and in which tragedy is compounded by society's emphasis on revenge rather than prevention. To consider new approaches we will note, on one hand, the present methods for handling pederasty in law, education, family, and religion. On the other hand we will describe several more visionary and radical proposals—which may represent long-range goals or ideas that deserve some scientific experimentation. Our principal aim in this chapter, however, is to propose some simple and more thoughtfully considered middle-range possibilities which realistically involve some compromise between law and order on the right and laissez-faire permissiveness on the left.

THE PRESENT SCENE

Americans are victims of a number of myths about law and law enforcement. The first of these is the notion that crime is somehow prevented by passing a law. Suppose, for example, a law was passed requiring men to wear undershirts during sexual intercourse. The enforcement of such a law would require a million new policemen and

213

a billion dollars in new expenditures—and all this would of course be to no avail unless police were allowed into each bedroom to enforce the law. And in most sex matters, the few men arrested would largely be those whose sex partners had filed charges, accusing them of not wearing undershirts. The passage of such a law, especially without specifying practicable methods for enforcement, would merely give the police and courts directions for handling such cases as came to their attention, with little real possibility of prevention at all. This brings us to a second myth, the popular notion that unpremeditated murders and sex offenses can be prevented by the strict punishment of offenders. Copious research has shown that in crimes of passion the offender is rarely deterred by thoughts of the electric chair, even if he is certain he will be apprehended. Historically, experiment after experiment has been attempted to prevent pederasty by the most horrendous punishments, but with little success. Where sex partners are equally desirous and consenting, and with compelling physical desires, the conviction quickly grows that the law is wrong and must be defied.

If society intends to rely exclusively on law and police to prevent sex offenses, then a police state will be required, wherein everyone can be watched twenty-four hours a day, with all bedrooms supervised. Even then the most spirited young people would take pride in finding ways to escape such surveillance and, as we have seen, most pederasts begin as rebellious teen-agers. If all persons guilty of pederast offenses were arrested, our prisons would be full of teen-age sex offenders. Ironically, the best means one could devise to manufacture pederasts would be to send more teen-agers to correctional institutions, as these seem in many cases to be more effective in turning youngsters into pederasts than in anything else they accomplish.[1] The same holds true for adults. Men come out of prisons more likely to practice pederasty than when they entered, so there should be a serious review of sending pederasts to prison at all, as long as prisons seem designed to reenforce pederast desires and habits. One may debate the effectiveness of prison in preventing crime, but our evidence makes it clear that it is largely a myth that long prison terms will prevent man-boy sex play. Perhaps prison terms reduce armed robberies or kidnappings, but correctional institutions increase pederasty as is most notable, for example, in the close relationship between reformatories and boy prostitution. Tax-funded juvenile institutions recruit and train the prostitutes, train the pimps, and nurture a central core of customers who consider a severe prison term as a price well worth paying in return for their sexual pleasures. To many persons, sex—like food—is considered a right not to be inhibited by law.

If society does not intend to prevent sexual deviance by massive expenditures of public funds on spies, secret police and reductions of freedom and privacy, then what are the alternatives? It is almost impossible for most teen-agers—and adults, for that matter—to understand the complex and inconsistent sex laws now on the books. They are aware that in our present laissez-faire situation, almost anyone with enough money for good lawyers can use the jumble of laws to his own advantage. When we examine the lives of those teen-agers now becoming tomorrow's pederasts it is clear that they do not know at what point they began to break the law. Real prevention will require spending funds on more adequate sex education, as well as on solving the family problems and poverty of life which nurture sexual and emotional sicknesses.

If we knew more precisely what causes pederasty, then intelligent programs of prevention might be devised. It is therefore a further illustration of our laissez-faire approach—an unofficial policy of tolerating and ignoring pederasty—that we spend so little on research to determine cause. A strict law, which was really intended to control or prevent pederasty, would begin with large expenditures on research. But, for purposes of discussion, let us assume that the Gebhart study[2] of pederasts in prison is accurate in its assessment of causes in many cases. This research indicates that pederasty is caused by "something disastrous" which happened between the sex offender's twelfth and fifteenth birthdays. Before that time the subjects studied tended to have "good socialization with females," which then suddenly and unexpectedly "deteriorated abruptly and their heterosexuality was nipped in the bud"[3] They turned to enjoy sex with younger boys instead of with girls. Why? The answer is that society inadvertently makes pederasts "by abruptly and powerfully repressing heterosexual behavior" *especially in girls*, who are no longer freely allowed to play with boys. Cross-cultural studies suggest a close correlation between the development of pederasty and the chaperoning of young adolescent girls. Society expects boys to be able to "wait out this period when he is robbed of girls" and a majority succeed in doing so, if they do not have "a great backlog of homosexual conditioning." However, the boy who has had a good deal of pleasurable homosexual experience does not and cannot wait, and in this crucial post-pubescent period of his sexual development he develops certain habits and tastes for homosexual pleasures which may come to dominate his life, or which in some cases may be simply repressed to crop up later in life at crucial or vulnerable moments. Our evidence supplements the Gebhart conclusions with the reminder that this young adolescent homosexual experience may largely be fantasy or imaginary, and yet may strongly cultivate or reinforce pederastic interests and later involvements.

VISIONARY PROPOSALS FOR THE FUTURE

The temptation is very real to conclude that society must choose between a) a continuing increase in deviant sex behavior such as pederasty or b) allowing young adolescents to have heterosexual intercourse. It may, however, be too late. Youngsters as well as adults are today strongly influenced by the permissive sexual culture (which now envelops and stimulates them) in which sexual pleasure is glamorized and which leads even 11-year-olds to conclude that the purpose of sex is to have fun and that almost any sort of sex play is fine so long as it is fun. The existence of effective birth control and disease-prevention methods, combined with an emerging minority sexual culture, has great impact upon the young—all this combines to create a new and entirely different sexual climate much more sophisticated than any that has existed previously. At the same time, modern diet and vitamins have made youngsters sexually mature and ready at a much younger age. Many boys of eleven are now sexually where their grandfathers were at the age of fourteen or fifteen. As suggested by the Gebhard study,[4] and illustrated by the boys we found involved with pederasts, a sizable percentage of adolescent boys will not long delay seeking the sex pleasures which the media praise, with a resulting great increase in heterosexual and homosexual promiscuity among junior-high-school-age youngsters even in many rural areas.

"Anyone is a fool," one pederast said after surveying such teenage behavior, "if he thinks adults can have a sexually permissive culture without youngsters also going along for the ride. The sexual pluralism of our world, which teaches the young that varied experiences are valuable and that no one moral view or style of sex behavior is right for everyone, is beginning to have an impact much as alcohol and drugs have also been passed down to high school, to junior high school, and into the upper levels of some primary schools. It is too late to stop the tide of sex freedom, but perhaps society still can direct it into more wholesome channels."

A neuropsychologist, reporting his research on the origins and causes of violence—which he says is "fast becoming a global epidemic"—finds little violence in cultures that allow sexual pleasures. In other words: "As either violence or pleasure goes up, the other goes down." He notes the irony in America of a culture that prefers sexual violence over sexual pleasure, often censoring, for example, those films that show people enjoying sex, while permitting those which show rape—almost as if "sex with pleasure is immoral and unacceptable, but sex with violence and pain is moral and acceptable." As a result, for example, many families are more tolerant of destructive drugs and alcohol than of sex pleasure. He concludes that America will continue to have a violent, sick society until "we recognize that sexuality is not only natural for teen-agers, but desirable." He suggests that families should allow youngsters to use the family home for sexual pleasure. [5]

Some would go even farther, advocating the repeal of all anti-sex laws. Laws against sexually deviant acts would be replaced with legislation of two types: on one hand, programs and experiments would be funded to develop a general climate of sexual health, including much more open debate on society's aims and policies on sex education. On the other hand, the emphasis in the law would be upon preventing force and violence. The crime of rape, for example, would be considered a crime of violence. A girl would no longer be humiliated with medical examinations and interrogation about her previous sex life—the issue would simply be whether or not she was forced to do something against her will. If she was forced into a car or was taken into a dark alley, she was kidnapped, which actually is more seriously punished under the law. Advocates of this kind of law reform say that if the sex taboos were removed from consideration as far as possible, youngsters would then not need to be emotionally damaged in interrogations and by the interpretations given by police and court.

Such a view suggests, on the basis of experience in other cultures, that if society's goal is to prevent pederast acts, the money now spent on court trials and prisons could better be spent supervising and chaperoning the young. Second, there does seem to be less pederasty in those societies which tolerate or ignore man-boy sex play. When not against the law, such play is often a passing phase, ending when a young man gets married or has access to women. In Western society, along with the other undergrounds, homosexual play presents a tempting and exciting realm for the young to explore, with all the excitement of forbidden fruit. Advocates of lowering the "age of consent" for legal homosexual activity assert that society creates the problem by making it a problem. "One does not create an appetite for healthy food by passing laws against candy," one observer said. "And certainly not in the context of forbidding youngsters to eat at all."

SOME PRACTICAL STEPS WHICH CAN BE TAKEN

Between visionary proposals which are far from obtaining general accpetance, and the present ineffective ways of handling pederasty, there are some middle-of-the-road, common-sense proposals which the majority of citizens might support. We begin with the assumption, right or wrong, that the majority of Americans do not in the near or foreseeable future intend to liberalize the sex laws, at least beyond tolerance for deviant sexual activity among consenting adults. The majority of American adults still support the legal prohibition of homosexual activity with boys under the age of sixteen, which suggests that society will continue to face recurring pederast arrests. Presented here are a series of proposals that would do much to alleviate the present chaotic and indefensible situation.

1. *Therapy.* A first proposal would be for more medical resources to be channeled into therapy, both for research and for treatment—especially of first offenders. These resources should be made more available for young adolescents. Medical insurance must be expanded to provide payment for treatment of persons who voluntarily seek therapy or who are assigned by courts. American society's lack of serious interest in preventing sex offenses is perhaps best illustrated by the shortage of centers and personnel for such therapy, such centers being almost nonexistent in some parts of the country. Since there is an onus and some shame involved in admitting pederastic tendencies, and because the roots of pederasty lie in the very early years, an adequate therapy program must make more medical resources available to young families and to schoolchildren. Also, the program should include a more adequate policy and definition of sexual health. There is no point in talking about preventing sex offenses until more therapy is provided and the necessary research is funded to make this therapy more effective in changing offenders. Certainly some of the radical substitute proposals which would replace prison with torture (aversion therapy) or medication and operations to remove sections of the brain or body, physically or functionally, are not yet validated as providing any humane solution or guaran-

tee against future offenses. On the other hand, the effectiveness of the new-style therapy centers is being demonstrated in the handling of drug addicts, other ex-prisoners and several different group therapy projects.

2. *Equipping Teen-agers to Cope.* Existing programs for lecturing and warning youngsters against sex offenders frequently fail, for they serve to inform many boys that there are men who will give them money, sexual pleasure, and other adventures. On the other hand it is almost impossible for pederasts to get far in a situation where adolescents close ranks against them. The most effective anti-pederast program exists where youngsters protect themselves from abuse and exploitation, as in some rough slum areas where boys immediately recognize pederasts and run them out. For example, the fatherless, impoverished street boy who is theoretically most vulnerable to pederasts, is in fact far more often better prepared by a rather brutal type of sex education in the streets than he would be by warnings and moral lectures. A stranger who merely smiles at a boy in such a neighborhood may come under verbal attack loud enough to be heard and serve notice for three blocks in every direction. Such street boys usually have much less tolerance for homosexuality than do middle- or upper-class boys, and if they get involved in sex play with a man or older teen-ager it is strictly on their own terms. Such boys may organize themselves to profit from pederasty by prostitution, blackmail, or mugging. Younger boys who are well protected against outsiders may be sexually exploited by members of their own gang. Their built-in defenses, however, provide clues for how all adolescents could be organized to protect themselves more effectively than is now possible by police or social agencies. Parents can shelter children up to a point, but finally neither society nor parents can protect them unless they are willing to be protected—which is what a lot of adolescent rebellion is all about. No youngster is as safe from sexual molesting as when he is with a group of self-disciplined, well-informed peers, who as a group are in control of their own situation. Youngsters can and will protect each other from strangers and outsiders, although they may not support behavior standards higher than those of the adults they respect. Nothing is so likely to push them into rebellious sex play as punishing them for sexual behavior common to their friends and parents.

As long as sexual morality is handed to them as law, however, without any chance for youngsters to think it through and make their own responsible decisions, they are not likely to do much to protect themselves or to accept the protection of the law. Note how two different upper-middle-class boys reacted to a prep-school coach who made sexual overtures. One said: "Get you hands off me and keep them off. If you touch me again without my permission I'm first going to kick you in the shins and then yell for the headmaster." The other one whispered to the coach: "Are you going to let me begin the game Friday night?" The first boy was raised with self-respect, not moral lecturing. When he was small his father never let anyone touch him without his permission, for he was taught that not even a parent, teacher, or doctor should violate his dignity without his permission.

3. *Changing the Supporting Structures.* Pederasty in the forms society most wants to eliminate rests upon the twin foundations of adolescent secrecy and rebellion. Perhaps there must be a major upheaval and radical change in society to end the alienation of the young who become involved with pederasts. But there are helpful and constructive steps which can be taken to reduce the support which adolescent society provides.

First, youngsters not only need sex education, values, self-respect, and the right to sexual privacy but they also most of all need money and jobs in an urban society. Burglary cannot be ended by courtroom lectures, imprisonment, or even therapy so long as the jobless youngster returns to a street where the fence who buys stolen goods provides him with his most constructive activities. So, also, man-boy sex play is—to many boys—related to the need for money and the desire for adventure. At present too many young boys from deprived sections of the community receive adult friendship, affection, and life-enriching experiences only from pederasts. A questionnaire to young adolescents asked, among other things, how they spent their time. Did they hike? hunt? fish? play music? look at TV?[6] A majority of them in a deprived community reported that they spent their free time just "hanging around." They were emotionally and culturally starved, their streets and neighborhood were drab and dull, their schools were failing them. The only fun and adventure open to them seemed to be through furtive delinquencies, drugs, and sex.

Second, a constructive change is under way in the enlargement of coeducational activities—with girls at the YMCA, in the Little League, in Scouting and other programs. Even those Little League managers who complain that a boy might accidentally touch a girl's breast if boys and girls were allowed in the sport together are aware of the value of providing healthy group activities for all youngsters and not merely for those who are financially privileged and athletically talented.

Expanding coeducational activities and making more jobs for deprived and rebellious youngsters are but first steps, however, toward helping the young people develop creative new structures for their own adolescent society. Adults who wish to oppose pederasty must volunteer their own time and money to assist the social agencies, and not merely rely upon passing laws to punish the victims of their previous neglect.

4. *Openly Facing Up to Pederasty.* How shall the schools, boy's clubs, and other youth-serving agencies handle the problem of pederasty among the men who are employed or who serve as volunteers on their staffs? At an organizational meeting for a new Big Brothers program, one man asked if thought had been given to psychological tests for volunteers in order to weed out sexual deviants. Considering the professional education and competence of many of the persons present, he was surprised to see how many were embarrassed by the question, getting off the subject as quickly as possible by announcing their intention to follow the guidelines laid down by the national Big Brothers organization. Also, a staff member of a boy-serving agency reported: "The volunteers in our agency who turn out to be pederasts are ordinarily not the shy, timid, sissy or feminine-looking types. Rather, they are more often the tough, cigar-smoking guys who love football, boxing, hunting, sex jokes, bragging, and put-downs. They are frequently the ones who make the most fun of 'fags' and 'queers,' or whatever label they may be using for the less athletic males. Often they are the most emotionally anti-homosexual, suggesting perhaps the thought that people are more likely to get uptight about their own temptations than about things that trouble other people. There's a vast emotional gulf between the gay who puzzles over his masculine identity and that sports enthusiast whose sex involvements are largely with women, and indeed whose sexual relationship with boys may most of the time go to abnormal lengths in his refusing to touch a boy, and in repressing and sublimating his pederast desires. We've had some rather sophisticated and well-educated staff members of this type, who have had nervous breakdowns, especially when they have found themselves unable to cope with cruel, sophisticated kids, who saw through them before they were conscious of their own problem."

There are constructive policy statements hidden in the middle of many staff manuals, and in booklets for lay persons who wish to develop programs for boys, to remind them that "good, well-intentioned men sometimes succumb to sexual temptation with boys without intending it." Some agencies take the leper approach, immediately discharging any man whom they suspect may be sexually interested in boys. Others have had success with the opposite tack. One pastor said, for example: "We know our Scoutmaster is a pederast, and so do the boys and their parents. The fact that everyone knows, and we have faced the problem openly and frankly, has created a very healthy situation. The boys in the troop are fond of him, and he does an excellent job. I am sure there is much less sexual hanky-panky among the boys than in the best typical situation. I know of one occasion in which the whole troop descended upon one younger member in force, scolding him severely for a minor bit of sex misbehavior far from any Scout activity. They said: 'Don't you know that someone might say it was our Scoutmaster's fault that you did that?' All around, it is a much healthier situation than I had once before when a pederast warned me against our Scoutmaster who later did get into hot water because he just couldn't admit his pederasty to himself or to anyone else."

NEW-DAY POLICY STATEMENT

The following policy statement, which has been approved and adopted by the board of a youth-serving agency but which, for various reasons, is not yet ready for official public release, suggests a sensible basis for an enlightened method of handling any pederast problem that may arise in the future:

a) Every new staff member will, at the time of his employment and periodically thereafter, be informed that many men are not aware of their own capacity to be sexually aroused by young boys, and that while such arousal is not necessarily an indication of abnormal homosexuality, this agency will not tolerate sexual contact between staff members and boys. New staff will be informed that if they find themselves so tempted we have counseling resources available to them at no cost, and with confidence respected, to help them understand and handle any problem which might arise.

b) Senior and more experienced staff are directed to educate themselves to be able to recognize warning signs and types of behavior which indicate that an adult is sexually interested in a boy. Such person should be called in for a friendly and confidential warning, along with the offer of counsel and help. Men who are seriously and sincerely interested in the welfare of boys will appreciate the opportunity to be forewarned and to anticipate any potential problem in their relationships.

c) Where there is reliable evidence that a man has sought, or has been involved in, any type of sexual activity with a boy, he is to be warned by the senior staff that a repetition of such behavior could lead to his arrest, and that he must either resign or enter into a program of counseling and therapy under the supervision of the staff. It will not be our policy to discharge able and competent men at the time of a first offense if they are responsive to direction, because every man makes mistakes, and some of the best men available for our type of work are especially sensitive to, and tempted by, boys. It is the judgment of this board that in many cases *the man who has such temptations and is aware of them is a better risk than the man who has such temptations and is not yet conscious of them*—if he is willing to be open and honest with himself and us about the subject.

d) We take it for granted that all boys will be delinquent on occasion, as in matters of sex, and that it is better if a boy is caught with his hands in the cookie jar by someone with the skill and point of view to be able to use the opportunity for growth and maturing. Therefore all members of this staff must participate in a workshop on "homosexuality and counseling," which shall have these objectives: (1) to prepare them to interpret to boys the point of view that they should avoid homosexual play because it is disapproved of by our society and can therefore lead them to unhappiness; (2) that they should not be surprised or let it be interpreted to them as an indication that they are homosexual, if they find they are aroused by male contacts or find some pleasure in homosexual acts, and (3) that homosexual tendencies are normal and can be discussed with our counselors without embarrassment. The staff cannot communicate these policies and attitudes to boys unless each staff member is personally convinced that these facts are true, for what we say by tone of voice and facial expression often communicates more than our words.

e) It is our intention by word and action to teach boys that sex is a personal and private matter. While sex play is to be discouraged among boys, especially at times when we are responsible for them, our style of handling sex play should be one which seeks to divert boys to more constructive activities, rather than scolding or lecturing them. Staff attitudes should make it clear that:

—we know all about such things and consider such sex play inappropriate at our activities,

—we will tolerate no sexual molesting of one boy by another,

—we consider it unimportant that all boys are sexually curious and experimental,

—the staff counselors are always available to talk with boys on sex problems or questions,

—just as we disapprove of staff members having sexual contact with boys, so we also feel it normal and natural for our staff to have some warm and reassuring physical contact with boys they work with.

We consider it equally inappropriate for adults in our program to be so uptight about homosexuality as to be unable to handle normal roughhouse or other natural physical contact with boys. A friendly pat, an arm around the shoulder, some playful wrestling is not taboo for homosexual reasons. If a man finds that he or a boy is aroused by such a contact, the energy should be channeled into empathy, appreciation, and affection of a type that will seek to guide the boy into healthy and wholesome sex attitudes. Such sexual arousal should be no occasion for shame, embarrassment or teasing, but, if necessary and noticed, can be dismissed with a remark like: "That's the way males are sometimes." In this way, the man who may be aroused or sexually attracted to a boy can perhaps be of more help to the boy who is aroused and sexually attracted to the man or the other boys, than the man who has not had the experience and has not learned to handle it in this way.

f) When a staff member or volunteer faces a special problem—such as a boy with a crush on him, or even explicit sexual overtures from a boy—he should bring the problem to a staff meeting for discussion, so that we can all offer counsel on what should be done both to avoid hurting and to make the experience a growing, maturing one for the boy. Since several members of the board and staff acknowledge that they are sexually attracted to boys sometimes, the subject can be discussed openly and naturally in staff meetings.

g) It is the policy of this agency to turn sex offenders over to medical authorities, rather than to the police, until such time as it appears that some adult who has violated the laws of the state and policies of this agency is not willing to undergo therapy. It is our conviction that teen-agers and adults can be helped with insights and strengthening therapy to adjust to the expectations of the community and to hold sexual impulses in necessary control. Therapy for adolescents is crucial if they are observed developing sexual interests in younger boys.

LAW AND COURT PROCEDURES

Even in advance of law reform there can be clarity and realism about what the law accomplishes. Laws do not prevent sex offenses, but provide structures for apprehending and dealing with offenders when a complaint is filed. Since many pederast first offenses are nearly unintentional or are unthinking careless continuations of adolescent habits, some courts provide suspended sentences with the requirement of therapy. Presumably more courts would prefer to handle first offenses in this way if such therapy were available. These efforts are frustrated, however, by the inadequacy of therapy resources in most places and by the tendency of the newspapers to punish in advance of trial. It would be a constructive step if publicity could be restrained in all first offenses, as with juvenile cases, so that everyone could have a second chance. At any rate, court sentencing, our evidence suggests, should take account of a much wider variety of motivations and behaviors than present procedure makes possible. Such a relaxed procedure—with the kindred recognition that pederastic offenses are in a different category from theft or rape— could make it unnecessary for youngsters to be threatened and hurt by police interrogations and court procedures. The court should, in many situations, recommend therapy for consenting youngsters also.

SOME CONCLUDING OBSERVATIONS

• There is no reason to expect any significant decline in the amount of pederasty in the foreseeable future. At present neither law, religion, nor community morals and pressures are effective in redirecting pederastic impulses and activities.

• New approaches are needed to enlist the cooperation of the adolescents themselves, but this will be a difficult job, especially among those adolescents who are rebellious on sexual matters. The world scene includes varied sexual customs and Western society itself is increasingly pluralist and permissive. Although there is considerable difference from one state or city or neighborhood to another, the taboo against homosexual play is declining, and there is a noticeable increase of acceptance of the "sex for pleasure" principle. This represents a major moral shift, the full impact of which has not yet been felt.

• Perhaps more blame is being placed on religious institutions than is really deserved for their lack of creativity in sexual morality, for their failure to stress the quality of loving relationships instead of moralism, and for their perpetuation of sexual myths rather than helping to bring about the higher standards that are demanded. It would seem that religious leaders must take initiative, however, in admitting that some of the present failure to deal with sexual deviance and sex offenders is rooted in what Richard Niebuhr called the "mistaken myth" of the human will when, in fact, human beings like those we have seen in the pederast underground are largely unable to rescue themselves. Punishing individuals makes little sense, unless they can be placed in a new supporting environment instead of being shoved back either onto a street which is organized to support delinquency or into an underground. Religious leaders can throw light into that underground so all can see that most pederasts are not vicious criminals, but that, indeed, many are teen-agers who desperately need help.

• As with alcoholics, drug addicts and others, no middle-of-the-ground solution to the problem is possible that does not begin with enlisting the cooperation of the pederasts themselves.

• We have examined only certain visible aspects of the pederast problem, much as one tentatively studies an iceberg by first noting what is visible. It seems quite clear, however, that all the authorities—in law, religion, and other concerned areas—should stop pretending to know the truth on sexual matters, and should begin to approach the subject of pederasty in the spirit of Isaac Newton, who said there is a great ocean of truth to be discovered, and all we know now may be compared to a pebble on the beach.

Notes

INTRODUCTION

1. Taylor (1975) validates autobiographical novels as reliable sociological data on pederasty.
2. Bernard (1974).
3. Linda Wolfe, *New York Times Book Review* (Jan. 19, 1975), uses this language to describe how books on sexual problems deal with faceless strangers.
4. Gebhard (1967), p. 229.
5. Vanggaard (1972), see chapter 18.
6. See Goodman (1966), Sorensen (1973), Duvert (1974).
7. See *Arcadie* (January, 1974), p. 37, and for a British organization's view, *Manchester Guardian* (May 18, 1974).

CHAPTER 1

1. For example, the Sydney (Australia) *Sunday Telegram* of Jan. 19, 1975.
2. Vanggaard (1972).
3. Freund (1967), p. 6.
4. See Forgey (1975), p. 22 ff.
5. McIntosh, in Bell (1972).
6. Eglinton (1971) is a 504-page defense of *paiderastia*.
7. Jones (1974), p. 95.
8. Other films with related themes include *The Victors, Germany Year Zero*.
9. Stewart (1972), Montherlant (1969).
10. Vanggaard (1972), pp. 59 ff.
11. Metzel (1973), pp. 8–20.
12. *Ibid.*
13. Sartre (1948) attributes adult fascism to a man's guilt over sex play with an older man when he was thirteen.
14. Moravia (1957).

15. Tournier (1972).
16. Bleuel (1973), Siemsen (1940).
17. Perrin (1955). On General Gordon, see Maugham (1972).
18. Fisher (1972).
19. Sorensen (1973), chapter 10.
20. Schofield (1965), pp. 21, 46.
21. For example, Dukhasz (1966).
22. Renault (1972).
23. Kazantzakis (1953).
24. Romains (1946), vol. 27.
25. Edwardes (1959), Mariani (1964), pp. 87 ff.
26. See "Boys for Sale," *Village Voice* (New York), Feb. 8, 1973.
27. Istrati (1926).
28. MacDougal (1968).
29. See Drew and Drake (1969), along with note 28 above, and Joyce Greller, "Baby Pros: The Child Hustler" in *Penthouse*, Feb. 1975.
30. Most pederasts consider themselves gentle with boys and disclaim sadomasochist books, but there is a large audience of readers whose fantasies revolve around such play, as is evidenced by such books as Robinson (1970), Duvert (1967, 1971, 1974), and hundreds of underground novels about rough play in reform school, and so on.

CHAPTER 2

1. Brake (1974).
2. Camus (1956), p. 65.
3. Pederastic incidents are found in all kinds of novels today. For example, mystery story: *Amis* (1973); spy story: *Freemantle* (1975); an autobiographical novel: *Del Castillo* (1959); a regional novel: *Rubin* (1971); historical novel: *Prokosch* (1968); a travel novel: *Favel* (1968).
4. For "gossip" see Davidson (1962), Peyrefitte (1961), Worsley (1967), etc.
5. In films: *The Conformist, Gates of Paradise* (Polish film about pederasty in children's crusade), the Polidoro *Satyricon* (the Fellini *Satyricon* tended to turn the pederast novel into a gay-homosexual film), *Los Olvidados, Lazarillo, Murmur of the Heart, If, Night Games, The Victors, Germany Year Zero*, and a passing incident in Z . . ., wherein a pederast stares at a boy standing on a balcony in his underwear. A friend asks: "Don't you ever think of anything else?" The pederast replies: "What else is there?"
6. Brongersma (1970), Karlen (1971), Ollendorff (1961), etc.
7. See *Arcadie* (September 1974) and *Medisch Contact* (February 21, 1975), pp. 205 ff.
8. The split was the result of the feeling of Guyon Society members that the Sex Freedom League neglected instructing and protecting youngsters from venereal disease.
9. 206 Railton Road, London SE 24.

10. Gerassi (1966.
11. For example, see *Time* Magazine (June 5, 1972).

CHAPTER 3

1. Gebhard (1972), p. 301.
2. Hatterer (1970).
3. Valente (1975).

CHAPTER 4

1. Gide (1950).
2. Blüher (1962).
3. Burton, "Terminal Essay, The Book of the Thousand Nights and a Night," in Cory (1969), p. 208.
4. Voltaire, "The Love Called 'Socrates,' " in Cory (1969), p. 351.
5. Mariotti (1952). This book contains only fragments of his research.
6. See also Vanggaard (1972), p. 71.
7. Ollendorff (1966), p. 45.
8. Friedenberg (1959), p. 121.
9. Ollendorff (1966), pp. 12–13, 44–46.
10. Eglinton (1971).
11. Olson (1974) gives a somewhat different interpretation of the Houston murders, but does confirm the difficulties of the police (p. 240), the lax and naive attitude of parents, the "hustling" of the boys ("They were male whores," said one policeman), and how youngsters involved were in a semi-underground to conceal sex and drug activities (p. 64, etc.)
12. Sartre (1951).

CHAPTER 5

1. Abood (1973), pp. 1–2; Libby (1974), p. 36.
2. For example, see DeMause (1974), pp. 503–576.
3. Kirkendall (1967), p. 125.
4. *Ibid.*
5. *Ibid.*
6. Sorensen (1973), and Rossman (1974), p. 171.
7. Saxon (1975).
8. Goodman (1960).
9. *Ibid*, p. 38.
10. The phrase is from Hanson (1957), discussing the pederasty of the French poet Verlaine, who in mid-adolescence was "broken to the sexual underlife" of his prep school.

CHAPTER 7

1. Taylor (1954).
2. Karlen (1971).
3. Cline (1936).

4. DeMause (1974).
5. See Renault (1972); Cory (1956), p. 31: "The Persians believed that *paiderastia* originated in the highlands of Armenia."
6. See Cory (1956), and on early Hindu society, Walker (1968), Vol. II, p. 199.
7. See Renault (1972).
8. Cory (1956).
9. Kenney (1968), p. 13.
10. A collection of classic erotic poetry about young boys. A new edition: *La Muse Garçonnière*, Paris: Flammarion, 1974.
11. See Schirman (1955).
12. For example: Romans 1:26, I Cor. 6:9.
13. On this subject see Achtemeier (1957), p. 103.
14. On this subject see Martignac (1975), p. 127, essay on the centurion, and Gillabert (1975), a book by a neo-Gnostic publisher.
15. Karsch-Haack (1906), cites hundreds of references from travelers.
16. See note 25, p. 84, in Daniel (1975).
17. Bousquet (1953), p. 36.
18. See note 35, p. 88, in Daniel (1975).
19. Daniel (1975), p. 93.
20. See historical records of Mehmed's secretary, Kritovoulous (1974; Miller (1921), p. 348; and Tralow (1947).
21. Gibb (1900).
22. Durant (1969).
23. McCarthy (1959).
24. See Lofts (1951); Oldenberg (1966), pp. 691–92; O'Meara (1967), etc.
25. Flaubert (1972).
26. Blüher (1962), Willets (1943), Laquer (1969).

CHAPTER 9

1. For example, McIntosh (1972).
2. Ford and Beach (1951), p. 130.
3. Davenport (1966), pp. 199 ff.
4. Suggs (1966). See also Levi-Strauss (1974).
5. Suggs (1966), p. 87.
6. Coffin (1966), p. 37.
7. Duvert (1974), pp. 99 ff.
8. See Corre (1894), Veze (1921), Thieuloy (1974), Wilson (1972), pp. 161 ff.
9. Grant (1974).
10. Malaparte (1952).
11. See Maugham (1971), Tavel (1968), Stewart (1973).
12. Maxwell (1966), pp. 175 and 287, etc.
13. The derivation is presumably from the North African Arab word for "anal intercourse" plus the French word for "whore."
14. Similar episode in Drew and Drake (1969), p. 77.

15. Coffin (1966), p. 37.
16. Barclay (1968), p. 177.
17. Michener (1963).
18. Meyendorff (1927), pp. 284–85; Dupree (1973), p. 198.
19. Mariani (1964), p. 87.
20. Peyrefitte (1959); Miller (1941), p. 185; Faralla (1963).
21. Drew and Drake (1969), p. 81; O'Callaghan (1962) and others; Oliver (1959), p. 119; Maxwell (1960).
22. Mariani (1964), p. 88.
23. See Daniel (1975), p. 9, on puritan measures in Tunisia.
24. For example, Duvert (1967), Duvert (1969), Duvert (1973).
25. See references cited in Drew and Drake (1969), pp. 33–47.
26. Nacke (1908).

CHAPTER 11

1. Zweig (1974.
2. Duvert (1974), p. 106.
3. Goodman (1962).
4. Sorensen (1973), Libby (1974).
5. Guersant (1953).
6. Duvert (1974), p. 100.
7. "Linda Lovelace" refers to a widely discussed film involving oral intercourse.
8. See Humphries (1970), Guersant (1953), etc.
9. This will not be published until after the death of the scientists and medical personnel involved.
10. Sorensen (1973), p. 303.
11. Sorensen (1973), Libby (1974).
12. Gebhard (1967).
13. Ibid., p. 316.
14. Ibid., p. 313.
15. Ibid., p. 231.
16. Ibid., p. 299.
17. Ibid., p. 321.
18. Merrill (1917).

CHAPTER 12

1. See, for example, Aaron (1972), pp. 40–41 as typical of autobiographical references to police payoffs by pederasts.
2. See Bernard (1974), p. 119.
3. This research by a clinical psychologist is not yet released for publication.
4. Worsley (1967).
5. See Ebermayer (1969), Jantzen (1969), Wyneken (1962).
6. For example, see Holt (1974), Pomeroy (1968), Fleischauer (1975).
7. For example, see Holland (1974), Davies (1974).

8. Brongersma (1974), p. 28.
9. See Peyrefitte (1954).
10. Swisher (1972).
11. Bernard (1975).
12. See Peyrefitte (1970), p. 20.

CHAPTER 13

1. Taylor (1974).
2. *Ibid.*, p. 61.
3. Duyckaerts (1970).
4. Stewart (1972), see pp. 177 ff., for example.
5. For example, Bender and Blau (1937), Bernard (1972).
6. This letter quoted was the source of the idea of a "ladder" to the underground as used in Chapter 3.
7. See *Better Life* (March, 1975), p. 9, for example.
8. For a similar statement, see Canfield (1974), p. 6, p. 13.
9. Lowen (1970).
10. See Walker (1968), Vol II, p. 199, etc.

CHAPTER 14

1. Bernard (1974), pp. 42 ff.
2. Brongersma (1970).
3. Bernard (1974), pp. 71 ff, and *T. soc. Geneesk*, no. 53 (1975).
4. Stewart (1972).

CHAPTER 15

1. See, for example, Palau de Lopez (1970), Martin (1953), Shaw (1969), Sykes (1958), Tannenbaum (1938), Jackson (1964), etc.
2. See Gebhard (1965), pp. 318 ff.
3. *Ibid.*, pp. 314–315.
4. *Ibid.*, pp. 301–304.
5. Prescott (1975), pp. 64 ff.
6. Rossman, Jean (1974), p. 623.

Definitions

There is much disagreement even among experts in the field as to the specific meanings of many of the scholarly terms used in this book. In order to avoid possible misunderstanding or misconception of their meanings, the author has thought it advisable to draw up this brief listing. Also included in the listing are a number of slang terms whose meaning might not be readily intelligible.

adventurer pederast: The "cruising prowler" who seeks out boy prostitutes or invites sexual experience with strange boys. Even when limited to voyeurism and flirting, it is essentially promiscuous in intent.

chicken hawk: See **adventurer pederast.**

chicken queen: A more gay type of pederast who plays feminine roles with young adolescent boys. See **gay-pederast.**

efebofilia, ephebofilia: European term for pederasty.

fetish- or fantasy-pederasts: Pederasts who substitute various psychic games for actual sex contact.

gay-homosexual: A homosexual person who is committed to an understanding of sexual relationships between consenting adults of the same sex as being normal, healthy and potentially as loving as heterosexual relationships, and who believes that his or her choice of such a gay life-style is determined by a homosexual nature which cannot or should not be changed.

gay-pederast: A **gay-homosexual** who seeks loving involvements with boys age 12 to 16, but generally only with boys who consider themselves gay. Of all types of pederastic relationships this type is likely to become passionate.

hebephile: Term used by Paul Gebhard in his book *Sex Offenders* to refer to men imprisoned for homosexual offenses against minors age 12 to 15.

homophobia: An emotional anti-homosexuality which characterizes some persons who may subconsciously be worried about homosexual tendencies in themselves. Presumably a well-adjusted person can be opposed to homosexuality without being terribly violent or emotional about it.

homosexual: (adjective) Sexual attraction or arousal by a person of one's own sex. (noun) A person who accepts an identity and sexual life-style which involves him or her in sexual relationships with his or her own sex because persons of the opposite sex are not sexually appealing.

homosexuality: Any sexual attraction, activity, or involvement with persons of the same sex.

Knabenliebe: German word for "boy-love," sometimes used in English to suggest something more romantic or gay.

paiderastia: Ancient Greek term is used for paternal or platonic man-boy relationships which admit erotic overtones and interest in boys aged 12 to 15, but seek to sublimate the eroticism into wholesome uses. Thorkel Vanggaard (1972) distinguishes between *paiderastia* (for the good of the boy) and *pederasty* (for the pleasure of the man).

pederast: Term used in this book to refer to any male above the age of eighteen who is sexually attracted to, or involved with, boys between the age of 12 (or puberty) and 16.

pederasty: The variables are so complex as to preclude any satisfactory definition of pederasty in terms of a particular sexual activity; or, on the other hand, to define it as mere temptation or sexual attraction between men and boys. We therefore use the term to encompass the whole range of sexual experience between males over age 18 and boys between puberty and age 16. A range which is playful rather than gay-homosexual, and therefore tends most often to be incidental rather than involving a life-style, which tends to be recreational sex rather than a quest for love, and which involves masculine horseplay sex rather than any feminization or feminine role-playing among males.

pedofilia: In America, and in this book, the term refers to an erotic attraction for, and sexual interest in, children below the age of puberty. In Europe the term **pedofile** is also used to include pederasty as discussed in this book.

"queer," "fag," etc.: Such terms have been used only in quotations and without precise definition in the text. For the most part, they refer to gay-homosexuals.

sensate-pederast: A man who has developed a taste for deviant sexual intercourse with boys who have had special training in erotic skills.

sex play: Any sexual activity for fun which is not essentially intended as lovemaking; determined more by attitude than behavior—that is, by the quality of playfulness. Ordinary sex play among males may consist of no more than teasing, joking, or masturbating; but it may move right on a continuum of experience into psychic games involving fantasy and the imagination, as well as into sports play (such as ejaculation contests) or wrestling and horseplay as substitute sexual activity. Or it may move into **perversion** (twisted, cruel sexual activity) or **vice** (the cultivation of degrading or excessive sensual pleasures); for example, to rape or be raped is no game, but to stimulate the imagination with talk or fantasy of raping another boy is a not uncommon type of psychic sex game.

sports-comrade pederast: A term used in this volume for the exaggeratedly-masculine man who seeks to repress and compensate for his pederastic desires through sports contact, or who seeks to express his pederastic eroticism only through mutual sexual horseplay with boys of his own type.

underground: A secret fellowship of rebels against society as it is organized.

underworld: Criminal organization or society.

Bibliography

*indicates a book which is a basic scholarly source
(f) indicates a work of fiction
(b) indicates a biography or autobiography

*AARON, WILLIAM. (b) *Straight: A Heterosexual Talks About His Homosexual Past*. New York: Doubleday, 1972.

ABOOD, E. F. *Underground Man*. San Francisco: Chandler and Sharp, 1973.

ACHTEMEIER, P. J. "St. Paul, Accommodation or Confrontation." Unpublished Ph.D. dissertation, Union Theological Seminary, 1957.

ACKERLEY, J. R. (f) *Hindoo Holiday*. New York: Viking, 1932.

*AMIS, KINGSLEY. (f) *The Riverside Villas Murder*. New York: Harcourt Brace Jovanovich, 1973.

ANDERSON, PATRICK. *Dolphin Days*. New York: Dutton, 1969.

*AUGIERAS, F. (b) *Le Voyage de Mont Athos*. Paris: Flammarion, 1970.

BAILEY, D. S. *Homosexuality and the Western Christian Tradition*. New York: Longmans, 1955.

BARCLAY, STEPHEN. *Bondage*. New York: Funk and Wagnalls, 1968.

BASTIN, GEORGES. *Dictionnaire de la Psychologie Sexuelle*. Brussels: Dessert, 1970.

BELL, R. R. *et al. The Social Dilemma of Human Sexuality*. Boston: Little, Brown, 1972.

BENDER, L. *et al.* "The Reaction of Children to Sexual Relations With Adults," *American Journal of Orthopsychiatry*, Oct. 1937, pp. 580 ff.

BERNARD, FRITS. "Nouvelle Enquête aux Pays-Bas," *Arcadie*, May 1973.

————. "Onderzoek van een groep pedofielen," *Medisch Contact*, Feb. 21, 1975, pp. 206 ff; and *Journal of Sex Research*, Aug. 1975.

*————. *Pedofilie*. Bussum: Aquarius, 1974.

————. "Pädophilie—eine Krankheit?" *Sexualmedizin*, Sept. 1972.

————. "Persooonlijkheitsaspecten bij pedofielen," *Medisch Contact*, March 14, 1975, pp. 313–334.

236

——— *et al. Sex met kinderen.* The Hague: Stichting Uitgeverij N.V.S.H., 1972.

BLEUEL, H. *Sex and Society in Nazi Germany.* Philadelphia: Lippincott, 1973.

BLÜHER, HANS. "The German Boy Scout Movement as Erotic Phenomenon." In *Die Rolle der Erotic in der Mannlichen Gesellschaft.* Stuttgart: Ernst Klett, 1962.

BORN, ERNST O. "Pedofiele Integratie" (pamphlet). Utrecht: Storm, 1973.

BOUSQUET, G. H. *La Morale de l'Islam et son ethique sexuelle.* Paris: A. Maisonneuve, 1953.

BRAKE, M. "The Skinhead—An English Working Class Subculture," *Youth and Society,* Dec. 1974.

BRONGERSMA, E. "L'Homophilie à visage couvert," *Arcadie,* Jan. 1974.

*———. *Das Verfemte Geschlecht.* Munich: Lichtenberg Verlag GmbH., 1970.

BROWN, DANIEL G. "Childhood Development and Sexual Deviations," *Sexology,* July 1972.

BUCHEN, IRVING, *et al. The Perverse Imagination.* New York: N.Y. Univ. Press, 1970.

*BURNS, JOHN H. (f) *Lucifer With a Book.* New York: Harpers, 1949.

BURTON, LINDY. *Vulnerable Children.* London: Routledge and Kegan Paul, 1968.

*CAMPBELL, M. (f) *Lord Dismiss Us.* New York: G. P. Putnam's Sons, 1968.

CAMUS, ALBERT. *The Rebel.* New York: Vintage Books, 1956.

CHESNEY, K. *The Victorian Underground.* London: Temple Smith, 1970.

CHURCHILL, W. *Homosexual Behavior Among Males.* Englewood Cliffs: Prentice-Hall, 1971.

*CLINE, W. B. *Notes on the People of Siwa.* Menasha, Wis.: Geo. Banta, 1936.

COFFIN, T. *The Sex Kick.* New York: Macmillan, 1966.

COON, EARL O. "Homosexuality in the News," *Archives of Criminal Psychodynamics.* Fall, 1957, pp. 843 ff.

CORRE, A. *L'Ethnographie Criminelle.* Paris: Library of Contemporary Science, 1894.

CORY, D. H. *Homosexuality: A Cross Cultural Approach.* New York: Julian Press, 1956.

*DANIEL, MARC. "Le Civilisation Arabe et l'amour Masculine," *Arcadie,* Jan. 1975, and subsequent issues.

DAVENPORT, W. "Sexual Patterns in a Southwest Pacific Society." In Brecher, Ruth and H., *An Analysis of Human Sexual Reponse.* New York: New American Library, 1966.

*DAVIDSON, MICHAEL, (b) *Some Boys,* London: David Bruce, 1970.

*———. (b) *The World, the Flesh and Myself.* London: Guild Press, 1962.

*D'ARCH SMITH, T. *Love in Earnest.* London: Routledge and Kegan Paul, 1970.

*DAVIES, PETER. (f) *Fly Away, Paul.* New York: Crown, 1974.

*DEL CASTILLO, M. (b) *Child of Our Time.* London: Knopf, 1958. More explict details in autobiographical novel, *Faiseur des Rêves.*

DE MAUSE, LLOYD. "The Evolution of Childhood," *History of Childhood Quarterly* 1, no. 4 (Spring, 1974).

DINGMAN, H. F. *et al.* "Erosion of Morale in Resocialization of Pedofiles," *Psychological Reports* I (1968), p. 792.

DORIAN, LEW. *The Young Homosexual.* New York: L. S. Publication, 1967.

DOSHAY, LEWIS J. *The Boy Sex Offender and His Later Career.* New York: Grune and Stratton, 1943.

DREW, DENNIS and J. DRAKE. *Boys for Sale.* New York: Brown Book Co., 1969.

*DUKHASZ, CASIMIR. (f) *The Asbestos Diary.* New York: Oliver Layton Press, 1966.

DUPREE, LOUIS. *Afghanistan.* Princeton: Princeton Univ. Press, 1973.

*DURANT, B. "L'amour Turc à Alger," *Arcadie,* Nov. 1968, and following issues.

*DUVERT, TONY. *Le Bon Sexe Illustré.* Paris: Editions de Minuit, 1974.

*————. (f) *Interdit de Sejour.* Paris: Editions de Minuit, 1971.

*————. (f) *Strange Landscape.* New York: Vanguard, 1976.

DUYCKAERTS, F. *The Sexual Bond.* New York: Delacorte, 1970.

*EBERMAYER, ERICH. (b) *Gustav Wyneken.* Frankfurt-am-Main: dipa-Verlag, 1969.

EDWARDES, A. *Jewel in the Lotus.* New York: Julian Press, 1959.

———— *et al. The Cradle of Erotica.* New York: Julian Press, 1962.

*EGLINTON, J. Z. *Greek Love.* London: Nevill Spearman, 1971.

*ELLIOTT, DAVID. (f) *Pieces of Night.* New York: Holt, Rinehart and Winston, 1973.

ERICKSON, R. J. "Male Homosexuality and Society," *Bulletin of the National Association of Secondary School Principals,* Nov. 1961, pp. 128 ff.

EVOLA, JULIUS. *Metafisica del Sesso.* Rome: Edizione Mediterranea, 1969.

*FARALLA, DANA. (f) *Children of Lucifer.* Philadelphia: Lippincott, 1963.

FINCH, S. M. "Effects of Adult Sexual Seduction on Children," *Journal of Clinical Psychology* 3, no. 1 (Winter, 1974).

FISHER, SUSAN. "Life in a Children's Detention Center," *American Journal of Orthopsychiatry,* April 1972.

FLACELIERE, ROBERT. *L'amour in Grèce.* Paris: Hatchette, 1954.

FLAUBERT, G. *Flaubert in Egypt.* London: Bodley Head, 1972.

FLEISCHAUER-HARDT, H. *Show Me.* New York: St. Martin's Press, 1975.

FLYNT, JOSIAH. "Homosexuality Among Tramps." In Havelock Ellis, *Studies in the Psychology of Sex.* Philadelphia: F. A. Davis, 1928.

FORD, C. S. and F. BEACH. *Patterns of Sexual Behavior.* New York: Harpers, 1951.

FORGEY, DONALD G. "The Institution of Berdache Among the North American Plains Indians," *Journal of Sex Research*, Feb. 1975, pp. 1–15.

FRAIBERG, S. H. "Homosexual Conflicts." In Lorand, S. *et al.*, *Adolescence: Psychoanalytic Approaches to Problems and Therapy*. New York: Paul Boeber, 1961.

FRASER, MAURICE. "Death of Narcissus." London, mimeographed, 1975.

FREUND, KARL. "Erotic Preferences in Pedophilia," *Behavior Research and Therapy* 5 (1967), pp. 335 ff.

———. "Diagnosing Homosexuality or Heterosexuality and Erotic Age Preferences by Means of a Pyschophysiological Test," *Behavior Research and Therapy* 5 (1967), pp. 209 ff.

FRIEDENBERG, EDGAR. *The Vanishing Adolescent*. Boston: Beacon Press, 1959.

GADPAILLE, W. J. "Homosexual Experience in Adolescence," *Medical Aspects of Human Sexuality* 10 (1968), pp. 29–30.

GAGNON, J. H. and W. SIMON. *Sexual Conduct: The Social Sources of Human Sexuality*. Chicago: Aldine Publishing Co., 1973.

———. *Sexual Deviance*. New York: Harpers, 1967.

GEBHARD, PAUL *et al*. *Sex Offenders: An Analysis of Types*. New York: Bantam Books, 1967.

*GENET, JEAN. (f) *Querelle*. London: Anthony Blond, 1966.

*———. (f) *Miracle de la Rose*. Paris: Gallimard, 1951.

*GERASSI, JOHN. *The Boys of Boise*. New York: Macmillan, 1966.

GIANOLLI, PAUL X. (b) *Roger Peyrefitte ou les clés du scandale*. Paris: Fayard, 1970.

*GIBB, E. J. W. *History of Ottoman Poetry*. London: Luzac, 1900.

GIBBS, J. *et al*. "Sex Education for Adolescent Delinquent Boys," *American Journal of Orthospychiatry*, Mar. 1969, p. 311.

GIDE, ANDRÉ. *Autumn Leaves*. New York: Philosophical Library, 1950.

———. (b) *Ainsi soit-il*. Paris: Gallimard, 1952.

*———. (f) *The Counterfeiters*. New York: Knopf, 1951.

———. *Fruits of the Earth*. London: Secker and Warburg, 1949.

*———. (b) *If It Die*. New York: Random House, 1934.

*———. (f) *The Immoralist*. New York: Knopf, 1930.

*———. *The Journals of André Gide*. New York: Vintage Books, 1956.

*———. *Urian's Voyage*. New York: Philosophical Library, 1969.

GILLABÉRT, E. *Le Colosse aux pieds d'argil*. Paris: Metanonae, 1975.

*GOODMAN, PAUL. (f) *The Break Up of Camp and Other Stories*. New York: New Directions, n.d.

*———. *Five Years*. New York: Vintage, 1969.

———. *Growing Up Absurd*. New York: Random House, 1960.

*———. (f) *Making Do*. New York: Macmillan, 1962.

*———. (f) *Our Visit to Niagara*. New York: Horizon Press, 1960.

*———. (f) *Parent's Day*. Saugatuck: 5 x 8 Press, 1951.

*GORHAM, CHARLES. (f) *McCaffery*. New York: Dial, 1961.

GRANT, JOHN. "The Vietnam Veteran," *Penthouse*, Jan, 1975.

*GRIFFIN, G. (f) *A Last Lamp Burning*. New York: G. P. Putnam's Sons, 1965.

GUERIN, DANIEL. *Essai sur la Revolution Sexuelle*. Paris: Editions Pierre Belfond, 1969.

*GUERSANT, M. (f) *Jean-Paul*. Paris: Editions de Minuit, 1953.

GULIK, R. H. *Sexual Life of Ancient China*. London: E. J. Brill, 1961.

HAMMOND, TONY. "Paidikon: A Paederastic Manuscript," *International Journal of Greek Love* 1, no. 2, pp. 281 ff.

HANLEY, JAMES. (f) *Boy*. New York: Knopf, 1932.

HANSON, L. and E. (b) *Verlaine: Fool of God*. New York: Random House, 1957.

HATTERER, L. J. *Changing Homosexuality in the Male*. New York: McGraw-Hill, 1970.

HENRY, G. W. *All the Sexes*. New York: Rinehart, 1955.

*————. *Society and the Sex Variant*. New York: Collier Books, 1966.

————. *Sex Variants*. New York: Paul B. Hoeber, Inc. (Medical Bk. Dept. of Harper & Bros.), 1941.

HOLLAND, ISABELLE. (f) *Man Without a Face*. Philadelphia: Lippincott, 1972.

HOLT, JOHN. *Escape From Childhood*. New York: Dutton, 1974.

*HOUGH, JOHN. (f) *The Two-Car Funeral*. Boston: Little, Brown, 1973.

HOUGH, RICHARD. (b) *Captain Bligh and Mr. Christian*. New York: Dutton, 1973.

*ISH-KISHER, S. (f) *Magnificent Hadrian*. London: Victor Gollancz, 1931.

HUMPHRIES, LAUD. *Tea Room Trade*. Chicago: Aldine Press, 1970.

*ISTRATI, PANAIT. (f) *Kyra Kyralina*. New York: Knopf, 1926.

JACKSON, C. (b) *Manuel*. New York: Knopf, 1964.

JANTZEN, H. *Jugendkultur und Jugendbeiwegnung*. Frankfurt-am-Main: dipa Verlag, 1969.

JONES, CLINTON. *Homosexuality and Counseling*. Philadelphia: Fortress Press, 1974.

KARLEN, ARNO. *Sexuality and Homosexuality*. New York: W. W. Norton, 1971.

KARSCH-HAACK, F. *Das Gleichgeschlechtlich Leben der Ostasien*. Munich: Seltz and Schauer, 1906.

KAZANTZAKIS, N. *Greek Passion*. New York: Simon and Schuster, 1953.

KENNEY, A. *et al. Symposium*. Boston: Houghton Mifflin, 1968.

KINSEY, A. *et al. Sexual Behavior in the Human Male*. Philadelphia: W. B. Saunders, 1948.

KIRKENDALL, L. A. *Sex Education and the Teen-ager*. Berkeley: Diablo Press, 1967.

KRITOBOULOUS. *History of Mehmed the Conqueror*. Princeton: Princeton Univ. Press, 1954.

LAQUER, W. Z. *Young Germany*, London: Routledge and Kegan Paul, 1962.

LEVI-STRAUSS, C. *Tristes Topiques*. New York: Atheneum, 1974.

LIBBY, R. W. "Adolescent Sexual Attitudes and Behavior." *Journal of Clinical Psychology* 3, no. 3 (Fall-Winter, 1974).

LICHT, HANS. *Sexual Life in Ancient Greece.* New York: Barnes and Noble, 1962.

LLOYD, R. *For Money or Love: Boy Prostitution in America.* New York: Vanguard, 1976.

*LOFTS, NORAH. (f) *The Lute Player.* Garden City: Doubleday, 1951.

LOWEN, ALEXANDER. *Pleasure: A Creative Approach to Life.* New York: Coward-McCann, 1970.

MAC DOUGAL, CHARLIE. "You Need Imagination in the Hole," *This Magazine Is About Schools* 3 (Summer, 1968).

*MALAPARTE, CURZIO. (f) *The Skin.* Boston: Houghton Mifflin, 1952.

MARIANI, FOSCO. *Where Four Worlds Meet.* New York: Harcourt, Brace, 1964.

*MARIOTTI, ETTORE. *La Neofilia.* Rome: Casa Editrice Mediterranea, 1952.

MARSHALL, D. S. and R. S. SUGGS. *Human Sexual Behavior.* New York: Basic Books, 1971.

MARTIGNAC, J. "Le Centurion de Capernaum," *Arcadie,* March 1975, pp. 117 ff.

MASTERS, R. E. L. *Forbidden Sexual Behavior and Morality.* New York: Julian Press, 1962.

*MAUGHAM, ROBIN. (f) *The Last Encounter.* London: Allen, 1972.

*_____. (f) *The Wrong People.* New York: McGraw-Hill, 1971.

MAXWELL, GAVIN. *Lords of the Atlas.* New York: Dutton, 1966.

_____. *Ten Pains of Death.* New York: Dutton, 1962.

MC CARTHY. MARY. *The Stones of Florence.* New York: Harcourt Brace, 1959.

MEAD, MARGARET. *Male and Female.* New York: William Morrow, 1949.

*MENEN, A. (f) *Fonthill.* London: Hamish Hamilton, 1974.

MERRILL, L. "Findings in a Study of Sexualism Among a Group of One Hundred Delinquent Boys," *Journal of Delinquency* 3, no. 6 (Nov. 1917).

METZEL, JOHN. *Sports and the Macho Male.* Dorchester, Mass.: Manifest Destiny Pamphlets, 1973.

MEYENDORFF, B. G. *Voyage d'Orenberg à Boukara.* Paris: Libraire Orientale, 1927.

MICHAUD, G. *Gide et l'Afrique.* Paris: Editions du Scorpion, 1961.

*MICHENER, JAMES. (f) *Caravans.* New York: Random House, 1963.

MILLER, HENRY. *The Colossus of Maroussi.* New York: New Directions, 1941.

MILLER, WILLIAM. *Essays on the Latin Orient.* London: Cambridge Press, 1921.

*MORAVIA, ALBERTO. (f) *The Conformist.* London: Secker and Warburg, 1957.

*_____. (f) *Two Adolescents.* New York: Farrar and Straus, 1950.

*MONTHERLANT, HENRY DE. (f) *The Boys*. London: Weidenfeld and Nicolson 1969.

———. *Paysage des Olympiques*. Paris: Grassat, 1940.

*MOTLEY, WILLARD. (f) *Knock on Any Door*. New York: Signet, 1951.

NÄCKE, PAUL. "Uber Homosexualitat in Albanien," *Jahrbuch fur Sexuelle Zwischenstufen* 9:325 ff. (1908).

NICHOLS. D. "Toward a Perspective for Boy Love." Unpublished, 97 pp. typescript.

*NORTAL, A. *et al.* (f) *Les Adolescents Passiones*. Paris: Curio, 1927.

O'CALLAGHAN, SEAN. *The White Slave Trade*. London: Robert Hale, 1962.

OLDENBERG, ZOE. *The Crusades*. New York: Ballantine Books, 1966.

*OLIVER, MARK. (f) *The Wanton Boys*. Garden City: Doubleday, 1959.

OLLENDORFF, ROBERT. *The Juvenile Homosexual Experience*. New York: Julian Press, 1966.

OLSEN, JACK. (b) *The Man With the Candy*. New York; Simon and Schuster, 1974.

*O'MEARA, WALTER. (f) *The Devil's Cross*. New York: Knopf, 1957.

*PALAU DE LOPEZ, A. *et al*. *En la Calle Estabas*. San Juan: Univ. of Puerto Rico Press, 1970.

PATTERSON, HAYWARD. (b) *Scottsboro Boy*. New York: Doubleday, 1950.

*PAYNE, ROBERT. (b) *Caravaggio*. Boston: Little, Brown, 1968.

*PERRIN, ANDRE. (f) *Mario*. Paris: Gallimard, 1955.

*PETERS, FRITZ. (f) *Finistère*. New York: Farrar and Straus, 1951.

PETRONIUS. (f) *Satyricon*. Los Angeles: Holloway House, 1970.

*PEYREFITTE, ROGER. (f) *Les Ambassades*. Paris: Flammarion, 1951.

———. (f) *Les Amours Singulières*. Paris: Jean Vigneau, 1949.

*———. (f) *Exile of Capri*. Paris: Flammarion, 1959.

*———. (f) *La Fin des Ambassades*. Paris: Flammarion, 1951.

*———. (f) *Jeunes Proies*. Paris: Flammarion, 1956.

*———. (f) *Notre Amour*. Paris: Flammarion, 1954.

———. (f) *Manouche*. London: Hart-Davis, 1973.

*———. (f) *L'Oracle*. Paris: Jean Vigneau, 1948.

*———. (f) *Special Friendships*. London: Secker and Warburg, 1958.

———. *Un Musée de L'amour*. Paris: Editions du Rocher, 1972.

POMEROY, WENDELL. *Boys and Sex*. New York: Delacorte, 1968.

PRESCOTT, J. W. "Body Pleasure and Origins of Violence," *The Futurist*, April 1975.

*PROKOSCH, F. (f) *The Asiatics*. New York: Harpers, 1935.

*———. *The Missolonghi Manuscript*. New York: Farrar, Straus and Giroux, 1968.

*PUNZO, GIORGIO. *Dialoghi dell'Amore Olarrenico*. Naples: Carlo Martello, 1964.

RADZINOWICZ, L. *et al*. *Sexual Offenses*. Vol IX in English Studies in Criminal Science, London, 1957.

*RANDOLPH, ALEXANDER. (f) *The Mail Boat.* New York: Holt, 1969.

RECLUS, ELIE. *Curious Byways of Anthropology.* New York: Robin Hood Press, 1964.

*RENAULT, MARY. (f) *The Persian Boy.* New York: Pantheon, 1972.

*ROBINSON, J, BRADBURY. (f) *A Crocodile of Choirboys.* San Diego: Phoenix, 1970.

*ROFEHART, MARTHA. (f) *Fortune Made His Sword.* New York: G. P. Putnam's Sons, 1972.

*ROMAINS, JULES. (f) *The Seventh of October.* New York: Knopf, 1946.

ROSSMAN, JEAN. "Remedial Readers." *Journal of Reading,* May 1974.

ROSSMAN, PARKER. "The Pederasts." In Goode, Erich *et al. Sexual Deviance and Sexual Deviants.* New York: William Morrow, 1974.

RUBENFELD, SEYMOUR. *Family of Outcasts.* New York: Free Press, 1965.

*RUBIN, MICHEL. (f) *In a Cold Country.* New York: McGraw-Hill, 1971.

RUITENBEEK, H. *et al. The Problem of Homosexuality in Modern Society.* New York: Dutton, 1963.

*SARTRE, JEAN-PAUL. (f) "Childhood of a Leader," In *The Wall.* New York: New Directions, 1948.

————. *Saint Genet.* New York: Mentor Books, 1964.

*SAXON, TROY. (b) *The Happy Hustler.* New York: Warner Books, 1975.

SCHIRMANN, J. "The Ephebe in Medieval Hebrew Poetry," *Safared* 15 (1955) pp 55 ff.

SCHOFIELD, MICHAEL. *Social Aspects of Homosexuality.* London: Longmans Green, 1965.

SHAW, OTTO. *Prisons of the Mind.* London: Geo. Allen and Unwin, 1969.

SIEMSEN, A. *Die Tragodie Deutschland und der Zukunft der Welt.* Buenos Aires: Cosmopolita, 1945.

*SORENSEN, ROBERT. *Adolescent Sexuality in Contemporary America.* New York: World, 1975.

SRIVASTARA, SHANKER S. *Juvenile Vagrancy.* Bombay: Asia House, 1963.

STERN, BERNARD. *The Scented Garden.* New York: American Ethnological Press, 1934.

*STEWART, ANGUS. (f) *Sandel.* London: Panther Books, 1972.

*————. (f) *Snow in Harvest.* London: Panther Books, 1971.

SUGGS, ROBERT C. *Marquesan Sexual Behavior.* New York: Harcourt, Brace and World, 1966.

SWISHER, VIOLA. "Generating the 'Genesis Children,' " *After Dark,* Sept. 1972.

SYKES, GRESHAM. *Society of Captives.* Princeton: Princeton Univ. Press, 1958.

*TAVEL, RONALD. (f) *Street of Stairs.* New York: Olympia, 1968.

TAYLOR, BRIAN. "Doesn't Apply to Me, Forster." Department of Sociology, Univ. of Aberdeen, Scotland. Unpublished typescript.

TAYLOR, G. RATTRAY. *Sex in History.* New York: Ballantine, 1954.

*TELFER, DONALD. (f) *The Corrupters*. New York: Simon and Shuster, 1968.
*TESCH, ARNOLD. (f) *Never the Same Again*. New York: G. P. Putnam's Sons, 1956.
THESIGER, WILFRED. *The Marsh Arabs*. London: Longman, 1964.
THIEULOY, J. *L'Inde des Grand Chemins*. Paris, 1974.
*TOURNIER, MICHEL. (f) *The Ogre*. Garden City: Doubleday, 1972.
*TRALOW, JOHANNES. (f) *Irene von Trapezunt*. Wiesentheid: Doremiersche Verlags, 1947.
ULLERSTAM, LARS. *The Erotic Minorities*. New York: Grove Press, 1966.
VALENTE, M. F. "On Homosexuality," *New York Times*, Jan. 14, 1975.
*VANGGAARD, THORKEL. *Phallos—A Symbol and Its History*. New York: International Universities Press, 1972.
VAZ, E. W. *Middle-Class Juvenile Delinquency*. New York: Harper and Row, 1967.
VEZE, RAOUL. *Baisers d'Orient*. Paris: Bibl. des Curieuses, 1921.
WALKER, B. *The Hindu World: An Encyclopedia*. New York: Praeger, 1968.
WEINBERG, GEORGE. *Society and the Healthy Homosexual*. New York: St. Martin's Press, 1972.
WELTER, G. E. *Bibliographie Freundschaftseros*. Frankfurt-am-Main: dipa Verlag, 1964.
WILLETS, FRITZ. "Vandervogel in Pre-Hitler Germany," *Journal of Criminal Psychopathology* 3, Jan. 1943.
*WORSLEY, T. C. (b) *Flanneled Fool*. London: Alan Ross, 1967.
WYNEKEN, G. *Jugend*. Frankfurt-am-Main: dipa Verlag, 1963.
YEBOR (anon.). "Reflexion sur la pedofilie," *Arcadie*, Sept., 1974.
ZWEIG, PAUL. *The Adventurer*. New York: Basic Books, 1974.

Index